International Marketing
in a Changing World

International Marketing in a Changing World

A Managerial Guidebook

M. Billur Akdeniz
Sebastian van der Vegt
S. Tamer Cavusgil

BEP
BUSINESS EXPERT PRESS
Leader in applied, concise business books

International Marketing in a Changing World:
A Managerial Guidebook

Cover design by Charlene Kronstedt

Interior design by S4Carlisle Publishing Services, Chennai, India

First published in 2025 by
Business Expert Press, LLC
222 East 46th Street, New York, NY 10017
www.businessexpertpress.com

ISBN-13: 978-1-63742-848-1 (paperback)
ISBN-13: 978-1-63742-849-8 (e-book)

Business Expert Press International Business Collection

First edition: 2025

10 9 8 7 6 5 4 3 2 1

EU SAFETY REPRESENTATIVE
Mare Nostrum Group B.V.
Mauritskade 21D
1091 GC Amsterdam
The Netherlands
gpsr@mare-nostrum.co.uk

Description

In today's volatile global business environment, international marketing is more complex, and more critical, than ever. This guidebook serves as a comprehensive yet concise roadmap for managing the intricacies of international marketing in a global marketplace, where rapid technological advancement, evolving consumer behavior, and fluctuating regulatory landscapes continuously reshape the playing field. Unlike traditional texts, which lean heavily on theory, *International Marketing in a Changing World* balances theoretical insights with practical application, offering immediately actionable strategies for professionals and students alike.

Authored by experts with decades of combined experience in academia and industry, this book incorporates feedback from over 100 global business educators and insights from executives engaged in international marketing. Its unique "3W-1H" framework (Who-What-Why-How) helps marketers understand complex concepts and identify key resources.

Through real-world vignettes, contemporary business cases, and a balanced approach toward international marketing theory and practice, this guidebook is tailored for executives, MBA students, professional master's students, and researchers needing a fresh, adaptable perspective on international marketing. Guided by the insightful notion that businesses should neither be mindlessly global nor hopelessly local, this guidebook provides a robust foundation to navigate and succeed in a world where change is the only constant.

Contents

List of Figures and Tables

Figures

Tables

List of Business Vignettes

Acknowledgments

Writing this book has been a journey of exploration and insight, and many have contributed to its fruition. We wish to acknowledge the following individuals and organizations to whom we are grateful for their inspiration, feedback, suggestions, and encouragement.

First, we sincerely thank John Riesenberger, president of Consilium Partners (ret.) and clinical professor at Thunderbird School of Global Management (ret.) for providing a detailed review and feedback on the previous versions of the book. Second, we greatly appreciate Seda Palaz Pazarbasi (advisor, Strategic Marketing Research, Consumer Insights, and Analytics), Selin Kahraman (head of data and insights, Innocent Drinks), Nadeem Zaman (category marketing head, Kimberly-Clark Corporation), Berk Talay (professor of marketing at the University of Massachusetts Lowell and former Fulbright Scholar at ESSEC Business School, France), and Simon Bartlett (partner, WBMV Consulting LLC) for providing feedback on the specific sections of the book.

Special thanks go to Elif Diler Ozsut (emerging markets region engagement director, GSK), Raymond Pettit (Chief AI & Analytics Officer, Neuro-AI Design), Pete Lankford (product designer, sustainability expert, and strategic leader), Cuneyt Evirgen (senior academic professional and faculty director, Georgia State University CIBER), Burcu Eksioglu (global price forecasting and early assets lead, AstraZeneca), and Ozge Ekmekci (portfolio innovation senior manager, 3M) for sharing their wisdom and wealth of experience in international business.

We are deeply thankful to all current and former students in the International Marketing course in the Paul College Online MBA Program who have been not only inspirational but also a source of motivation in the conception and writing of the book. We also owe great gratitude to Frank Armstrong, whose sharp editorial skills and thoughtful suggestions have been pivotal in refining the manuscript.

Finally, we appreciate the financial support from the Center for International Business Education and Research (CIBER) at Georgia State University and from the Faculty Scholars Program at the University of New Hampshire. We also appreciate the support from the Peter T. Paul College of Business and Economics. The commitment of these institutions to advancing knowledge has been crucial to the culmination of this book.

Preface

Welcome to a world in flux—the international business landscape of the twenty-first century. Here, rapid technological changes intersect with evolving consumer behaviors and changing competitive and regulatory landscapes, creating both opportunities and challenges. In response, we have crafted this Managerial Guidebook to provide practical strategies and insights for navigating the complex and dynamic realm of international marketing.

Our motivation to write this book springs from the pressing need for modern, clear, and accessible guidance that resonates with business professionals. Traditional textbooks, often extensive in their approach, sometimes fail to capture the essence and changes of the contemporary business environment. This book aims to fill that gap—a need for a guide that is both concise and comprehensive, catering to professionals seeking practical insights alongside theoretical underpinnings.

The uniqueness of this book lies in its foundational approach. From the outset, we focus explicitly on international marketing, aiming to simplify complex concepts, enhance decision-making, and improve the professional marketing experience. The authors' collective expertise in research, teaching, and practical application brings a rich, synergistic perspective to each chapter.

To ensure relevance and utility in preparing this guidebook, we surveyed over 100 international business educators globally, seeking their perspectives on what is currently lacking in the field. Additionally, we interviewed executives responsible for international marketing in their organizations, gaining firsthand insights into their challenges and areas for improvement. This diverse blend of perspectives provided the foundation for our book and helped shape it into a relevant and robust resource.

We also prioritized a balance between theory and practice, a feature often missing in conventional texts. We ensure that readers can easily understand and apply key concepts and strategies through contemporary business vignettes and real-world cases, alongside our innovative 3W-1H framework (Who-What-Why-How).

Compiling this guidebook was a journey of continuous discovery, shaped by recent significant shifts such as digital transformation, the COVID-19 pandemic, and advances in AI. These experiences not only influenced our perspectives but also reflect the broader changes impacting the field of international marketing.

This book is tailored for a broad spectrum of readers. Executives navigating the global market, MBA students delving into international business nuances, professional master's students, and practice-oriented researchers will find this book a valuable addition to their go-to resources. We aim to support professionals by helping them avoid common pitfalls and identify competitive advantages. In a broader sense, we hope anyone intrigued by the evolving world of international marketing will discover insights and strategies immediately applicable to their endeavors.

Guided by the insightful notion that businesses should neither be mindlessly global nor hopelessly local—but rather seek a balanced approach somewhere in between—our guidebook explores the delicate balance between global strategies and local insights. We hope this perspective guides our readers navigate the complexities of the international marketplace. As you dive into this book, we invite you to share your thoughts as you go along—we are eager to hear your perspectives. There is always something new around the corner, and we are excited about what the future holds. We hope you find the journey insightful and engaging. Enjoy your exploration into the fascinating world of global marketing!

Reviewer Quotes
and Endorsements

"So many books, often extensive in their approach, fail to capture the essence and changes of the contemporary business environment. In contrast, this manuscript serves as a guide that is both concise and comprehensive, catering to professionals seeking practical insights alongside theoretical underpinnings. The authors have done a great job of conveying the excitement and intricacies of going international through a highly readable book."—**Ahmet Bozer, president of Coca-Cola International (Ret.), Atlanta, Georgia**

"In an era marked by profound transformations in the global business landscape, this executive guidebook introduces the reader to the increasingly complex and dynamic world of international marketing. The authors successfully bridge the gap between theory and practice in offering thoughtful and practical advice in going international."—**Peter Buckley, 200th Anniversary Chair in International Business, Alliance Manchester Business School, University of Manchester, Manchester, U.K.**

"This innovative book will serve a diverse readership. Whether you are an executive navigating the global market, an MBA student, or a practice-oriented researcher, this book is a valuable addition to go-to resources. It will support professionals through their growth in avoiding common pitfalls and identifying competitive advantages. Congratulations to Tamer Cavusgil and his coauthors, Billur Akdeniz and Sebastian van der Vegt."—**Maria Tereza Fleury, full professor Fundação Getulio Vargas, FGV Brazil, São Paolo, Brazil, and fellow and past president of the Academy of International Business**

"The authors of this book have masterfully stroked a balance between concepts and applications, which is a rarity in traditional textbooks. This is done through fresh business vignettes and real-world cases from business

professionals. Through their combined expertise and backgrounds in research-ing, teaching, and executing international marketing, they offer a wealth of knowledge and experience, creating a synergistic effect between academia and practice. The book provides a unique blend of perspectives in every chapter."—**Bodo B. Schlegelmilch, PhD, DLitt, PhD (hon.), professor emeritus, WU Vienna University of Economics and Business, Austria; Bualuang ASEAN Chair professor, Thammasat University, Bangkok, Thailand**

"Conventional international marketing textbooks often repurpose or build on general marketing content with an international twist. In contrast, this author team begins with a clear focus on international marketing from the outset. With this mindset, they simplify the shifting realms of the field, increase the probability of a more informed decision-making, and enhance the inter-national marketing experience for professionals. Managers as well as academics worldwide will find this book an authoritative guidebook for navigating global markets."—**Professor Peter Liesch, president of the Academy of International Business, and professor of international business, UQ Business School, The University of Queensland, Australia**

"This executive guidebook offers important strategies and insights for profes-sionals grappling with the nuanced realms and challenges of international marketing today and tomorrow. A must reading for practitioners and aca-demics alike."—**Professor Jagdish N. Sheth, Emory University, Atlanta, Georgia**

"Finally, a book that can enlighten practitioners responsible for international marketing in their organizations, gaining firsthand insights into their chal-lenges and areas for improvement. A unique blend of academic and practical viewpoints offered in this book will please any reader interested in relevant and robust guidance in international marketing. Congratulations to this author team for giving us a highly accessible reference book."—**Ying Zhu, professor of international business, University of South Australia, Adelaide, South Australia**

"This book caters to the pressing need for contemporary, clear, and accessible guidance that resonates with business professionals. The shifts and transformations of the current world we live in demand a new kind of resource, one that is both concise and comprehensive, to navigate the complex realities of international marketing. In an authoritative and highly readable manner, the authors respond to this challenge."—**Ayşegül Özsomer, professor of marketing, Koç University, Istanbul, Turkey**

CHAPTER 1

Introduction

FIFA Men's World Cup

In November 2022, the world gathered in Qatar for the FIFA Men's World Cup. For the first time in its illustrious history, the FIFA World Cup was to take place in the northern hemisphere's winter, during the European club football season. Also, for the first time, the FIFA World Cup was to be held in a Middle Eastern country, with different cultural values and traditions than many Westerners had ever been exposed to.

The run-up to the FIFA World Cup was anything but smooth. Awarded the rights to host the FIFA World Cup in 2010, in 2017, Qatar was accused by Western media of a bribery scandal before the vote to host the competition. The country was also in the spotlight for its treatment of migrant workers, which was claimed to be less than optimal. A small army of largely Asian men helped build the FIFA World Cup's eight stadiums, carefully constructed within a 35-mile radius, and Western governments and NGOs widely criticized their treatment.

As a result of this criticism, Qatar offered significant changes and concessions to its labor code. It reassured that not only were its workers treated fairly but also that it was committed to *an inclusive and discriminatory-free* World Cup. With public displays of homosexuality subject to a 3-year prison term, this was a significant departure from the norm. Another change promised by Qatar was its treatment of alcohol consumption. Normally available in only a few select 5-star hotels, alcoholic beverages were slated to be available in and around stadiums in designated zones.

Budweiser, owned by AB In-Bev, welcomed the policy change: They had been sponsoring the World Cup since 1986, and their latest sponsorship deal for the 2022 World Cup reportedly cost $75 million. To satisfy anticipated demand, they shipped beer to Qatar in a massive logistical project. Peter Kraemer,[1] AB In-Bev's chief supply officer, said they had to ship it by ocean freight and find refrigerated warehouses to keep beer cool in Qatar's hot temperatures. Trucks were loaded indoors overnight and then sent to serve alcohol the following day.

So far, so good, until Qatar announced a change in policy just 2 days before the day the World Cup was set to kick off. Beer was to be no longer available in and around the stadiums. Instead, only non-alcoholic beverages were to be sold. Quickly, Budweiser, which had so much vested in this operation, sent out a global tweet that simply read, "Well, this is awkward." The company deleted the tweet shortly after, but its sentiments were plain: It was not happy.

Faced with an impossible situation, the company reevaluated its marketing plans for the World Cup in real time. On November 19, the day after deleting its earlier tweet, it tweeted a photograph of many cases of beer in a warehouse in an indeterminate location. It said— *New Day, New Tweet,* and *Winning Country Gets the Buds. Who will get them?*[2] Later, the brewer announced that the winning nation would also receive "a celebration on us" and unveiled a cunning new slogan that could be seen inside the stadiums: *Bring Home the Bud.*

Before the World Cup, the company had announced plans to roll out its multiplatform campaign—*The World Is Yours to Take*—during the World Cup, which was an evolution of its *Yours to Take* marketing platform launched earlier in 2022. To ensure its success, the company had even enlisted globally renowned football stars, such as Lionel Messi and Neymar, to feature in its commercials under this theme. However, now, with only a few hours to go before the tournament began, they decided to switch their digital slogans to *Bring Home the Bud.*

Even though most spectators were not happy that only Budweiser ZERO was sold at the stadiums, the company understood that in-stadium sales were only a small portion of its anticipated revenue from the World Cup. This new slogan allowed Budweiser to pivot and stay relevant in real time despite the restrictions on beer sales.

After Argentina famously took home the World Cup trophy, Budweiser made good on its promise and set up distribution points in cities around Argentina where citizens could pick up a free beer. The company had turned bad news into good news and still had a chance to celebrate Argentina's win, leveraging both the Budweiser Anthem music video, performed by Lil Baby *The World Is Yours To Take*, and its global *#BringHomeTheBud* campaign.

Budweiser's new impromptu *Bring Home the Bud* campaign became its largest-ever global campaign. "This has been an incredible journey. It's a historic moment, not just for me, but for all of Argentina. *The World Is Yours to Take* has been a great way to tell my story to achieve this dream. I'm excited that we're able to celebrate and Bring Home the Buds to all the fans that supported us." Lionel Messi said in a statement released by Budweiser after the World Cup.[3]

The Budweiser World Cup marketing case study illustrates many cultural complexities managers face while marketing their products and services across borders. In this case, Budweiser had to face a myriad of challenges, including different regulations and customs, changing on-the-ground conditions, targeting a real-time (in-stadium) and a virtual (online and TV) audience simultaneously, and managing many different vested interests.

While this case is unique, some of Budweiser's challenges are not. Many companies struggle with building a global brand while remaining locally relevant. In fact, many international marketers would argue that this is their biggest challenge—finding the correct balance between local and global (some use the word *glocal*, which refers to global, yet local). Creating an international brand capable of resonating with global and local markets is no easy task. It requires careful planning and consideration of various factors, such as cultural differences, language barriers, customer preferences, and local regulations. Similarly, international marketers need to comprehensively understand the target market to implement their marketing strategy effectively.

Finding a balance between global and local needs often requires compromises to ensure the brand remains appealing to the broadest possible audience. The goal should be to create a brand identity that is easily recognizable and appealing to customers from all corners of the world. Doing so will increase the brand's visibility and help it establish a strong presence in both global and local markets. To achieve this, companies must create a consistent brand identity that resonates across borders and boundaries. This process involves developing effective marketing strategies tailored to the local market, considering customer preferences, language barriers, and cultural differences while remaining consistent with the global brand identity. Recognizing and appreciating these cultural nuances and adhering to each country's laws and regulations are important to ensure your brand is represented correctly.

All international companies must adhere to local regulations, customs, and the desires of stakeholders such as suppliers, investors, employees, and customers, which can be daunting. This is true whether you are a company that sells directly to consumers, an Internet-based start-up, or a business that provides services to other businesses. Take Netflix, a global unicorn that expanded to 190 countries in just 7 years. The company invested heavily in creating locally relevant content embedded in the local language, culture, and artistry to strengthen its presence in each region. It also had to abide by local regulations for content. To tackle these issues, Netflix prioritized creating local and regional content and invested heavily in great local voiceovers and translations for all its programming. As a result, synergies between consumer tastes became apparent, and unlikely global hits made in different regions were born. This commitment enabled the company to build a robust presence in all its markets, cementing its position as a global leader.[4]

In short, marketers who work in foreign countries or for companies with a presence abroad often have a very challenging job. To successfully create a powerful brand image that resonates across borders, they must implement an effective *glocal* marketing strategy that preserves the global brand's core value proposition but remains tailored to the local context. This requires conducting competitive research, being familiar with local culture and customs, hiring the proper agencies, and managing alliances and partnerships strategically. Our book addresses all these topics.

Yet, what was already a very complex job has been made more so by rapid technological advances, increased competition, and a seemingly never-ending array of disruptions and crises. Some of these disruptions result from predictable megatrends, while others are unforeseen. These disruptions can negatively impact international operations and derail the best-laid marketing plans. For example, Budweiser had to contend with changing government regulations, while specific industries have suffered in recent years due to the COVID-19 pandemic.

The COVID-19 pandemic provided a unique case study for marketers who had to adapt and adjust their plans quickly. Some thrived, and others survived, often due to circumstances beyond their control. For example, Netflix took advantage of the pandemic as people stayed home and watched more of its content. Another company that benefited was Etsy, an e-commerce platform beloved by craft enthusiasts worldwide. It weathered the pandemic remarkably well, not just because more consumers were shopping online, spending time at home, and picking up new hobbies. It also picked up new customers and sellers looking for masks, sanitizers, and other related items.

The pandemic severely impacted companies in the global hospitality industry and those reliant on disrupted supply chains. Even the most advanced international marketing strategies and tactics could not have prevented these companies from experiencing the impact of this disruption. Fortunately, some managed to reduce the severity of the crisis by emphasizing customer loyalty programs, catering to local customers and events, and building up the resilience of their organizational structures.

Having the right strategies in place can be the key to successfully navigating both predictable and unpredictable events and disruptions. With operational agility, supportive global networks, and the right global marketing strategies, companies can survive and thrive in the long term. In this book, we will explore how to build brand love, create global resilience, understand global megatrends, and enhance a company's reputation through mitigating strategies that will help it weather any storm.

The World We Live in

The world in the twenty-first century is more complex, innovative, and unpredictable than any business or organization, big or small, has ever inherited. Change is constant and rapid, as an unprecedented level of technological transformation and the digital revolution continually evolve the ways we eat, play, watch, search, and travel. Complexity, involving multiple layers, channels, and stakeholders, can make any business decision more complex and more challenging to detangle. Even though we live in a volatile, uncertain, complex, and ambiguous (VUCA) world, the essence of marketing is still the same as Peter Drucker put it more than 50 years ago: "To know the customer so well that the product or service fits them and sells itself." As far as international marketing goes, the aim for an organization is to identify, assess, and respond to opportunities while managing risks abroad. Yet, this volatility, uncertainty, complexity, and ambiguity impact professionals like you and your ability to strategize, practice, and lead your organization's international marketing efforts in an entirely new and different way. While it is usually everyone's responsibility to create a better value proposition and customer experience in foreign locations, this responsibility increases for marketers and the number and variety of stakeholders you need to consider. Notably, while international expansion brings with it tremendous opportunity, it also increases company risk and leads to a decrease in the amount of control you can exercise.

By becoming more knowledgeable about international marketing and the available tools and resources, you can create a genuine international marketing strategy suitable for your organization's goals and needs, allowing you to navigate complexity and uncertainty. Creating an international marketing strategy involves leveraging your organization's competitive advantages, resources, and global experience while also considering the distinct characteristics of each local market. Additionally, you can gain insights from different markets that can help accelerate your organization's internationalization process.

As we mentioned earlier, to succeed in international marketing, it is important to balance standardizing your company's products or services for global efficiencies and allowing some flexibility to adapt them to local markets. With the sizeable shift from traditional marketing channels to online, mobile, and digital marketing efforts and the proliferation of consumer trends and habits, international marketing requires a deep understanding of customers, cultures, and trends. This book aims to help marketers and other business leaders interested in marketing:

- Feel confident and comfortable in their next cross-border marketing venture.

- Ensure that the global brand they are trying to build resonates with its target audience.
- Understand the tools necessary to pursue opportunities and mitigate risks in international markets.
- Ensure that their organization uses its resources and capabilities efficiently and effectively to create sustainable practices and minimize errors in international marketing.

Indeed, in recent years, the role of marketers in an organization has grown more relevant and important, putting the onus on marketers to be well-informed, well-rounded international business leaders who can help make or break a company's success. To equip modern-day international marketers with the necessary skills and tools to make informed, evidence-based, and data-driven decisions, we offer a unique take by synthesizing research with practice. After all, it is only by understanding and responding to customers' needs in different countries, cultures, and contexts that organizations can succeed in their international marketing initiatives.

Flow of the Book

This guidebook offers a comprehensive overview of international marketing by combining research and practice. It emphasizes providing readers with the skills and tools to make informed decisions. The selection of the topics we covered in this book was not random. In the early stages, we conducted an online survey through a network of over 100 international business academics and practitioners worldwide. Also, we interviewed many practitioners and executives responsible for international marketing within their organizations. We asked them where they felt least prepared to resolve the international marketing issues in their organizations and what they deemed the most helpful to improve international performance. Based on the feedback we collected, we set out to create an outline that goes from big picture to execution.

In Chapter 2, we look at the big picture of where the world is going, *Navigating Megatrends*. Every enterprise must adapt to the megatrends that are gradually reshaping our world. These include major technological and scientific shifts, climate change, the rise of individualism and entrepreneurship, empowerment and equity, the growing importance of mega cities, as well as shifting demographic and consumer trends.

In Chapter 3, we evaluate *Market Opportunities and Entry*. Before entering any foreign market, it is crucial to understand its potential and the different ways of entering a market. We look at how you can capture global market opportunities and build an international brand presence while marketing products and services abroad and provide a risk–benefit analysis of foreign market entry modes to help guide the best entry mode in your internationalization efforts.

In Chapter 4, we address one of the most popular topics in international marketing, *Managing across Cultures*. In international marketing, recognizing the significance of culture is crucial for successfully establishing business operations in foreign markets. Understanding and integrating cultural nuances into marketing strategies is essential for building strong relationships and achieving success abroad, same as deciding that you are okay with being at a competitive disadvantage.

In Chapter 5, we dive deep into one indispensable aspect for the success of international marketing, *Market Research*. As we delve into the essential aspects that executives should prioritize to ensure effective market research outcomes, we focus on the key considerations for executives when it comes to collecting, analyzing, and interpreting data.

In Chapter 6, we focus on *Brands and Company Reputation*. One of the most critical responsibilities of any marketer is building and protecting a brand that will stand the test of time. In relation to this, we discuss topics like standardization versus adaptation, glocalization, brand guidelines, responding to crises, and safeguarding your company image and rights.

In Chapter 7, we concentrate on *Marketing Execution*, encompassing key elements such as products and services, pricing, communications, and channel strategy and tactics. Additionally, we specifically discuss how companies can effectively utilize marketing execution and tactics to work toward a more sustainable future.

In Chapter 8, we focus on the rise and importance of *Digital Marketing* strategies and tactics within the realm of international marketing. We will explore how organizations can navigate digital transformation effectively, highlighting the necessary digital marketing skills, capabilities, and tools that are essential for international marketers.

In Chapter 9, the final chapter, we provide an *Outlook into the Future* of international marketing with an emphasis on emerging and evergreen trends. The global marketplace represents a constantly changing environment characterized by diverse cultures, emerging trends, and rapid technological advancements. We specifically discuss that successfully navigating these dynamic international markets necessitates more than a set of strategies; it also requires adaptability, resilience, empathy, and collaboration.

Before You Begin

Technological advances are upending the world of international marketing. What is valid today regarding our capabilities may not be valid tomorrow. Advances in artificial intelligence, data collection, real-time communication and feedback, A/B testing, social media, geotargeting, large language models (LLMs), and others are quickly reshaping how the world is organized and how companies operate and communicate holistically. For as much as possible, we tried, in this book, to stay true to the things that will likely still be valid in the foreseeable future, despite the rapidly changing landscape that is facing today's international marketers.

It is true that only a few years ago, you could not ask an AI tool to create a sales funnel for a pharmaceutical product in Spanish for a Columbian audience or to ask help from an advanced software service provider for insights into consumer sentiment toward certain products in real time and respond simultaneously with a targeted advertising campaign that is sure to resonate. Today, you already can. As these tools continue to improve, they will make some of marketing agencies' work obsolete, especially those that do more transactional work.

It is also true that future marketers will need to understand and appreciate where this world is going, what tools are out there at their disposal, and what can be done creatively to capture the tremendous opportunities we now have. That means not just being able to understand the tools and their capabilities, but also being able to ask the right questions, thinking creatively, collaboratively, emotively, and out of the box. For those well-rounded individuals, who understand and appreciate the differences in the world, an AI-enriched environment will present more opportunity than ever before. Those merely relying on these new tools to carry out campaigns will gain efficiency but lose efficacy.

Understanding cultural nuances, how reputations and brand love can be built on an emotional connection, how megatrends will shape our future world, and connecting the dots between seemingly unrelated things will be increasingly important. It is also work that technology will be unable to perform for the foreseeable future. For those marketing professionals looking to gain a competitive edge, this book will provide you a solid basis for grounding yourself, even as you take advantage of the many new opportunities the world of international marketing now offers.

CHAPTER 2

Navigating Megatrends

DHL in Unprecedented Times

We are living in a time of infinite possibilities to create outcomes that inspire and improve the way we work and live. As the world's leading logistics company, we make every effort to stay on top of the logistics trends and ahead of new developments. We outline the five mega trends shaping the logistics industry as follows: Digital Technology, Diversity & Inclusion, Customer Experience, Future of Work, and Sustainability.[1]

At the beginning of 2023, DHL proudly proclaimed its commitment to navigating the *Era of Logistics*. As a division of the German logistics firm Deutsche Post, DHL's success as an international courier, package delivery, and express mail service relies on responding to global megatrends. This is more than a slogan for the company; an opportunity to attract potential customers and gain efficiency while staving off threats such as theft, natural disasters, and political unrest.

DHL's proactive approach to understanding the changing global environment and utilizing cutting-edge technology allows it to remain competitive in a rapidly evolving market. Its focus on megatrends enabled it to navigate the COVID-19 pandemic successfully. Businesses from agriculture to automotive, to energy, to retail—all leveraged DHL's platforms during the crisis to manage their risks and plan for contingencies. "Mega trends provide challenges and opportunities for all of us. I'm excited about the future and all of us entering the Era of Logistics." says Katja Busch, chief commercial officer and Head of CSI at DHL.[2]

As far back as 2014, DHL incubated a spin-off company, Resilience360, in its Global Innovation Center. This was part of the company's efforts to become more resilient to long- and short-term threats by leveraging the increased capability of AI and digitalization. The aim was to transform supply chain disruption and global, environmental, and sociopolitical volatility into a competitive advantage. To achieve this goal, the Resilience360 digital platform provided companies with a holistic, real-time view of their end-to-end supply chains and real-time risk visibility.

In 2021, DHL-backed Resilience360 merged with Riskpulse to become Everstream Analytics, launching a new platform that combined the unique capabilities of two global supply chain risk analytics solutions. According to David Shillingford, chief strategy officer of Everstream Analytics:

> Our solution utilizes AI and proprietary data at scale together with our team's deep expertise in supply chain risk analytics. We believe that risk analytics should be embedded in supply chain digitization and data-driven decision making across all functions, and our API-centric approach enables this. Our clients can use this to transform risk into a competitive advantage—as our tagline says, "Get in Front of What's Ahead."[3]

For DHL, the impact of managing megatrends goes beyond managing their clients' risk; it is about staying ahead and anticipating what is coming next. From simple things like advising its smaller customers on their digital marketing campaigns to complex global initiatives, like its global *Go Green* campaign, the company has integrated megatrends in both its operations and its marketing activities. DHL has also prioritized sustainability, investing in renewable energy to reduce its carbon footprint and establishing a global goal of zero emissions by 2050. In 2021, its parent company, Deutsche Post, announced it would invest €7 billion in green energy initiatives by 2030.

An Age of Changing Dynamics

Wayne Gretzky, the Canadian ice hockey player with the best winning record of all time, was once asked about the secret of his success. "Simple," he replied. "I don't skate to where the puck is, I skate to where it's going to be." As we note in the earlier example, DHL actively looks to capitalize on the opportunities presented by megatrends; it leverages new technologies, trends, strategies, and partnerships. The company's incorporation of megatrends is by no means limited to marketing activities. It has fused the trends to its core business strategies, and, by doing so, it stands to benefit from improved relations with its customers, logistical efficiencies, and increased ability to compete now and into the future.

Companies of all sizes must adapt to the megatrends gradually reshaping our world. These megatrends include major technological and scientific shifts, climate change, the rise of individualism and entrepreneurship, empowerment and equity, the growing importance of megacities, and shifting demographic and consumer trends. All these megatrends significantly affect organizations as they navigate drastic changes while striving to stay competitive.

Managing a complex and ever-changing consumer space in the context of these drastic changes is a major challenge for companies. Traditional segmentation and targeting approaches are no longer enough in the age of digital transformation, as consumer mindsets become more convoluted and subject to manipulation, thanks to multifarious emerging digital platforms and the ease of accessing them. To effectively manage this complexity, marketers must take on the primary role of managing perceptions across this universe of noise, managing their brand, and being aware of changes in consumer sentiment, both short term and long term.

At the same time, consumers have evolved into highly discerning decision-makers. They crave diversity in product offerings, flexibility in purchasing channels, and swift delivery. They need to know if the product they have selected is the one they are looking for, whether it is available, and if so, in what quantity. And if not, what are the alternatives, what are the extra costs (if any), and when can they expect delivery? Not just on what date, but during which timeslot. This phenomenon, initially observed in customized consumer products, has spread across industries.[4] Stepping back, the fact that consumers have become increasingly demanding is directly tied to the rise in technology and individual empowerment, megatrends we will discuss later in this chapter. While some companies can barely keep up with the rapid changes affecting our world, others stay ahead of the curve and even assert an advantage. First-mover advantage in new and complex spaces brings high rewards for some organizations. In contrast, those who fail to adapt may be unable to compete in an ever-shifting global economy.

Take Tesla, for instance. Once a shaky electric vehicle start-up founded by Elon Musk, the company transformed itself and became one of the leaders in the global auto industry. In 2020 alone, the company claimed that its sold vehicles helped avoid 5 million metric tons of carbon dioxide emissions,[5] equivalent to taking 1.1 million cars off the road. The company defines itself as a complete energy and transportation ecosystem driven by the future of renewable energy and self-driving cars. That said, even transforming an industry will not keep a company immune from ever-changing global conditions into the future. As of 2023, investors began viewing the brand as more like a regular car company than one of the world's fastest-growing tech giants since competitors have started taking a share of the electric vehicle market by introducing a range of new models. In response, Tesla started cutting prices across its models sold in the United States, which was also seen as defensive because of a lack of new models. Tesla waited 3 years before launching a new model, *Cybertruck*, a long gap based on the U.S. automotive industry standards.[6]

On the other hand, there are a few corporate blunders as staggering as Kodak's missed opportunity in digital photography, a disruptive technology that, ironically, the company invented in 1975.[7] Or who can forget Blockbuster? At its peak, Blockbuster employed 84,000 people worldwide, with over 9,000 outlets. Yet, the video rental store failed to transition to the digital economy. Jonathan Salem Baskin, the company's former marketing communications leader, explained, "Digital changed Blockbuster's business, for sure; however, it was not its killer; that credit belongs to Blockbuster itself."[8] He meant that the company identified the megatrend, digitalization of on-demand movies and the rise of streaming services but failed to change its business model to cope with the challenge. As these examples show, executives often recognize that their industry is changing, yet they do not implement the significant changes required in their business models to adapt to this new reality. Consequently, they may eventually go out of business altogether due to the disruptive influence of megatrends.

Victoria's Secret Redefines "Sexy"

Inspired by an uncomfortable trip to a department store to buy underwear for his wife, American businessman Roy Raymond ventured to create a place where men would feel comfortable shopping for lingerie; essentially, a women's underwear shop targeting men in 1977.

Forty-five years on, and after many transformations, the former head of international business, now the CEO of the brand, Martin Waters, told the *New York Times* that when the world was changing, they were too slow to respond. The company has struggled with declining sales, market share, and ratings since the mid-2010s, yet it is still an influential brand determining cultural trends in its industry. Nonetheless, the brand has failed to keep pace with a transforming culture, changing demographics, and consumer preferences, hence losing its relevance, especially in the wake of the *#MeToo* movement worldwide. In addition, it faced competition from brands with more body-positive messages, such as Aerie and ThirdLove.

A broad societal desire for the depiction of more realistic and inclusive body images and role models has prevailed. Victoria's Secret *angels* no longer entice from a societal or consumer standpoint in the United States but also fail to do so in foreign territories. The brand must move forward with what women want instead of trying to fulfill a male fantasy. In June 2021, Victoria's Secret launched VS Collective to replace its once-famous angels.

The brand ambassadors are now women from diverse backgrounds, ranging from sports to social activism. They include Megan Rapinoe, the 35-year-old pink-haired soccer star and gender equity campaigner; Eileen Gu, a 17-year-old Chinese American freestyle skier who will promote the brand to the world through various social media channels; and Priyanka Chopra Jonas, a 38-year-old Indian actor and tech investor.

The company overhauled its brand image, website, and marketing message worldwide. In October 2022, it introduced a global campaign named "Undefinable" designed to boost the brand's commitment to championing women's voices and unique perspectives. The global campaign takes inspiration from authentic stories and reflects a dedication to evolution and listening to shifting consumer tastes. It reinforces the idea that beauty is always for the individual to define. Additionally, as the brand continues with its commitment to listening and learning, Victoria's Secret invites all women into the conversation to use their voices to share their stories of what makes them *#Undefinable.*

With nearly 1,400 retail stores worldwide and over 30,000, a predominately female workforce, Victoria's Secret aims to boast the largest team of trained bra-fit experts worldwide to inspire women and advocate for positive change. But will potential consumers consider it authentic for Victoria's Secret to jump on the individual empowerment megatrend? Is it too late? There is still some uncertainty around whether this shift in brand image and marketing strategy will be sufficient to help the world's largest lingerie retailer stage a successful comeback and regain market share.

What Is a Megatrend?

A term coined by John Naisbitt in the 1980s, a megatrend is a large social, economic, political, and technological change that influences individuals, businesses, and societies for an extended period.[9] The defining characteristics of megatrends are threefold. First, megatrends are gradual changes, distinct from short-term changes known as black swan events or game-changers, which are more disruptive and unpredictable.[10] For example, while climate change is classified as a megatrend, the COVID-19 pandemic is often called a black swan event. Second, megatrends are transformative in their global reach, broad scope, and dramatic impact. They compel individuals, enterprises, organizations, societies, and governments to rethink their future and make better-informed decisions about current strategies. Third, megatrends are interconnected; they can either reinforce each other's impact or counteract it. Identifying these interlinkages between megatrends is essential when designing policies, strategies, and interventions to address them; thus, they should not be examined in isolation.

Why should marketers be concerned about megatrends? The answer is clear: Megatrends are incredibly powerful and long-lasting, influencing and reshaping the world's agenda. For example, in today's ever-changing global climate, disparities in income and opportunity have become more pronounced. Emerging markets (EMs) that once drove growth now face struggles, and trade relationships have become increasingly fractured. While the nature of long-term trends may alter, and EMs will recover, the crucial point is that marketers cannot ignore long-term global trends.[11]

Megatrends are driving significant changes to how multinational companies and industries manage their operations and resources, such as shifts in supply chains, new waves of innovation, and shifts in the skillset required from their employees. This has a profound and sustained impact on consumer and business-to-business (B2B) markets and how companies operate and compete at home and abroad.

For instance, in supply chain management, the COVID-19 pandemic and digital technology have had a profound impact, accelerating the impact of megatrends. Consequences include increased use of software-as-a-service products hosted in public clouds, the adoption of robotics process automation to automate high-volume and repeatable tasks such as examining carrier websites for appointment scheduling, and mass personalization and on-demand manufacturing practices to keep less physical inventory on hand.[12]

Blockchain, a financial technology, promises increased transparency in supply chains. However, this could mean major changes in financing and how supply chains are structured. Some intermediaries might even disappear. On the bright side, technology will likely open doors for new and innovative financing solutions.

The emergence of ESG standards is gaining momentum as leading companies find new ways to build their brands and connect with customers in meaningful ways. As a result, businesses will be increasingly held accountable for their actions in terms of social responsibility. Moreover, with the rise of ESG investing and a heightened focus on corporate social responsibility, many companies are proactively evaluating and addressing their environmental and social impact to remain competitive. For instance, they may take steps to reduce their carbon footprint or invest in community projects that benefit society.

Megatrends create opportunities and risks, often simultaneously, regarding how a business interacts with its customers, competitors, and stakeholders. Despite their potential to disrupt "business as usual," relatively few companies fully understand and apply megatrends to their current and future strategy. These disruptions can provide excellent opportunities for change, creativity, and innovation. However, they can also be damaging to some companies. Therefore, businesses need to consider the potential consequences of megatrends before acting on them.

Like human beings, companies naturally tend to resist disruptive change and prefer to maintain the status quo. While many international organizations are aware of emerging megatrends, they may lack the necessary skills or have an inertia that prevents them from adapting and taking advantage of the opportunities these trends present.[13] As a result, they risk falling behind their rivals, who act quicker and gain a competitive edge. If they fail to be first movers in their industry, they must recognize the need for adaptation and proactively make the necessary changes to stay ahead of the ever-evolving landscape. By doing so, they can remain competitive despite lagging the early movers.

How Do We Identify and Act upon a Megatrend?

What should a company do to identify megatrends, and how can it ensure it has the right strategy to address them? Certainly, these are not simple questions; however, identifying megatrends is arguably easier than finding the appropriate strategy to capitalize on the opportunities and mitigate the associated risks. Table 2.1 provides a comprehensive list of tools and resources for companies to identify and understand megatrends. Megatrends can be perceived as long-term events but have implications that can impact everyday operations. For companies, benefiting from megatrends starts with asking thought-provoking and uncomfortable questions to thoroughly understand what a megatrend implies for their business, brands, customers, and society.

It is also essential to examine the interactions between different megatrends. What does each megatrend mean and what do several of them imply for your company? Megatrends present a great deal of risk for many businesses, and improving risk management capabilities remains an arduous task for multinational enterprises (MNEs), which, by definition,

Table 2.1 The 3W-1H of megatrends

Understanding megatrends (who—you[!])	Key tasks for international marketing practitioner (what)	Explain why important (why)	Tools and resources (how)
Stay ahead of trends and navigate through disruption * Identify and understand the different types of megatrends * Conduct environmental scanning * Develop market intelligence and generate insights	Identify the megatrends likely to affect your industry in the next 10 years * Monitor macro events in the global economy and understand implications for your industry and business * Regularly check your competitors'/ adjacent industry landscape. Are others moving in a different direction to capitalize on megatrends? * Capitalize on megatrends with revised business models, marketing, products, services, and processes that increase resilience	Assessing megatrends and their impact on your business is an important and sometimes overlooked task * It can disrupt business practices and require companies to devise new strategies and business models * Since they are pervasive worldwide and can manifest as opportunities or threats, they have important implications for international marketers	Bain and Company Insights * Deloitte Megatrends * Edelman Trust Barometer * globalEDGE Global Insights * Google Trends * McKinsey and Company Insights * The CMO Survey * The Economist World in Figures * The World Bank * The World Economic Forum Global Risks Report

are multicountry, multi-industry organizations subject to many national, regional, and geopolitical influences. Over three decades ago, Bartlett and Ghoshal identified three strategic objectives for MNEs: to be efficient, to be flexible, and to exploit learning worldwide.[14] One can argue that despite the vicissitudes of the current and future times, these primary objectives still apply for multinational companies to build resilience despite global disruptions. Furthermore, a balance between agility and resilience is essential for companies that must rapidly analyze opportunities and make swift decisions to adjust their organization in response to mega-trends. While many build resilience into their strategic plans, they often fail to implement the changes soon enough.

Companies can also seek guidance in new markets from various organizations, such as management consulting companies like Ernst and Young, McKinsey & Company, PricewaterhouseCoopers, and Boston Consulting Group, as well as other international organizations, for example, the World Bank and the World Economic Forum. These organizations regularly review the world's megatrends and publish their findings in reports and white papers, addressing these watershed developments that often offer highly attractive opportunities for managers and businesses. This is one reason why it is essential to stay abreast of the work of management consulting companies, as they often precede academic literature in recognizing major events in the global economy.

For instance, McKinsey Consulting anticipated a fundamental shift from nations or countries to cities and regions being the unit of analysis. It acknowledged the heterogeneity within large economies such as the United States and China. Given this heterogeneity from region to region and from city to city, McKinsey Consulting argued in favor of a more focused approach to cultivating national markets. Hence, it advocated for firms to adopt a city- or region-based marketing approach rather than an entire nation and allocate resources accordingly.[15] First, companies should regularly examine and review the impact of megatrends on their international business. Managerial questions about megatrends would include:

- What are some of the megatrends that are affecting your industry?
- What types of opportunities, headwinds, and actions are associated with each trend?
- Are these trends relevant to countries and regions where your company conducts business?
- How well is your company positioned to deal with these opportunities and threats, and what changes do you foresee that you must make?

What Are the Megatrends That Will Change Our World?

While many in academia, think tanks, media, and consulting groups have attempted to cluster and categorize megatrends, no single approach works best. In this chapter, we will review five of the most influential megatrends that have the most profound impact on business and will continue to do so in the future. These megatrends are not mutually exclusive, and some of them, such as technological disruptions, have far-reaching consequences for nations, industries, and individuals around the globe.

While various sources consider numerous long-term trends, there is a broad consensus among academics, practitioners, and consultants on these five megatrends. This makes them especially pertinent to the purpose of this book. The current and future impact of these fundamental shifts in international marketing practices, and in business in general, should be borne in mind when formulating a strategy.

Table 2.2 summarizes the five megatrends discussed in this chapter: rise in technology, environmental stress, urbanization, economic power shift, and individual empowerment. Below, we provide a brief overview and discuss each one's impact on businesses, including the opportunities, risks, and implications that will follow.

Rise in Technology

The rise in technology, which is driving what many now describe as the Fifth Industrial Revolution, is perhaps the most examined megatrend. Building on the Fourth Industrial Revolution, which relied heavily on data, machine learning, and improvements in communication, the Fifth Industrial Revolution more closely intertwines technology with our daily lives (see Table 2.3). This era is characterized by synergy between human intelligence and machine application. For example, during our writing journey, LLMs began revolutionizing the way we work. Soon, advances in medicine and other aspects of daily life that seem akin to science fiction will likely become a reality. This includes, for example, the transformative potential of brain-to-computer interfaces, such as implantable brain chips, enhancing our capabilities in ways we can only imagine.

Table 2.2 Megatrends: Opportunities, headwinds, and actions

	Opportunities	Headwinds	Actions
Rise in technology	Artificial intelligence Big Data Hyper-connectivity Digital revolution Global workforce	Fine line between what is public and what is private Cyber-attacks, security issues Job losses	Responsible data management practices Embracing new technological opportunities Advocate for consistent regulations
Environmental stress	Less resources More resilient supply chains and operations Lower costs Conscientious and connected capitalism	Unpredictable changes in ecosystems Resource scarcity Accusations of greenwashing	Greater role in strategic operational and investment decisions ESG prioritization Stakeholder capitalism Regeneration
Urbanization	The rise of megacities Increased concentration of customers Decreased length of supply chains Diverse workforce	Environmental stress Complex demographics within cities Traffic congestion	Cater to different market segments Provide products and services that improve life in cities Partner with other businesses on innovative solutions
Economic power shift	Rise in middle classes with greater purchasing power Increase in the number of ultra-wealthy individuals	Rising inequality Regional disparities Disappearance in the social safety net for the bottom of the pyramid	Provide products and services for the new middle class Cater to ultra-net-worth individuals Encourage even economic growth
Individual empowerment	Improved living standards Increasing opportunity to be heard Rise of the platform economy	Increased polarization Complex consumer space Rising expectations Online noise	Address rising expectations from brands Communicate in a personalized, authentic, and transparent way Align the company's core values with consumer expectations

Table 2.3 Evolution of industry and technology over time

Industry	Time period	Key technologies
Industry 1.0	1750–1850	Steam and waterpower Primitive mechanization
Industry 2.0	1850–1930	Electricity Chemical engineering Mass production
Industry 3.0	1930–2000	Binary computers Automated production Electronics
Industry 4.0	2000–2020	Datafication of economy Internet of Things (IoT) Machine learning
Industry 5.0	2020–Present	Human–computer collaboration Human intelligence with AI

The one inarguable aspect of this technology megatrend is the acceleration, distribution, and application of computing power, coupled with the exponential growth of data and machine learning, enabling extraordinary technological advances in the twenty-first century. The unprecedented rate of change we are currently witnessing indicates profound and far-reaching shifts in scientific discovery, production, management, and governance. These changes reshape nature and the speed of progress in ways never experienced before.

The amount of data that are currently being collected is staggering. The Internet of Things (IoT), which emerged as a concept 20 years ago, is now a commonly used phrase. It is defined as the networking capability that allows information to be sent to and received from objects and devices such as fixtures and kitchen appliances using the Internet. Practically speaking, we are talking about a seemingly endless number of devices, gadgets, phones, computers, machines, buildings, and more. By 2025, an estimated 75.44 billion IoT devices will be installed worldwide. All these devices collect data, but as of 2023, 90 percent of these data were untapped.[16] With investment in data engineering and analytics growing, this is likely to change.

Impactful technologies that make sense of all these data provide a myriad of incredible opportunities for businesses. From artificial intelligence and quantum computing to autonomous vehicles, virtual/augmented reality, biotechnology, blockchain technologies, wearable technologies, drones, robots, and beyond, the use of algorithms to predict human behavior, diagnose disease, write articles, trade stocks, and deliver customized learning is rapidly progressing.

Yet, there are significant challenges associated with this megatrend as well. For example, the spread of technology is not equitable worldwide, leading to a digital divide between those without access to technology. This technological revolution has also created a skills gap in many areas, often leading to increased inequality and job displacement for those without the necessary qualifications. Moreover, it has generated several other issues, such as cybersecurity threats, privacy concerns, unauthorized use of proprietary information to train LLMs, polarization of society and politics, and job automation. All these challenges must be addressed to make the most of this technological revolution and ensure its benefits are shared equitably across society.

The necessary call to action for any firm responding to these technological advancements starts with an in-depth understanding of how it influences your business and those in your industry and related industries that your company relies on. This is no simple feat, as it includes, for instance, analyzing marketing agency support, internal and external use of AI to support your business, use of technology for logistics and customer data, and even software-as-a-service support companies. Once this is achieved, the next step should be to create a comprehensive plan outlining the changes needed to effectively manage the effects of technological advancement.

While some industries and companies are bound to become less relevant, others are likely to be born and rise. Right in between these two extremes are the ones that fundamentally need to shift their business models to stay relevant in changing technology, shifting industry standards, and diverging customer expectations. With the evolution of skills required for the new types of jobs, it will be essential to recognize the value humans bring to businesses with their potential for innovation, creativity, inspiration, and other unique qualities. By leveraging these characteristics, companies can develop a competitive edge that will enable them to remain successful in this evolving environment.

How will individuals, corporations, and governments renegotiate their expectations of one another in an era of hyper-connectivity, big tech companies, and rapidly changing economies? The rise of big tech has brought widespread access to vast data resources and enabled global reach, while various digital platforms have become essential infrastructure for our societies. This also gives big tech immense economic and political power. To ensure a sustainable and equitable balance of power in the years to come, it is essential that individuals, corporations, and governments consider a variety of factors when regulating, including but not limited to privacy concerns, freedom to innovate, and taxation. By taking a comprehensive, collaborative approach to regulation, all stakeholders can work together to create a balance that is fair to all.

From a practical perspective, in the short term, multinationals operating across borders must be aware that data rules and regulations will vary between countries and regions. For example, certain marketing practices may be prohibited in the EU due to a failure to comply with data privacy laws. Therefore, multinationals need to review local data regulations before engaging in marketing activities in a foreign market. In the long run, it is in the best interest of multinationals to advocate for harmonized regulations that create a level-playing field between domestic companies and multinationals that must comply with higher standards when required.

Environmental Stress

Even as technology advances, humans and other living beings will always depend on clean water, air, food, and shelter. Climate change is no longer a prediction; it is our current reality. We are witnessing oceans heating, glaciers melting at unprecedented rates, and increased intensity of weather-related events, all of which are having a devastating effect on our planet. Population growth, use of polluting and carbon-based technologies, and wasteful practices have all put immense strain on the natural resources available to us. Multinationals are a major contributor to the production of greenhouse gases and pollution worldwide and must continue to focus on finding a balance between economic and environmental well-being. The environmentalist's paradox is important when looking at how rising consumption and growing waste can be managed without depleting our ecosystems. To improve the general well-being of humans, it is necessary to use more resources while avoiding putting excessive strain on our ecosystems.

Yet, it is no longer possible to continue business as usual as our Earth has passed a climate change threshold with an increasing global biodiversity crisis pushing species into extinction, increasing extreme temperatures, droughts, floods, and pressure on critical life resources like water. For instance, changing climate variability is a key driver of global increase in food insecurity as both climate change and desertification are detrimental to agricultural productivity.[17]

It takes a lot of optimism to extract the opportunities related to climate change and depleting resources. One company poised to profit is Beyond Meat, available in approximately 118,000 retail and food service outlets in over 80 countries worldwide. They have developed faux-meat products to contend with our current appetite for meat and to satisfy picky palates. A peer-reviewed *Life Cycle Analysis* from the *University of Michigan* assessed Beyond Burger's environmental impact compared to a standard quarter pounder. It determined that the Beyond Burger generated 99 percent less impact on water scarcity, 93 percent less impact on land, and 90 percent less greenhouse gas emissions compared to its beef counterpart.[18] Another example of a company making drastic changes is Google, which committed to harnessing only carbon-free energy by 2030. One of its first steps was to examine its energy supply and create carbon heat maps for its individual data centers. In 2019, Google managed to match 100 percent of its global annual electricity consumption with renewable energy. However, hourly, only 61 percent of all the electricity used was matched with regional, carbon-free sources due to variations between sites. For instance, Google's lowest clean energy percentage is in Singapore, where most grid electricity comes from natural gas, while the highest percentage is in Oklahoma, where wind power accounted for 96 percent of the company's data center's energy requirements.[19]

Our economies currently depend on natural resources to maintain economic growth. It is incumbent on businesses and governments to embrace more conscious, connected, and sustainable approaches. This will surely lead to an increased focus on renewable energy sources and ESG to create a more responsible and equitable economic system. Neville Isdell, the former CEO of the Coca-Cola Company, spoke of *connected capitalism* as a way for companies to better engage with their stakeholders wherever they do business. More recently, Paul Polman, the former chief of Unilever, described *conscious capitalism* as a more sustainable form of capitalism.[20] Multinationals, especially those in EMs, see rising pressure to integrate with broader societal aspirations. Achieving more in this area will ultimately require a shift away from traditional business models toward more innovative and disruptive approaches that actively engage all stakeholders in the decision-making process.

For marketers, the world of ESG and sustainability presents various opportunities and risks. On the one hand, they are usually not involved in decisions around production, transport, and sourcing of materials. Instead, they are typically asked to promote positive aspects of a company's efforts such as reducing carbon footprint and water use and adopting solar energy and other sustainable sourcing methods. This can, however, lead to accusations of "greenwashing" if those efforts are overstated or do not truly reflect the environmental impact of the company's actions. To avoid this negative fallout, marketers should be engaged early when company leadership makes strategic operational and investment decisions. This way, companies can reap the benefits both from their actual ESG-related efforts and the positive public relations (PR) associated with them. Innovative marketing campaigns can then authentically communicate these efforts to the public.

Moving beyond the ESG-related sustainability trends, many forward-looking companies look to our natural environment for inspiration. They are beginning to incorporate concepts such as biomimicry, biodiversity, and regeneration into their operations. Biomimicry is the imitation of natural biological designs or processes in engineering or invention. This idea, that the best solutions come from nature, can be both profitable and in-tune with the environment, providing economic and financial incentives.

Biodiversity, the incredible variety of animals, plants, fungi, and microorganisms that make up our natural world, is essential for healthy ecosystems. MNEs in cosmetics, pharmaceuticals, nanotechnology, food, agriculture, and fashion merchandise increasingly engage in biodiversity prospecting. This process scans the environment for bioactive compounds that they can use in their operations. Unfortunately, this practice is ethically dubious because it often disregards the rights of access to land and fails to remunerate indigenous people for the commercialization of genetic and biochemical resources.

Regeneration, on the other hand, is defined as "the renewal or restoration of a body, bodily part, or biological system after injury or as a normal process." In contrast to a circular economy, in which materials, products, and services are kept in circulation for as long as possible, forward-thinking companies are now striving to incorporate regenerative processes that can be a net positive for the environment. While this goal requires significant research, development, and investment, the potential rewards could be enormous for multinationals that get it right.

Urbanization

Urbanization can best be described as the population shift from rural to urban areas, with an increasing share of people in any given country living in urban areas. According to the *World Bank*, 56 percent of the world's population lives in cities. This trend is expected to continue, with the urban population projected to surpass its current size by 2050.[21] This megatrend, closely related to the world's demographic shifts, will be particularly significant in fast-growing African and Asian cities.

High-Speed Train versus Kingfisher

The first high-speed train began operations in Japan in 1964 and is known as the Shinkansen, or bullet train. However, it had a big problem. When the trains zoomed through a tunnel, air would compress around the front before releasing a tremendous booming noise once the train exited the tunnel.

In the 1990s, the chief engineer, using biomimicry, solved the problem. What helped him? Birdwatching. The kingfisher is a small bird with a long beak that dives into the water for its prey. The engineer redesigned the front of the train to be shaped like a kingfisher's head, allowing the train to slice through the wind rather than trapping it inside the tunnels, thereby fixing the booming sound. This radical innovation has diffused to many countries, such as France, China,

Russia, and Korea. High-speed rail is economically viable for a mass transportation system, saves energy by reducing the number of cars on the road, and offers lower greenhouse gas emissions than most transport alternatives. High-speed rail can offer the triple bottom line many policymakers have called for over the years.

Triple Bottom Line (TBL), a term coined by John Elkington in the 1990s, is a sustainability framework that examines a company's social, environmental, and economic impact (i.e., Profit, People, Planet). As these are aligned with the United Nations' 17 Sustainable Development Goals (SDGs) and many governments', institutions', and businesses' sustainability strategies and actions, many international marketing scholars and practitioners now recall the term. Moreover, based on a conservative estimate by the United Nations, SDGs will help generate market opportunities worth over 12 trillion dollars annually by 2030.

As a result, concepts like net positive, social return on investment (ROI), carbon footprint, circular economy, cradle-to-cradle products, and biomimicry have sparked new ideas, strategic thinking, and implementation, sharpening the two other *P's* for MNEs worldwide.

Factors such as increased economic opportunities, improved healthcare and education, and better transport, infrastructure, and communication networks have driven urbanization. Generating more than 80 percent[22] of global GDP overall, cities serve as a primary engine of economic growth and offer many opportunities for MNEs. Cities offer numerous advantages and are generally ideal places for an international marketer to be based. For instance, they boast larger talent pools, diverse sets of consumers who may be willing to try your product, a range of places of entertainment, housing options, infrastructure, financial institutions, support agencies, and a vast professional network. Moreover, they allow MNEs to significantly reduce their supply chain and logistics support, as customers are based in close geographic proximity. Making the most of these advantages can be key to business success.

Yet, as urbanization continues to accelerate, the many challenges associated with this megatrend need to be addressed imminently. These include increased pollution; environmental stresses; demand for new infrastructure to bring power and water and remove waste; increased need for housing and employment; congested infrastructure; and more. It has been estimated that cities are responsible for 75 percent of global carbon dioxide emissions, with transport and buildings being the largest contributors. Therefore, the rise in megacities has the potential to exacerbate global environmental pressures further.

Nevertheless, for MNEs operating in foreign countries, this megatrend is mainly positive. In general, larger cities offer higher wages and attract educated workers, due to their greater productivity and higher levels of innovation. Big cities can also contribute to sustainable development, focusing on innovation, efficient building infrastructure, and a recent emphasis on *smart cities* that lower the cost of services and reduce environmental impact.[23] An opportunity for companies lies in developing products and services that improve the quality of life and reduce environmental stresses. MNEs such as IBM, Microsoft, Siemens, and Cisco have invested heavily in the *smart city* concept, seeking to advance clean energy usage, innovation, mobility, security, and urban planning. However, this is only the beginning. Companies of all sizes are busy creating new and innovative ways to plan, build, and lead better cities that enhance the quality of life of their inhabitants, harnessing a tremendous commercial opportunity. This includes improving healthcare access, developing infrastructure, and introducing cutting-edge technology into cities.

One such example is Amsterdam. The city has implemented green initiatives such as energy-efficient buildings, bicycle-sharing programs, and smart grids to reduce emissions. Montreal is another city that has embraced sensors and artificial intelligence to better serve its citizens. In partnership with Waze, a crowdsourced Google traffic app, Montreal uses over 500 traffic cameras and 700 smart signals to prioritize public transport and reduce commute times. Montreal was the first Canadian city to share this information openly with Google, and the results have been mainly positive.[24]

Building truly green, resilient, and inclusive cities will require intense policy coordination and investment decisions from all stakeholders, including national and local governments, MNEs, civil society, and ordinary citizens. Companies can take advantage of the urbanization trend by participating in discussions and offering products and services that improve the lives of people living in cities. Doing so would significantly impact the future of global cities for the benefit of everyone while allowing companies space to grow their business, a win-win situation. Even when your company's product or service does not appear directly linked to the urbanization trend, partnering with other companies with that connection can present many advantages. For example, you could team up with a new ultrafast urban delivery service to increase the speed of access to your product.

Economic Power Shifts

The shifts in economic power between countries and people are as old as time itself. Historically, inflation, war, or discovering new resources have often triggered economic power shifts. A classic example is that of the Roman Empire, whose focus on diluting the purity of its coins to increase circulation resulted in rampant inflation. This contributed significantly to the decline of the Roman Empire, as it drastically diminished the purchasing power of its middle class, widening the gap between those who had access to wealth-preserving assets, such as land, and those who only possessed coins or currency, rapidly losing value.

In late Renaissance Europe, an influx of silver from the *New World* and an increasing population led to significant inflation across Europe, though its effects varied from country to country. Similarly, during the twentieth century, the world experienced a drastic redistribution of wealth as fortunes were made during the *Roaring Twenties*, only to be lost during the Great Depression of the 1930s. Then it regained following World War II in postwar Western Europe.

The effects of redistribution and wealth creation can have far-reaching implications for MNEs. Economic power shifts can change the global balance of power, create new economic growth and development opportunities, and shape how countries interact. Slow-burning events, such as steady but rapid economic growth or sustained inflation, can trigger shifts in economic power. Other factors that influence these include new trade agreements and alliances, climate change, conflict between nations, global pandemics, birth rates, access to natural resources, and migration patterns.

Currently, three sizeable economic power shifts are underway. First, a significant rise in the middle class, primarily in EMs, is occurring. This trend is happening unevenly from country to country and varies from region to region, yet the overall trend remains upward. Second, an increase in wealth concentration among the top 1 percent of the population has been observed for years and is expected to continue. This has led to a widening in the gap between rich and poor, creating a seemingly spiraling disparity in socioeconomic status worldwide. Third, multipolarity has risen, leading to a divisive, conflicted, and eventually less stable world. This trend has led to fragmented social cohesion within societies, an increased distrust in institutions, and an upsurge of nationalism.

About half of the world's wealth is concentrated in just 1 percent of the population's hands, and this wealth shift to the rich is only expected to accelerate. According to Oxfam, a respected British Charity, during COVID-19, the wealthiest 1 percent captured 26 trillion dollars (63 percent) of all new wealth and 16 trillion dollars (37 percent) went to the rest of the world.[25] Regional disparities are also likely to remain, but the dynamics will change. While developed countries experience aging populations and uneven growth, areas with greater population centers in the developing world will likely see sustained periods of economic growth and increased volatility. Asia, home to around 60 percent of the world's population, is rapidly gaining economic ascendancy, empowered by increased regional trade.

These long-term economic power shifts can positively and negatively impact MNEs. On the one hand, they open opportunities to cater to the tastes of the newly wealthy and growing middle class. On the other hand, they can also lead to instability, unrest, and protectionism that can damage any business. Therefore, marketers need to understand both the short- and long-term economic power shifts to be successful.

Individual Empowerment

One of the most remarkable trends in recent years has been the rise in the power of the individual due to advances in technology, connectivity, and education. Now, more than ever, peer-to-peer business opportunities, digital marketplace, idea-sharing platforms, and influencer tools are available to just about everyone. As of 2023, there are about 7.1 billion mobile phone users worldwide, with projections reaching 7.49 billion by 2025.[26] The immediate repercussions for marketers are readily apparent. With the growth in mobile phone usage comes a shift in how people shop and view content, and, hence, consumers can be targeted using sophisticated tools like geotargeting and mobile ads.

Social media platforms like Instagram, TikTok, and X have revolutionized communication and interaction. Technology companies such as Netflix, Baidu, Flipkart, and Spotify have transformed how people consume goods and content, making life easier and more convenient. Meanwhile, gig economy companies like Airbnb, Didi, and Etsy have opened access to various goods and services. Platforms like Kickstarter, Google Hangouts, and Zoom have led to new avenues for collaboration and connection between people from all walks of life. These technological advances have reshaped our lives.

With increased individual empowerment comes greater expectations. For instance, Millennials and Gen Z have different expectations regarding ownership, mobility, and connectivity. Even in countries where these digitally native generations lack access to necessities like a bank account, electricity, or clean water, they still have access to mobile phones and the information that comes with them. This access has serious implications for marketers who can now actively interact and influence them through tailored experiences and customized products and services.

By now, you will have noticed the connection between the five megatrends. For example, individual empowerment is related to advances in technology and the rise of ESG-related inclusion initiatives that allow individuals from marginalized communities to have a voice and be heard, like never before. Individual empowerment is also linked to economic power shifts. Not all regions or socioeconomic groups have the same level of access to education, technology, and connectivity. Those at the back end of the curve will likely feel disempowered, which could lead to greater disparities. Moreover, as social platforms and media organizations invest in new ways to draw people into their ecosystems and refine their targeting techniques, this could lead to further polarization in politics and a tendency for people to live in virtual bubbles, only exposed to others with similar viewpoints.

This raises an important question for companies: To what extent should they work to decrease the negative effects of technology, including political polarization, in their marketing efforts? Recent *CMO Survey* results[27] indicate that marketing leaders differ significantly in their opinions on the responsibility of marketers to promote unity and inclusion. While some organizations are actively seeking ways to bridge the divide between opposing perspectives, many others reported that they prefer to sit on the sidelines of any debate that may be viewed as political for fear of alienating one side over another. Efforts to promote unity could also backfire if companies are seen as inauthentic or insincere in the eyes of the consumer and as prioritizing profit over genuine unity.

Many consumers remain unconvinced that engaging in social dialogue should be the primary role of a company and prefer to focus on the quality of the product or service itself. Hence, marketers believe unity messages can be perceived as opportunity exploitation to serve a company's primary role, so it is often a better strategy to avoid overt political stances rather than join in. Companies have a long history of marketing efforts promoting unity and comfort after crises that affect everyone, like hurricanes, floods, or terrorist activities. As we mentioned earlier in the chapter, managing a complex and ever-changing consumer space is a major challenge for companies. With increased individual empowerment comes increased complexity and sometimes unwanted noise, requiring more active management and monitoring of brands by marketers. But it also comes with plenty of opportunities. As this newfound empowerment is transforming how people view themselves and their role in society, companies can now interact with their consumers more meaningfully and personally.

Conclusion

In reviewing the megatrends, the most crucial lesson marketers can draw is that none of these trends are happening in isolation. Urbanization trends are related to climate trends, and individual empowerment is strongly connected to technological advances. There are many other links as well. Perhaps the most impactful tool marketers have at their disposal is to capitalize on more than one of these trends regarding how they relate to their product or service. Connecting with your customer on an emotional level means understanding what is going on in their world—which is rarely achieved by focusing on a single factor influencing their lives. All of us live in a complex world influenced by many different trends, and the ability of marketers to speak to what is going on in our daily lives will directly impact the emotional connection they have with their customers. Businesses staying ahead of the curve can reap the benefits in a rapidly evolving landscape. Analyzing megatrends can provide valuable inputs into idea generation, market definition, and sustained innovation. It can also help businesses create a framework for innovating from high-level strategic to low-level tactical decisions.

Bites for Thought

Benetton Group (UCB) was ranked by Greenpeace as one of the Detox Leaders in 2015, thanks to its global commitment to protecting the environment, product safety, and supply chain transparency.[28] The Italian clothing brand renowned worldwide for its vibrant colors, knitwear expertise, and social commitment has not been foreign to approaching sustainability as a strategic objective since long before ESG became a megatrend. However, this is not the only area the company has purposefully created a societal impact.

UCB is perhaps best known for its "United Colors" advertising campaign, launched in the early 1980s. Luciane Benetton, one of four siblings who founded the company, prevailed on the Italian photographer Oliviero Toscani, as creative director, to create the first multiracial advertisement for the brand. As an early leader, UCB has long promoted diversity, inclusion, and belonging as core values.

Fast forward to the 2020s, companies are now asked to provide nonfinancial indicators like ESGs, in addition to financial figures. Many are adjusting their core values, marketing communications, and performance metrics to remain competitive to include environmental, societal, and governance-related factors. As more organizations respond to this megatrend and, hence, competition kicks in, Benetton's

ESG still outperforms its industry peers, signifying that it pays to stay ahead of the curve when it comes to megatrends.

Questions
1. *Identify the top three megatrends for your company and the sector you are in.*
2. *How are these trends affecting, and will continue to affect, the global environment, the business you are in, and your company?*
3. *What does your company do to minimize the risks and pursue the opportunities generated by these megatrends?*
4. *Elaborate on two or three out-of-the-box thinking elements necessary to deal with disruption from a strategic and execution point of view.*

CHAPTER 3

Evaluating Market Opportunities and Entry

Acıbadem Health Group

Founded in 1991, Acıbadem Health Group quickly made its mark in Turkey's private healthcare sector by combining high-quality care with affordability. With a reputation that grew stronger by the day, the company strategically embarked on a path to international expansion, leveraging its domestic success to enter new markets.[1] Their global journey was initially spurred in the late 1990s by unsolicited inquiries from the Turkish diaspora and others with cultural ties to Turkey. Recognizing the growing demand for its services from foreigners, Acıbadem began collaborating with independent intermediaries to facilitate medical tourism to their hospitals, marking the first stages of their international outreach.

As the flow of international patients grew, Acıbadem established a dedicated international department to manage healthcare marketing more effectively. The CEO explained the rationale behind creating the department: "We saw internationalization, first, as a means to enhance our brand visibility, and second, as a way to diversify commercial risk by not putting all of our eggs in one basket for the company's future." After establishing its international department, Acıbadem Health Group expanded its outreach by setting up offices abroad and actively promoting its medical capabilities and services through diverse channels. The company developed a sophisticated hybrid communication and marketing strategy that included three main outlets: (1) independent sales representatives working on a commission basis; (2) owned subsidiaries called *Acıbadem Information Offices*; and (3) *Acıbadem Health Points*, which are clinics designed to serve local communities directly.

Through this strategy, the company rapidly expanded its presence into 30 countries, spanning diverse regions from the Middle East to Europe. In each country, Acıbadem tailored its operations to suit the local context, demonstrating considerable adaptability in establishing the most suitable business models for each target market. Acıbadem also innovated by establishing diagnosis centers in foreign markets. These centers not only offered a lower-risk form of investment but also helped the company gauge market potential and build brand equity. Typically, the new centers would conduct routine medical procedures and refer more complex cases back to Turkey, enhancing patient flow and international visibility.

Taking a bold step further, Acıbadem ventured into direct foreign investment by opening hospitals in Macedonia and Bulgaria and later in Amsterdam.

> Given that healthcare is inherently local, it is necessary to pay a lot of attention to the local dynamics. For that reason, we usually have native partners, like in Macedonia and Bulgaria. Yet, there are exceptions, such as our Amsterdam facility, where we still own 100% of the shares. Currently, we are focused primarily on developing countries. Depending on our success in that space, we will take a further step to expand into the developed markets. (CEO of Acıbadem)

Acıbadem's journey underscores the importance of strategic marketing, meticulous planning, and flexibility for service firms expanding internationally. By diligently assessing market opportunities and tailoring its entry strategies, Acıbadem expanded its international presence and attracted additional partners and investors, fueling further growth (Table 3.1).

Venturing Abroad

Traditionally, firms that sold tangible goods were the first to enter the international market, offering their products to a global audience eager for novel items. However, a significant shift has occurred in the last few

Table 3.1 The 3W-1H of market opportunities and entry

Understanding megatrends (who—you[!])	Key tasks for IM practitioner (what)	Explain why important (why)	Tools and resources (how)
Decide on the foreign market to enter and the most suitable entry mode * Estimate market potential * Assess the tradeoff between different market entry modes * Manage partnership and business negotiations and agreements	Analyze company readiness to internationalize * Assess the suitability of products and services for foreign markets * Screen countries and regions and measure market potential * Analyze the transferability of company experiences, products, services, and learnings to new markets * Assess the costs and benefits of different entry modes * Establish benchmarks for a company's international business objectives	Entering a foreign market involves risk; companies need tools to minimize risks and maximize returns as they expand internationally * Companies need to measure the degree of control versus the degree of risk in various entry modes * Marketers need to understand the advantages and disadvantages of different entry modes from a brand/product perspective	BBC Country Profiles * B-Ready by the World Bank * CAGE Country Comparator by NYU Stern * Compare Countries at TheGlobalEconomy * Corruption Perceptions Index by Transparency International * globalEDGE Market Potential Index (MPI) * Global Market Opportunity Assessment (GMOA) by Harvard Business Publishing * International Business Guides by HSBC * McKinsey Global Institute Global Connectedness Index * OECD Business Insights on Emerging Markets

decades, enabling service firms, such as the medical company Acıbadem described earlier, to actively engage in international markets actively. This transformation was spurred by a new phase of globalization in the 1980s, encouraging even traditional local service providers to seek opportunities beyond their national borders.[2] Advances in technology, digitalization, and the deregulation of service agreements have further fueled the internationalization of large service providers across various industries, including management consulting, advertising, engineering, banking, and medical services.

Today, firms across all sectors continue to actively pursue international expansion, despite facing numerous barriers to trading goods and services. These challenges, often arising from protectionist policies and trade restrictions set by governments or intergovernmental alliances, are fueled by regional conflicts, economic uncertainties, and a shift toward nationalistic agendas. Nonetheless, firms of all sizes persist in overcoming these hurdles to tap into global markets. When they do so, they must consider a variety of factors when assessing potential opportunities. These include local market conditions, socioeconomic/political environment, resources/infrastructure availability, expansion/timing, and a company's long-term growth strategy. Any location chosen should also provide favorable circumstances (e.g., supportive regulatory framework, large and growing consumer base, access to innovative technologies).

Companies venture abroad for a variety of reasons. Most seek a combination of growth, revenue, expansion, business partners, skilled labor, increased efficiency, or reduced cost of operations in new markets. Whatever the reason, acting in a calculated and strategic manner is key to success. This chapter taps into two important activities that help prepare organizations: (a) to enter foreign markets or expand their international presence and (b) to assess foreign market potential and decide on the entry mode.

Here, we depart from the more traditional view of market potential assessment and entry mode decisions in mainstream international business books. Instead, we approach both topics more from the marketer's perspective and discuss global market opportunities, mainly regarding how to build an international brand presence and market products and services abroad.

Expanding internationally usually implies a major strategic shift for an organization, so market potential assessment and entry mode decisions cannot be pursued in a vacuum. Both activities need to be aligned with a company's high-level strategy, which typically provides answers to the following key questions:

- What business are we in/do we want to be in?
- What is our core competence?
- Where do we want to go from here?
- Who do we target?
- With whom do we compete?

The marketer's input into a company's high-level strategy has grown over the years because of the digitalization of business models, the increase in consumer data inflow and competitive value offerings, and the change in consumer targeting strategies. As a higher percentage of CEOs view marketing as a major driver of growth, its contribution to company strategy and internationalization has become paramount.[3] Hence, the marketing team can significantly influence foreign market expansion decisions, timing, and entry modes. With its status in the C-suite secure and new technology enabling ever-better marketing campaigns, the influence of the marketing team will continue to grow. In this chapter, we will explore the various factors that marketing managers should consider before the internationalization process, including:

- How ready is the firm to expand internationally?
- How can a firm identify the most promising international markets for its products or services?
- When establishing a local presence in a foreign market, what factors should be considered in selecting the optimal entry mode (e.g., joint ventures, franchising, exporting, wholly owned subsidiaries) and how can a firm minimize the risks associated with each entry mode?
- What is the role of segmentation, targeting, and positioning in assessing global market potential?

Global market opportunities offer the prospect of building brand equity and enhancing a company's performance far beyond what it can achieve in its home market. At the same time, the international expansion and the presence of an enterprise or a brand in a foreign market can affect the company's reputation, perceived quality, and image in the home market. Hence, the complexity of business operations and the stakeholders/constituencies your company attends to increases with each expansion into a foreign market. Any manager desiring to enter a new market is confronted with numerous questions. These include, among others, how to estimate the market size for a product or service in a foreign country, select the right partner, and assess the risk–return–control scenario for your international operations.

Conducting a market potential assessment prior to a company's international expansion refers to examining the favorable combination of circumstances, locations, and timing that market offers for various entry modes such as exporting, investing, sourcing, and partnering in foreign markets.[4] This in-depth exercise provides companies with an essential component of their international marketing strategy.

Motivations for Expanding Operations to Foreign Markets

Motivations for international expansion often stem from a mix of active and passive factors influenced by strategic objectives and external conditions. Understanding these motivations and aligning them with company goals is essential for effective market entry and long-term success.[5] Active motivations are usually the ones driven by the firm's strategic orientation, while passive motivations result from a firm's response to its environment or competitor's actions. Marketing strategy plays a greater role in active motivations; and yet, its role in passive motivations—especially in terms of targeting physically proximate consumer locations and responding to competitor strategies—cannot be underestimated.

The active motivations to enter a foreign market include the following: (i) to provide products with unique value to global markets, (ii) to grow the business, and (iii) to increase profitability. From a marketing perspective, identifying unmet needs (i.e., white spaces) in global markets and targeting the right customer segments at the right time can provide a competitive edge. However, success is not guaranteed, as consumer perceptions, competitive dynamics, and rapid technological changes can challenge market positioning. For instance, when Volkswagen first entered India in the early 2000s, they positioned their VW brand as a more premium car than Honda and Toyota. They attempted this by leveraging German engineering excellence through local market insights.[6] However, this backfired as one of their other brands, Skoda, was seen as a higher-end label than VW by Indian car buyers due to its history in India.

When the Skoda brand was first launched in 2001, it led with the Octavia model, a premium car that immediately became the car of CEOs and senior executives. Its subsequent models, such as Laura and Superb, were even more premium and had diesel engines, which were considerably more expensive than their Japanese petrol-engine counterparts. As a result, Skoda established a reputation as a premium car that was not easy to shake off despite VW's best efforts to position its own brand as superior. This case reinforces the argument that consumer perception of quality is more difficult to change than the actual quality of a product.

Passive motivations to enter a foreign market are: (1) to respond to competitive pressures, (2) to create growth opportunities for mature products in the domestic market, and (3) to get closer to target consumer markets. In these cases, analyzing competitors' strategies and adapting accordingly is critical. Companies must also assess readiness to avoid premature market entry, which can lead to poor outcomes. Foreign markets can provide new opportunities for declining domestic products, allowing firms to prolong their lifecycle or innovate for established markets while expanding internationally. This type of internationalization strategy is usually less aggressive than those driven by active motivations. Many companies that employ this strategy prioritize maintaining market share over growing the entire product or service category.

Cultural, geographic, and economic proximity can also influence passive motivations. Neighboring countries with shared heritage or systems (e.g., Canada and the United States) may offer easier entry points. Tools like the CAGE framework (Cultural, Administrative, Geographic, and Economic Distance) can help managers assess market similarities and make informed decisions about expansion strategies. By clearly identifying their motivations, companies can align their internationalization strategies with their overall objectives, enhancing their chances of success in foreign markets.

Airbnb Wants You to "Live" in (and Not Just "Go" to) the 200+ Countries It Operates

Airbnb is perhaps one of the truly born-global startups among Silicon Valley's mega unicorns. The company currently operates in about 6 million active listings in 100,000 cities in 220 countries and manages its website in numerous languages, all while aiming to provide authentic local travel experiences for guests. The 3Hs—homes, hoods, and hosts—have defined the core Airbnb experience since 2008. Airbnb prides itself on being a "glocal" company (global, yet local). While its value proposition is simple—*rent your home for a short time, we take a small cut, and everyone wins*—there are many challenges to market entry in the short-term rental facing the market leader. Local occupancy regulations, travel restrictions, language barriers, fee transparency, safety, and hygiene are just to name a few of them.

There are four key factors to consider when thinking through internationalization; why, when, where, and what do you need to adjust in terms of product offering and business model to achieve global scale. Perhaps, the most crucial is why you should go international, and the rest will follow. For some business models like Airbnb, which targets marketplaces, international growth is more of a must-have than a nice-to-have. It allows for raising supply and demand to a far greater scale. For others, it is often presented as an opportunity—rather than a requirement—to sustain top-line growth through pursuing new markets and fending off competition early on.

When Airbnb enters new markets, it is agile and quick to communicate with local authorities and communities. In its interactions with city officials, providing useful information is integral to its strategy. In London, for instance, Airbnb provides the mayor's office with information about the growth of tourism in the city's outer boroughs to help it spread the economic benefits of tourism across the city. Airbnb's main argument in defending its position as complementary rather than in opposition to hotels is that its average host provides this service in their home or only when they are away.

Airbnb portrays an image of global citizens who "Don't Go There. Live There." Yet, the central issue to their long-term global growth and foreign market entry remains: How can a company build a global brand while simultaneously remaining a locally relevant one that inspires people worldwide to change their travel habits?

Global Market Potential Assessment

No matter what motivates a company's decision to expand abroad, the goal is always the same: to capitalize on a beneficial combination of factors, locations, and timing to improve performance beyond what they can achieve domestically. Whether through exporting, investing, sourcing, or partnering in foreign markets, companies can reap great rewards by taking advantage of the opportunities available in international markets.

Opportunities present themselves in many forms. You could sell your products or services, expand your digital business platform into a foreign market, establish production facilities to manufacture products more cost-effectively and efficiently, outsource raw materials and other services, or enter into strategic alliances with foreign partners.[7]

Technological advances have made it easier and more cost-effective for companies to go abroad. Digitalization, technological innovations in business models (such as sharing economy, app-based business models, subscription services, and user/contributor platforms), and advances in information technology can provide competitive advantages to firms by connecting geographically distant locations with comparatively low costs and high performance. Cloud-based services further improve data collection, storage, and management, while new communication technologies facilitate interaction among partners in pursuit of global market opportunities.

The ever-increasing ability to share information through digital platforms has opened unprecedented opportunities for large and small companies to connect with each other and their target consumers. Even the smallest businesses can reach a global audience by creating a virtual presence. Therefore, every firm should consider global market opportunity assessment in light of these new technological advances.[8]

In later chapters, we will revisit some of the technological tools that firms now have. This section focuses on global market potential assessment from an international marketing perspective by explaining its various components. We discuss six key tasks managers can perform to assess global market opportunities and how marketing can contribute to these tasks. These provide a comprehensive yet flexible approach for companies entering foreign markets or expanding internationally. Whether companies choose to follow all the steps and in what order will depend entirely on the individual circumstances of the firm. For a summary of these tasks, activities, resources, and tools available to marketers, please refer to Table 3.2.

Table 3.2 A systematic process of global market potential assessment

Task	Activities	Tools	Role of marketing
1. *Assess your firm's readiness to pursue international expansion*	Conduct a SWOT analysis and evaluate resources, skills, competencies, and organizational commitment for international expansion	PESTLE framework, internal market analysis, and SWOT analysis	Input into company expansion strategy and readiness
2. *Evaluate the suitability of the firm's offerings for foreign markets*	Perform STP analysis to identify key factors for international customers, assess competitors, and adapt products to preferences, regulations, and distribution channels	Market segmentation, focus groups, interviews, adaptation to laws and regulations, legal analysis, and trade channel analysis	Provide insights into customer preferences, market trends, and competitor positioning
3. *Screen countries and identify the best ones to target with the chosen company offerings*	Identify five high-potential markets based on size, growth, purchasing power, openness, ease of business, and risk	GDP per capita, domestic consumption, demographic data, purchasing power, economic forecasts, and ease of doing business	Provide input into what trends are driving growth across possible target countries

Task	Activities	Tools	Role of marketing
4. *Estimate the market demand in selected target markets*	Forecast short- and long-term industry sales for each target country, considering market size, growth, competition, lifecycle stage, and entry barriers	The host country's rules, regulations, entry barriers Market potential indicators Economic forecasts (inflation, growth)	Assess similarities and differences between trends in the specific industry in the host versus the home country
5. *Identify foreign business partners where necessary*	Identify value-added activities needed and the top five traits of potential partners. Evaluate and select partners based on industry expertise, international experience, and capabilities in manufacturing, marketing, R&D, or distribution	Organizational readiness to collaborate, risk analysis of the partners in the channels, cultural and organization fit, and identifying the desirable attributes in partners according to the value-added activities	Determine the value-added marketing-related activities and specific marketing goals, such as the firm's market penetration timeframe
6. *Estimate the company's sales potential in each target market*	Develop conservative and liberal scenarios for product acceptance in the foreign market, evaluating pricing, investment, risks, distribution access, and competitive intensity	Assess perceived benefits of the firm's offerings, competitive positioning, costs of products landed in foreign markets, and custom margins	Size and profile of target customer segments Assessment of the relative strength of the products and brands Pricing strategy

Source: Adapted from Cavusgil, Knight, Riesenberger, and Yaprak. 2009. *Conducting Market Research for International Business.*[9]

Step 1: Analyze and assess your firm's readiness to pursue international expansion

As previously mentioned, when assessing your firm's readiness to internationalize, you need to examine organizational motivation, resources, and necessary skills; in other words, it is the organizational readiness to engage in international expansion.

Organizational readiness is a dynamic concept, and the process to evaluate it is ongoing and ever-changing. You need to continuously check and confirm your company's ability to perform in ways that maximize outcomes in foreign markets. There are diagnostic tools that can help guide this process. At a minimum, it is important to answer these questions during the assessment stage:

- What is it that we hope to gain?
- Is international expansion consistent with the other high-level strategic and marketing objectives of the company?
- What types of additional demands will international expansion place on the firm's resources and capabilities?
- What is the core competence and the competitive advantage/source of differentiation for your firm in international expansion?

Step 2: Evaluate and assess the suitability of your firm products and services—for foreign markets

Once you have confirmed your firm's readiness for international expansion, you need to determine which brands, products, or services are the most suitable for international expansion. This task is probably intimately connected to the company's marketing strategy, and it will depend on the success of your products and services at home and their potential to be well received abroad.

In the next section, we delve deeper into this topic when we discuss the segmentation–targeting–positioning (STP) framework. Most companies offer a portfolio of brands, products, and services, but not all may be suitable for foreign markets. As with determining a firm's readiness, some key questions can help determine the suitability of your offerings for these foreign markets:

- Why do people buy your products and/or services?
- What are the key benefits sought?
- What factors can enhance and/or limit sales in the target market?
- Are the products already standardized?
- Where do people purchase the product or service?

- What stage of the product lifecycle is the product or service at?
- Are the products competitively priced?
- Will the product comply with local regulations?

Step 3: Screen countries and identify the best ones to target with the chosen company offerings

Once you have selected suitable products and services, the next task is to screen countries to identify which target markets have the most potential. This can be both the most time-consuming of tasks and potentially the most impactful, as market potential assessment involves resource allocation and opportunity costs.[10]

Several databases and frameworks can help companies with this mission in the international business and marketing literature and practice. In addition to the CAGE model mentioned earlier, there are an abundance of secondary data sources that index countries based on various metrics/indices such as Ease of Doing Business, Corruption Index, Political Stability, and Global Connectedness. During this assessment, managers should consider the following questions:

- What are some of the methods that help screen, rank, and eliminate the target countries (e.g., size of the market, distance to home market, GDP)?
- What are some of the key factors that can enhance or limit country attractiveness for foreign direct investment (e.g., growth rate, degree of economic development, demographic characteristics)?
- What factors would most help or hinder your firm's ability to sell goods and services, find the right partners, and be a cultural fit (e.g., level of competition, degree of government intervention, market sophistication).

Step 4: Estimate the market demand in selected target markets

Once the number of countries is reduced to a manageable number, then your company is ready to conduct a more in-depth examination of the specific industry and focus on industry-level indicators. Typically, most firms forecast industry and company sales potential in both the short- and long-term timeframes through quantitative methods such as market size analysis, competitive landscape analysis, pricing trends analysis, and customer segmentation analysis. Additionally, qualitative research such as interviews with customers, competitors, and industry experts can help you gain insights into the dynamics of a sector. During this examination, here are some critical questions that managers can ask:

- What is the size and growth rate of the industry?
- What are the consumer trends in this industry? How frequently do they change?
- What are some industry-specific market potential indicators?
- What is the level of competitive intensity in the industry?
- What pricing/marketing strategies are being used by your competitors?

Step 5: Identify foreign business partners where necessary

Once the company has selected a target market, the realization sets in that usually some kind of partnership with a local player is warranted. This could take many forms. For instance, local partners could include suppliers, wholesalers, joint venture partners, franchisees, and even distribution-channel intermediaries. Initially, the company should pinpoint the types of partners essential to its foreign market venture, engage in negotiations to establish terms with them, and subsequently provide ongoing support while monitoring their conduct. Partners are not always necessary, but, when they are, they become vital to your international expansion success.

The process of screening and evaluating business partners can be complex and overwhelming, and different criteria should be taken into consideration, including tradeoffs and synergies, independently and conjointly. Moreover, sought-after characteristics may not be present in potential partners, making it necessary to craft a strategy for handling an imperfect partner. The type of foreign market entry mode chosen also influences the nature and selection of partnerships. Here are some questions to consider when choosing your partner for a foreign venture:

- Can you rank all your selection criteria for potential partners in order of importance (e.g., traits essential for the success of the venture)?
- What are some of the legal frameworks and guidelines that need to be established with foreign partners?
- How can you ensure that potential partners have "skin in the game" and will be committed to the success of the partnership?
- What types of assets, both intangible (e.g., relationships, brands, goodwill) and tangible (e.g., technology, plant, equipment, personnel), do the potential partners bring to the table?
- How can you develop a culture of trust, transparency, and collaboration with potential partners?
- How can companies navigate through an unsuccessful partnership and develop an exit strategy?

Step 6: Estimate the company's sales potential in each target market

The last, but certainly not the least, step in market potential assessment is estimating the company's sales potential. This is an estimated share of the industry sales the firm expects to generate in a particular foreign market. Figure 3.1 provides a framework that illustrates the key factors for estimating the sales potential of a company in a foreign market. The key factors include: (i) customers, (ii) competitors, (iii) cost and pricing of offerings, and (iv) utilization of the right channels for the promotion of products and services. A more in-depth discussion of customers and competitors is provided in the next section, which covers the role of segmentation, targeting, and positioning in assessing the global market potential of a company.

Estimating sales potential can be challenging and depends on the availability of information and assumptions on which sales projections

```
                    ┌─────────────┐
                    │  Customer   │
                    │ Profiling and│
                    │  Targeting  │
                    └─────────────┘
                           │
┌──────────────┐   ┌─────────────┐   ┌──────────────┐
│              │   │  Revenue    │   │              │
│ Sales Channels│──│  Potential  │──│ Competitive  │
│ and          │   │     in      │   │ Positioning of│
│ Communications│  │  Foreign    │   │ Brands and   │
│              │   │  Markets    │   │ Products     │
└──────────────┘   └─────────────┘   └──────────────┘
                           │
                    ┌─────────────┐
                    │    Cost     │
                    │ Structures  │
                    │ and Pricing │
                    │  Strategy   │
                    └─────────────┘
```

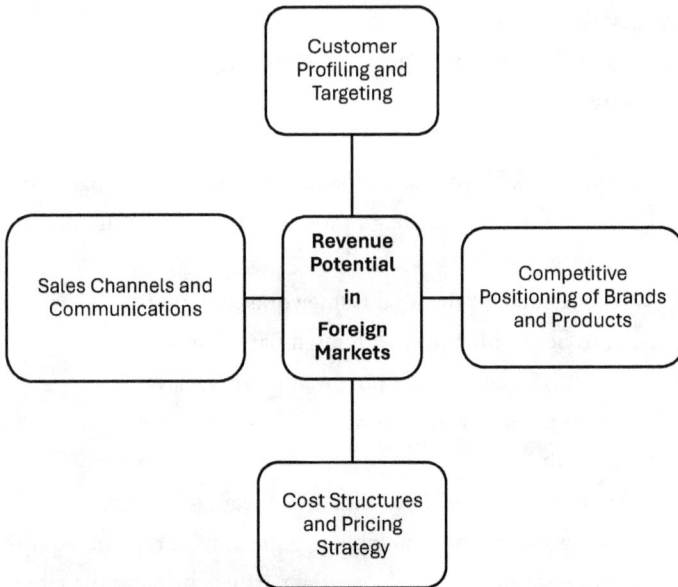

Figure 3.1 *The factors of company sales potential estimate in a foreign market*

are based. However, with the increased level of data now available about consumers, suppliers, and competitors, as well as advanced statistical models, managers have the ability to make reasonable estimates around best-case, worst-case, and what-if scenarios. To ensure a sound and un-biased estimate is available to guide a company's international expansion efforts and investments, it is important to employ several approaches in conducting such an assessment. Some questions to consider in estimating sales potential are as follows:

- What is the company's sales potential in the target market as compared to other markets?
- What are some of the assumptions you used to determine the sales potential?
- What are the tools you utilize to determine sales potential?
- What is your timeline to achieve the estimated sales?
- What are you willing to accept as a worst-case scenario?
- What type of marketing strategy and investment would you need to achieve the sales potential in a local market?

The Role of Segmentation, Targeting, and Positioning in Assessing Global Market Potential

The Segmentation–Targeting–Positioning (STP) framework is one of the most popular tools in any marketer's toolkit. It is centered around the customer and focuses on identifying and targeting the right consumer with the right product at the right time. Whether in domestic or international markets, STP can help marketers identify attractive target market segments and the ideal consumers within those markets. STP is composed of three relatively straightforward components: market segmentation, targeting, and positioning. Market segmentation involves dividing the market into smaller groups based on the extent to which their needs are similar or different, such as country or consumer group. Targeting builds on the results of segmentation and helps companies evaluate the attractiveness of each segment, allowing them to choose one or more targets. Finally, positioning attempts to create a competitive positioning map in the minds of the target segments of consumers, so that they associate certain products and brands with specific benefits.[11] The STP framework can help a marketing manager pursue a more informed customer strategy in home markets and sensibly position products/services in foreign markets. In this section, we will discuss how STP can help a company's international expansion efforts.

Segmentation

Segmentation is the art and science of identifying smaller groups of individual consumers, businesses, or countries with similar needs and wants to a company's offerings. It is scientific, as various statistical analyses (e.g., cluster analysis) use data to provide the optimal number of segments, and it is also an art form as it requires managerial interpretation, experience, and insights to interpret the results and determine the correct number of segments with unique characteristics.

When creating viable segments, certain characteristics should be taken into consideration: measurability, accessibility, substantiality, differentiability, actionability, and stability. In practice, segmented data from the population are needed to identify subgroups and pursue a segmentation strategy. This data can range from consumer-level (e.g., demographics, behavioral traits) to business-level (e.g., product benefits), and even country-level (e.g., geographic) data.

In international marketing, the first step in segmentation is often segmenting and selecting individual countries or clusters of countries. Geographic segmentation is easier, yet also more limited compared to individual- or business-level segmentation. This is because the statistics needed for country-level segmentation are obtained on a country-by-country basis and, usually, countries that belong to the same segment are physically closer to each other.

Geographic segmentation allows companies to transfer their learnings and experience from one country to another that belongs to the same cluster, assuming that the country will respond similarly to the company's offerings. That said, a marketing manager needs to be cognizant that differences within countries and differences between neighboring countries can still be highly significant. Furthermore, some countries have varying levels of economic development and stability. Hence, country-level segmentation might produce more stable results for those countries that are more developed. Countries categorized as emerging or developing markets are typically more unstable and vulnerable to global changes.

The next step is understanding international consumer segments. The most popular means of segmenting international consumers are through demographics, psychographics, behaviors, and benefits. Geographic-, demographic-, or psychographic-based segmentation is descriptive in the sense that these criteria prioritize certain characteristics of the consumers for segmentation.

On the other hand, behavior- and benefit-based segmentation goes one step further by examining how consumers behave in response to certain offerings and then segment them based on such criteria to better predict consumer behavior in similar contexts and offerings in the future. This allows marketers to gain a deeper understanding of their target audiences and create more effective strategies for reaching them.

By leveraging digital and social media platforms, segmentation can now be more easily applied as a powerful predictive tool rather than just a descriptive one. Using digital analytics, companies can segment e-commerce consumers at a global level based on their activity, referrals, time spent, purchase amount, etc. on a website or social media platform.

This type of online consumer behavior is especially important for those businesses that rely solely on digital platforms or use an omnichannel strategy. New AI tools or web analytics services can help companies better understand digital consumer behavior and gain insights into different segments of consumers, based on demographics, interests, geography, mobile device usage, and other behavioral patterns.

Another trend in market segmentation is the consideration of megatrends, which we discussed in the previous chapter. Especially in the areas of technology and environment consciousness, it is now easier to identify *global segments*. Indeed, thanks to advances in technology and digital platforms that have made the world more connected than ever before, many industries have seen a decrease in the need for complex market segmentation.

A global market segment consists of customers that share common characteristics across multiple national markets, such as people using smartphones, smart home assistants, electric cars, and sustainable and green products.[12] Companies offering benefits that are tailored to the needs and wants of these global market segments can target them with standardized marketing programs, even across borders. To ensure effectiveness, marketers should create a unique and consistent value message for their offerings in the minds of consumers. Finally, another important, yet often overlooked, area of segmentation is business-to-business (B2B) segmentation. There are a variety of bases that can be used to segment B2B markets, such as geographic location, demographics, and customer behavior. Additionally, industry-specific variables like firm size, product usage, and customer ratings can also be used to identify key segments of potential and existing clients.

In summary, while the internationalization of trends and the use of advanced digital tools have made segmentation easier, it remains a critical tool for screening countries, markets, and consumers. By grouping countries, markets, or consumers into more manageable sizes, companies can systematically and effectively assess the potential of each group.

Targeting

Once you identify the relevant potential segments, the next step is to decide which ones to target. Depending on the segmentation approach (from macro, country-level segmentation, to global segments, to more micro, consumer-level, and firm-level segmentation), targeting may involve selecting one or two niche or micro segments (niche marketing), a few differentiated segments (differentiated marketing), or an entire market (mass or undifferentiated marketing). With careful consideration of their resources and goals, companies can then make an informed decision as to which segment they will target. The more you choose to focus on niche marketing or smaller segmentation, or even the outlier scenario of a segment of one, the more costs you will likely incur. Quite simply, the cost of capturing the unique requirements of individuals to provide highly customized offerings is high.

To better address individual needs and tailor products according to individual needs, companies are increasingly pursuing open innovation efforts in which customers or potential users of a product play an integral part in the development process. By tapping into the collective knowledge and experience of outsiders, companies can gain valuable insights into their target market's needs and preferences, enabling them to create more effective and tailored products and marketing campaigns.

Crowdsourcing platforms, conducted both internationally and in local markets, provide an invaluable resource for open innovation efforts. Through competitive processes, users can submit their ideas and products can be evaluated by other users (e.g., Starbucks, Threadless) or by company professionals (e.g., LEGO). This can lead to the production and implementation of user-generated ideas and products on a global scale. In assessing the attractiveness of foreign market segments, marketing research has identified various criteria, which are not necessarily very different from the criteria used for choosing segments in a home market.

Usually, the criteria are grouped into three categories as follows: size and growth, structural characteristics, and product–market fit. These are normally analyzed on a single-country basis, as the attractiveness of various segments is unlikely to be the same across various target countries. For example, a segment that is large and growing in one country may be small or shrinking in another.

The size of a segment and its growth potential should be assessed by considering factors such as the population size, spending power of households, growth rates, and prospects of the country in which the product offering is being considered. Furthermore, the presence of other similar products or services, and their respective market shares, should also be considered. The structural characteristics category looks at factors such as concentration of competitors, ease of access, government regulations, barriers to entry, and environmental risk. These factors can affect the competitiveness of the market and, thus, influence a company's ability to gain market share.

Finally, the Product–Market Fit criterion assesses the degree to which a company's products or services match the needs and wants of the population—in other words, the suitability of the company's offerings to the market. Marketers should consider aspects such as product benefits, pricing, competitive positioning, and the relationships across product segments (synergy, cannibalization) when assessing the product–market fit.

Positioning

One of the primary goals of marketing is to identify and meet consumer demand. There is an old saying that good marketing makes the company look good, but great marketing makes the consumer feel good. To this end, positioning strategies are incredibly powerful tools to create meaningful connections with current and potential customers. By positioning products and services to address physical or emotional demand, companies can successfully create perceptions in the minds of consumers about their product (e.g., Volvo is the safest car, as well as in relation to its competitors). Positioning strategies effectively create a mental map in consumer minds about certain products and their characteristics within a competitive landscape—making it imperative for marketers to understand how they can use such strategies to drive sales.

Positioning a product, service, or brand name on an international scale is an incredibly complex task. Companies must take into consideration not only the cultural differences and preferences but also the competitive landscape in different countries. For instance, the soft drink market and players vary significantly between the United States and the Middle East, meaning Coca-Cola may need to develop different positioning statements tailored to each country.

Companies often use price-versus-attribute positioning statements (such as quality, convenience, and exclusivity) to effectively reach their target markets. However, doing so consistently across borders is a difficult task, as the most relevant product attributes for one market may not apply in a foreign market. For example, the amount of pulp in orange juice, or the amount of protein in a cup of yogurt, may differ depending on the desired consumer preferences.

At a global level, one of the most important tools a company possesses to drive its consistent reputation and image is its positioning statements. As the firm's stakeholders expand overseas (e.g., consumers, investors, competitors), the firm's responsibility in addressing the differing needs of the enlarged group of stakeholders also increases. Building a global image while maintaining or improving its image at home can present additional layers of complexity. To develop successful positioning statements, firms need to pay attention to their communication strategy and deliver their core values consistently. However, they must also show flexibility and be able to adjust their positioning statements to accommodate the unique characteristics of individual markets.

It is no exaggeration to say that building your company's reputation and brand image both at home and overseas can be extremely challenging. Country-of-origin (COO) effects, consumer ethnocentrism, religious practices, and rules and regulations, all contribute to the difficulty of establishing a successful presence in foreign markets. For instance, some companies may struggle to enter or remain in a market despite having a high-quality product to sell if their core values do not align with consumers or the government in the new market. On the other hand, consumers may be willing to pay more or buy more based on certain COO or made-in labels (e.g., German car brands, Italian clothing brands, or Japanese consumer technology brands).

Finally, consumer ethnocentrism is also a challenge that must be addressed when considering positioning statements for your product, service, or company brand in international markets. Consumers with high levels of ethnocentrism are likely to prefer local market labels over foreign ones, perhaps due to a belief that manufacturing standards are superior in their country than others. Nationalism or animosity toward foreigners can further fuel ethnocentrism, making it more difficult for foreign brands to succeed. However, if marketers are able to navigate these complex dynamics, they can create successful positioning strategies that can contribute to the success of the foreign venture.

Pioneering Digital Segmentation and Positioning in Emerging Markets

In 2014, one of the largest pharmaceutical companies in the world embarked on an initiative to enhance its digital engagement on a global scale. However, the uptake of this initiative was uneven across different regions, particularly in emerging markets (EM), where digital adaptation started slowly. It was not until late 2015 that a significant change occurred with the appointment of a new head for EM Commercial Digital Operations.

The new hire faced a challenging landscape. At the time, the concept of digital engagement was not readily accepted by the traditional general managers (GMs) within the company. They were resistant, uniformly arguing that customers preferred traditional face-to-face interactions with medical representatives over interaction across digital channels.

The makeup of EMs, from Latin America to Asia, represented another challenge. The company's total reach was limited to its 10,000 medical representatives across this vast and complex geographic and cultural terrain. Realistically, these representatives could engage with only 20 percent of the total physician population capable of prescribing the company's extensive and diverse product range. Simply increasing the number of representatives by fivefold was deemed unrealistic.

To address these challenges, the new Head of Digital posed two compelling questions to the 30 or so general managers:

What if I told you that your customers are already digital, and that digital segmentation could increase your customer coverage to 60 percent? What happens to your top line if we can convey our product message to an additional 40 percent of active physicians?

This approach led to the implementation of a behavioral segmentation strategy across all EM countries, utilizing just eight questions derived from European publications. These questions were designed to identify attitudes, beliefs, and behaviors, revealing that a significant portion of customers were either digitally savvy or active on digital channels. By 2016, it was clear that only about 20 percent of the EM remained conventionally nondigital.

The strategy focused on efficiency and increasing "the share of voice" (SOV). In the pharmaceutical industry, conventional potential segmentation (A, B, C, and D) is typically used to identify target physicians for visits. Visit frequency, another key parameter, is adjusted based on the potential of these physicians. By identifying digitally savvy customers through behavioral segmentation, the company was able to reduce the frequency of face-to-face visits, supplementing these in-person visits with digital SOV campaigns for products in mature stages of their lifecycle. This not only saved time for medical representatives but also allowed them to allocate more time to new customers.

The strategy further evolved to focus on the quality of engagement. The introduction of brand-engagement-level segmentation (aware, not aware, knows, advocate) allowed for the customization of brand messages for each segment. This led to a 3D segmentation approach, combining brand, message, channel, and customer potential.

In summary, the conventional segmentation identified target customers, brand engagement segmentation customized the message (what to say), and behavioral segmentation dictated the delivery method (how to say it). As a result, the multinational pharmaceutical company achieved over a 150 percent increase in customer coverage in EMs, enhancing both "Share of Voice" and "Share of Quality" in customer engagement through effective 3D segmentation.

Entry Mode Decisions

Now that you have undertaken the analysis of which country to target, alongside which segment of the population, and the company, brand, and product positioning, it is time to tackle how you will enter the market. Following the global market opportunity assessment, one of the most critical decisions that management makes in international expansion is the foreign market entry strategy.

Typically, there are three types of foreign market entries: (i) export or import of products or services, (ii) contractual relationships such as franchising and licensing agreements, and (iii) equity-based international business activities such as joint ventures or wholly owned subsidiaries. For each type of entry option, there are both advantages and disadvantages that need to be evaluated when deciding on which entry strategy is best suited to your organization.[13]

In the nonequity market entry modes, there are different options, such as exporting, importing, and global sourcing as well as contractual relationships. For many companies new to conducting business abroad, these nonequity modes are the go-to choice, due to their relative cost-efficiency and lower risk compared to equity investments. The main reasons behind choosing these nonequity entry modes, including contractual relationships such as licensing, franchising, and co-marketing, are usually speed and cost-efficiency, as it enables companies to quickly expand their presence in a new market without having to invest large amounts of capital or resources.

The equity-based foreign market entry is more time-consuming and difficult to execute. However, while it entails higher risk and increased investment, it also provides a higher level of control and involvement. In joint ventures, for instance, firms can hold a minority, majority, or equal partnership status along with the foreign partner(s), which can offer advantages such as ease of access to local markets, knowledge about those markets, domestic culture, and laws and regulations through a local partner. As mentioned, the equity option also carries significant risks, including potential conflicts between partners, changing local market conditions, shifting objectives, cultural differences, and costly dissolution of a possible failed venture. These are all considerations that must be considered.

In entry modes such as wholly owned subsidiaries (WOS), where the company can fully acquire a local firm or establish a new greenfield investment, the resource requirements are highest. Consequently, in the typical internationalization stage models, WOSs are not typically the first stage of entry into a foreign market. Instead, firms initially explore more cost-effective alternatives.

Each foreign market entry mode has its advantages and disadvantages and will result in varying levels of risk, reward, control, and investment. It is important to note that these four components of a foreign market entry mode are intertwined. For instance, a firm's ability to influence the decisions, operations, and resources involved with the foreign venture is directly related to the level of control it holds over the venture.

As the local firm/partner delegates substantial responsibility for decision-making to its foreign partner, this also implies low resource commitment and low level of risk. As mentioned, this is typically the case in entry modes such as exporting, importing, or global sourcing, which provide quick access to foreign markets. On the other hand, a foreign market entry mode such as direct investment in a plant or a wholly owned subsidiary requires the firm to commit more resources, as it involves establishing a permanent base in the foreign market. While this mode brings increased risk, it also gives the firm more control over its foreign operations. Thus, it is essential for firms to carefully weigh the risks against the rewards before committing to any foreign market entry strategy.

Selecting an entry mode is not a simple or isolated decision. Managers need to factor in many variables and consider the company's long-term strategy, business goals, and strategic objectives. Some of the critical factors in selecting an entry mode are as follows:

- Company objectives such as desired profitability, market share, or competitive positioning.
- The degree of risk the company can live with and the level of control it desires to maintain.
- The financial, technological, and other resources that the firm can commit.
- Conditions in the target market such as competitive intensity, availability of partners, institutional frameworks, and infrastructural resources.
- The amount of time the company is willing to take to find success in the target market.
- Specific characteristics of the product or service offerings (e.g., fragility, perishability, high-tech vs. low-tech, B2C vs. B2B, and price)

While the final decision on which mode of entry to use lies with the firm, the marketing department has an integral role in helping to choose the right strategic option that will bring the most success and value to the firm in the long run. For example, the marketing team must consider the strength of potential partners' brands, assets, and the marketing resources they can provide. It is also important to consider other aspects such as the use of partner brand ambassadors, operational control over pricing, and other executional details. Before deciding on how to enter a country, it is essential for marketers to carefully evaluate the pros and cons of each mode of entry from a marketing perspective to help the firm make an informed decision.

Planning to exit a foreign market is also important when things do not work out as planned. The plan should involve setting clear goals and a defined timeline and understanding the resources required. When leaving a country, marketers should strive to maintain relationships that were built in the country and recognize that a company's reputation in one market may influence its reputation in neighboring countries. Additionally, the partner you leave in one country could be a potential or existing partner in another, thus remaining key to the success of that region's marketing operations.

One should remember Bill Gates's famous dictum: "It's fine to celebrate success, but it is more important to heed the lessons of failure." Companies can improve their chances of success in other markets by reflecting on what went wrong and learning from failure. Lastly, Table 3.3 provides a useful way of understanding the tripartite resource–risk–control approach to foreign market entry decisions.

Conclusion

Your organization's decision to venture abroad may have been driven by a saturated market and declining margins in the home market, but, more often than not, it results from wanting to replicate the success in the local market and expand it. However, success in the home market does not guarantee success abroad. Careful planning, consideration of a multitude of factors, and making informed decisions will be key to a smooth start in the foreign market. The process starts with an honest and realistic look

Table 3.3 *Foreign market entry mode types and their resource–risk–control structures*

Type of entry mode	Entry mode examples	Partner	Advantages	Resource needs	Risk level	Control level
Trade of products and services	Importing, exporting, and global sourcing	Yes	Quick market entry with low risk	Low	Low	Low
Contractual relationships	Licensing, franchising, project-based (nonequity) ventures, and co-marketing	Yes	Low investment and low relative risk	Medium	Medium	Medium
Equity-based international business activities	FDI, WOS, IJV (minority, majority, and 50/50 IJVs)	Yes / No (WOS)	High control and high reward	High	High	High

inward at your products, aptitude, and resources. It then extends to a broad evaluation of potential markets, using frameworks such as PESTLE. Once you have selected your target market and segments, you need to decide which strategy to pursue (e.g., go alone, go with partners, setting up operations in the country). Each of these strategies has its pros and cons that will impact on the speed of market penetration and your chances of eventual success.

Finally, it is important to remember that while a scientific and considered approach to assessing foreign markets is invaluable, not all elements can be predicted or controlled. Marketing is as much an art as it is a science, and sometimes experience, intuition, and a bit of luck can make all the difference. Unexpected events or unreliable information can derail even the best-laid plans for international expansion. As such, having a team that is resilient in the face of adversity and ambitious in the face of opportunity will be key to the firm's long-term success.

Bites for Thought

Among the prominent players in the U.S. restaurant industry—Subway, McDonald's, and Starbucks—Subway stands out as the sole entity with a larger domestic presence than international. Despite this, Subway, known for its foot-long sandwiches and quick-service restaurants, is experiencing significant international demand, and has strategically formed partnerships with established operators dedicated to expanding Subway's global footprint. "In 2022, the company signed eight development agreements with big global franchisees across Asia Pacific, Europe, the Middle East, Africa, India, Latin America, and the Caribbean regions, committing to building a total of 5,300 restaurants by 2027," said Mr. Chidsey, the chain's first CEO from outside the founding families, since 2019.

The key goal in their expansion strategy is to leverage their partners' local expertise to navigate cultural and regulatory differences so that the company can grow quickly and efficiently. For instance, across the 50 EMEA countries where Subway operates, the company adeptly tailors its growth strategy to accommodate diverse geographic, cultural, and economic distinctions.

In different regions like Latin America and the Caribbean islands, Subway's adaptable format allows it to cater to diverse consumer preferences. In areas where restaurants generally serve as family-friendly dining destinations, larger-format premises are developed to meet this demand. While in large cities, such as São Paulo, since guests are looking for a quick, convenient option, the company is experimenting more with grab-and-go, third-party delivery, and curbside options. Also, across the region, Subway has seen an increase in digital and online orders and is focused on bringing third-party delivery, curbside, and drive-throughs to more of the locations using learnings from other markets. For example, in Puerto Rico, half of the restaurants now include drive-throughs, which have successfully brought business to the locations.

Questions

1. *How do you assess your company's readiness to internationalize?*
2. *How should your company evaluate and customize its foreign market expansion strategy and execution according to varying host market conditions?*
3. *What are the criteria in selecting the right partnerships for your international operations?*

CHAPTER 4

Managing Across Cultures

K-Pop

There is perhaps no more passionate love than that of a teenager for a pop idol.[1] One of the masterstrokes of the Korean government was to recognize this love and transform it into a cultural brand to promote their values. In Seoul, the capital of South Korea, just north of the Han River, stands an office tower home to SM Entertainment, the inventor of one of the most potent cultural movements of the twenty-first century: K-pop. SM's Korean pop entrepreneur, Lee Soo-man, studied computer engineering in the United States in the 1980s and returned to his home country with a dream—globalizing Korean music. Soo-man claims that the Korean entertainment industry has created a new paradigm for cultural export. In the past, he suggests what effectively cultural exports from the West, mainly the United Kingdom and the United States, followed in the wake of economic empire building. The Korean model, by contrast, was *culture first and economics second*.

"The way BTS connects with its fans is truly remarkable," says Tamar Herman, author of *BTS: Blood, Sweat & Tears*.[2] Since their debut in 2010, the Korean pop band has built an army of global fans (dubbed A.R.M.Y.) that has propelled them to global success.[3] BTS's overwhelming popularity has helped popularize Korean culture worldwide, spurring increased tourism and interest in learning the language. Their impact is so great that it is estimated to have contributed up to 0.5 percent of South Korea's GDP. No wonder they are more than just a boy band; they are an economic force for Korean culture.

The *Korean Wave* or Hallyu is a cultural phenomenon in which South Korean popular culture's global popularity has risen dramatically over the twenty-first century. BTS has been a leading force of Hallyu. Their chart-topping songs and dynamic performances have become a global force transcending national boundaries and captured worldwide interest in K-everything, including K-pop, K-beauty, and K-dramas. Their success has even contributed, albeit indirectly, to the first non–English language film, "Parasites," winning the Academy Award for Best Picture, and "Squid Games" becoming the most-watched global series on Netflix in 2022. The power of BTS, and other *hallyu* elements, has created a strong "Korean brand image" worldwide.

BTS has also made a massive impact on social media and in the way audiences engage with music. Their songs are personal and emotional, emphasizing storytelling that captures their A.R.M.Y.'s attention and passion. Unlike Western record labels, K-pop focuses on fan participation rather than streaming numbers, creating a sense of involvement and ownership among fans who engage in sumseuming; Korean slang for streaming 24/7 as one breathes. This attitude is echoed in what the West calls Meet and Greet events, known as fan service in the East. The message is that the artist is fortunate to meet the fan and not vice versa. While K-pop may have been at the center of everyone's attention, consuming one aspect of cultural content usually entices the desire to consume more from the same culture. Hence, the export of *Korean cool* allowed companies like Samsung, LG, Hyundai, and Kia to reap the benefits.

South Korea's BTS is a shining example of an aspect of Asian culture that has gained popularity among Western audiences. The success of their shows, music, and other cultural content is also testament to how foreign languages are not always an obstacle to achieving mainstream success. With the right offering presented to the right audience at the right time via the right channel, content can significantly influence global consumer culture. In South Korea's case, it remains to be seen whether this trend will be sustained in the long term (Table 4.1).

Culture Matters and Human Nature, Too

At the core of international marketing lies an ever-present tension between standardization and localization. To achieve economies of scale and

Table 4.1 The 3W-1H of culture

Managing across cultures (who—you[!])	Key tasks for IM practitioner (what)	Explain why important (why)	Tools and resources (how)
Manage across cultures through understanding cross-cultural differences * Understand consumer culture theories, trends, and generational differences * Manage institutional, legal, economic, and political differences in relation to cultural differences * Stress the importance of cultural sensitivity and ethics in international marketing and avoid cultural stereotyping	Engage local experts and build multicultural teams to understand cultural nuances * Adapt to different communication styles, nonverbal cues, and negotiation tactics * Increase your cross-cultural competence to minimize bias, maximize inclusivity, and make informed and ethical decisions across different cultures * Expand your professional network to include individuals from diverse cultures and stay informed about global trends and their impact on different cultures	Cultural competence aids in building trust and credibility as well as enriching communication with partners, clients, and team members in international business settings * Awareness, sensitivity, and willingness to learn cultural nuances lead to effective leadership and improve the business environment * Cultural competency helps to mitigate risks and increase competitive advantage by providing deeper insights into consumer behavior amidst rapid technological advancements	Hofstede Insights * GLOBE Project * *Kiss, Bow, or Shake Hands* by Terri Morrison and Wayne A. Conaway * Pew Research Center * *The Culture Map* by Erin Meyer * The International Social Survey Program * Culture for Business tool by Trompenaars Hampden Turner

scope across foreign markets, multinationals must find a balance between standardizing their products and services, advertising, and messaging, while also localizing to cater to different national or regional markets. There are advantages and drawbacks to both global standardization and local differentiation. For international marketers, consistent global success will involve a combination of the two approaches—finding the right balance between both. Yet, finding the right balance is not easy, and many multinationals try to solve it in different ways.

Take the French cosmetics brand L'Oréal for instance. L'Oréal has developed a portfolio of brands with different COOs, catering to the local market in each region and country. Their prominent brands include L'Oréal Paris (France), Stylenanda (South Korea), Niely (Brazil), Maybelline New York (United States), Shu Uemura (Japan), Armani (Italy), and Magic Mask (China).

The fast-food retailer McDonald's, on the other hand, has just one main brand, while operating in 100 countries. However, it has customized and localized its menus, even while leveraging some of its most popular global products like Big Mac in different countries; so much so that *The Economist* invented the Big Mac index back in the 1980s as a light-hearted guide for the individual purchasing power of different countries, as this product exists worldwide in a standard size, composition, and quality.[4]

Netflix, the big tech giant in entertainment services allows members to stream TV series, documentaries, and movies that appeal to a more global audience as well as content that caters to local cultures and tastes with original content productions. Keep in mind that there are more similarities than differences among the approximately 8 billion human beings who inhabit our world. The instincts and emotions that define us as human beings are what we call human nature. Happiness, sadness, anger, fear, hunger, thirstiness, pleasure, respect, interaction, and love are all examples of universal emotions that are hard-wired in all of us, and these can be highly instrumental in building relationships. Along with these emotions, the "when," "how," and "toward what" we feel can be the product of one's national culture or any other cultural conditioning of a person within a group. Unlike human nature, culture is a collective phenomenon affected by societal values and norms. When building relationships and opening operations in foreign territories, the cultural conditioning of human beings matters a lot, as there are differences and similarities that should be considered.

International marketers have a responsibility to help alleviate some of the tension between global standardization and local responsiveness. A great asset in this regard is an understanding of cross-cultural differences and leveraging them into opportunities to serve local consumers better. For some multinationals, this means that accentuating differences in culture, religion, values, taste, and aesthetics has become the central goal, and they tailor their offerings in different countries around the world, accordingly. For others, emphasizing cultural similarities can bring opportunities driven by the alignment between the universal aspects of human nature and the core value proposition of the firm.

No marketer can aspire to be an expert in every culture. Still, it is plausible to be actively aware of cultural similarities and differences to achieve a more inclusive approach to conducting international marketing. This requires marketers to actively observe how different cultures can affect the psychology of the human mind and our emotions and be aware of societal norms and interactions that emerge from distinctive cultures. While easier said than done, this type of awareness and sophistication is necessary for multinationals to market their products and services across different cultures successfully.

What Is Culture?

Culture may be described as a combination of the beliefs, values, attitudes, norms, and behaviors shared by a particular nation or a group of people. It comprises the language, thoughts, communications, actions, customs, beliefs, values, and institutions of racial, ethnic, religious, or social groups. Culture is learned through socialization within a society and is transmitted from one generation to the next. It can also evolve over time in response to environmental changes. One of the most cited descriptions of culture in international marketing defines it as the collective programming of the mind that distinguishes members of one group from another.[5]

Culture is multilayered, with the individual and their profession at the core, expanding into the organization, nation, and world region (see Figure 4.1). Each layer has its unique set of norms, values, symbols, and artifacts. These layers are interconnected and, hence, rely on one another to form a cohesive bond for a certain group of people. No matter how many layers you decide to examine or in what context they exist, all layers need to be considered to truly understand the culture of a person or group.

National culture varies along specific cultural spectrums, such as individualism versus collectivism or power versus distance. We will discuss

Figure 4.1 The nested view of culture

each of these in more detail later in this chapter. For marketers, understanding these cultural dimensions will allow them to better adjust their international marketing strategy to suit local contexts.

At a fundamental level, there are two primary roles that culture plays in the context and conduct of international marketing. First, to understand and resolve the challenges of external adaptation of companies and, second, to address the problems associated with internal integration.

External adaptation involves setting goals and strategies and recognizing opportunities and threats in the external environment in which you operate. It is essential for understanding consumers, competitors, and the political and regulatory systems of potential target markets. By taking an adaptive approach to their external environment, organizations are better able to recognize and capitalize on opportunities that arise.

On the other hand, internal integration involves the firm's relationship with its employees and other internal stakeholders.[6] This can include developing effective communication systems, training local staff, and promoting shared values throughout the organization. Through these efforts, the company can create a successful corporate culture in a foreign market, stay more attuned to the needs of its customers, and cultivate positive relationships with its partners.

The Multiple Components of Culture

Any culture has various components, and international marketers must observe and understand how a particular culture shapes the day-to-day lives of target consumers. Language, religion, and time orientation are three of the most important aspects to consider when forming marketing strategies.

All languages contain significant nuances, so it is insufficient to merely do a literal translation when conveying a message across different cultures; one must ensure that the true meaning of the message is retained. Numerous examples exist of international marketing campaigns that have gone wrong due to confused language. Even global marketing giants such as Coca-Cola have experienced this. When the company wanted to adapt the name of its flagship product to the Chinese language, it used the written characters *ke kou le la*, which literally translated to *bite the wax tadpole*. Coca-Cola failed to understand that each syllable in Chinese has numerous homonyms. After studying 40,000 different characters to find a phonetic equivalent that could effectively represent the brand and product in a meaningful way, they changed the Chinese product name to *ke kou ke le*, which means *happiness in the mouth*.[7]

Religion has a considerable effect on how people interpret messages and products, as religious values and beliefs can shape consumer behavior. Religion, a system of faith and worship usually operating between the individual and a deity or deities, establishes certain beliefs and values for society as a whole and is an integral part of most cultures. It has direct implications for lifestyles in terms of the consumption of food and beverages, holidays, and clothing.

Secrets of a Cultural Icon: The Yellow Boot

First produced in Newmarket, New Hampshire, in 1974, Timberland's culturally iconic product is known simply as the "yellow boot." Once established as a functional and stylish wardrobe staple, "the boot" was embraced and culturally redefined multiple times over its half-century history by distinct consumer groups worldwide. The designer Virgil Abloh once famously said, "You can't set out to make an icon. Culture returns it to you." The design team responsible for seasonal color up-dating of the pattern came to understand different consumer groups, and their unique interpretation of Timberland's icon, as mirrors of cultural change.

There were straightforward rules at play for this golden goose: The color was malleable and fair game for seasonal interpretation. How-ever, the quality of the material and the build formula standards could not be compromised; you could view the product through colored glasses of any shade so long as the quality and authenticity remained. The boot, made of premium-grade heavyweight waterproof nubuck, nylon Taslan laces, brass hardware, and a sturdy rubber sole, is built to be waterproof and maintains durability standards to this day.

The yellow boot originates from the general-purpose work boots of the 1960s. The padded color, height, and lacing pattern were not unique but borrowed from other established designs. Yet, it was the first guaranteed waterproof leather work boot sold. Timberland didn't just raise the quality and performance of their product; it delivered a more stylish offering that became popular not only for how it worked but also for how it looked. What it said about the user's tastes became a reason to buy. It is no coincidence that the wheat-colored nubuck on Timberland's icon matches the stitching on a pair of Levi's. That it was simultaneously being sold in Saks and workwear channels revealed its chameleon-like qualities.

During the 1980s, Timberland expanded its distribution to Europe. In many countries, especially Italy, it was perceived as an expression of pragmatic American style—a refreshing and youthful counterpoint to Milan high fashion. Expensive and worth it! In the 1990s, the yellow boot was adopted by key Hip-Hop celebrities in the music industry and soon became an identifiable component of urban wear. New fans of the brand understood the boot not as camping gear but as invincible, bulletproof armor for the urban trail. In your *Tims* you could stand tall, tough, and impenetrable. In the early 2000s, Timberland began its expansion into the emerging Chinese market but was met with sluggish sales. Later, to counter this trend, Timber-land was reframed as TeeBooLang, kicks but doesn't break. A happy coincidence between meaning, pronounced phrase, and its phonetic similarity to "Timberland," TeeBooLang was picked up and used in the successful Strong Boot marketing campaign. During the 2010s, Japanese culture began taking an interest in it, leading to appropriating twentieth-century *old-school* American clothing and apparel.

Timberland's iconic boot was created when today's environmental issues had little or no influence on a product's design. For many of today's consumers, however, the brand has become synonymous with the outdoors, whether as gear that equips you to go there or the brand's commitment to the environment via product initiatives like Earthkeepers. The boot has managed to keep up with the brand's evolution while retaining its prized authenticity. Real-time tuning of the product and how it is messaged are essential to a successful and sustained product lifecycle abroad. Timberland had to center its story around durability and authenticity—and their icon remains the original, the real deal, around the world.

Like language, there are popular blunders concerning religion as well. In 2015, Pringles, a Kellogg's brand of stackable potato chips that is popular all over the world, decided to release a new smoky bacon-flavored potato chip. In London, United Kingdom, in a Tesco store, Pringles created an aisle display to promote this new flavor with the phrase "Ramadan Mubarak" above the chips during the Ramadan holiday. Individuals who practice Islam do not eat any kind of pork in accordance with rules outlined in the Qur'an. Although this didn't happen in a predominantly Muslim country, the store was located near the East London Mosque, which serves the country's largest Muslim community. News of this failed marketing campaign spread quickly and negatively impacted both Tesco and the Pringles brand. To try and address the situation, Tesco issued a statement saying—"We are proud to offer a wide range of meals and products to meet the needs of our customers during Ramadan."[8] Nevertheless, this had little effect, as the damage had already been done.

Finally, time orientation refers to how different cultures view and interact with time. It is one of the most consequential constructs in any culture, and international marketers need to understand how a society perceives it. For example, monochronic time characterizes societies in which time is seen as a rigid resource, with individuals adhering to strict schedules and focusing on completing one task at a time. On the other hand, polychronic time cultures perceive time as flexible and fluid, allowing for multiple tasks to be carried out simultaneously. Canada, the United States, and some European countries such as Germany and Switzerland are typically monochronic. In contrast, other European countries like Italy, Spain, countries from the Middle East, Africa, and Latin America have a more polychronic time orientation. These time orientations can immensely impact collaborations and business relationships including camaraderie, meeting schedules, and projects.[9]

Cultural Orientations and Enculturation Versus Acculturation

There are a few important constructs that every international marketer should be aware of pertaining to culture. These include cultural orientations, and the concept of enculturation versus acculturation. Understanding these constructs will allow you to tailor your strategies, as well as products and services, to better serve the needs of your customers and help your company's expansion plans. Let's start by exploring cultural orientation. To effectively market products and services, it is essential for marketers to understand the cultural orientations of their target audiences and of their own internal company culture.

The four types of cultural orientations are ethnocentric, polycentric, regiocentric, and geocentric orientations. Ethnocentric orientation is the most domestic market-oriented approach, in which a firm focuses exclusively on its home market. In ethnocentric firms, international marketing managers consider domestic culture, values, strategies, and processes to be superior to foreign ones. Ethnocentrism is sometimes reflected in the preference of individual consumers and reflects the belief that purchasing foreign products is wrong, because it hurts the domestic economy, causes job losses, and is broadly unpatriotic.[10]

Polycentric orientation involves viewing each foreign market as unique and, thus, tailoring products and marketing strategies specifically to each market. With this orientation, managers are more aware of the importance of recognizing different international markets and cultures. Regiocentric and geocentric orientations share an even greater international outlook, with the only difference being that the former treats the world as divided into regions with similar cultural traits (e.g., Latin America, Middle East), while the latter perceives the entire world as one potential homogeneous market. While none of these orientations are static, shifting the orientation of the firm is not an easy task. For larger companies, this may even seem akin to changing the direction of a supertanker, slow and steady, in real time. However, while understanding the orientation of the firm is only half the battle, it means that you can now think of strategies to target an orientation that are most likely to result in success.

Finally, enculturation and acculturation are both important processes that help in understanding how cultures interact and evolve over time. Enculturation involves internal learning of a culture's language, customs, values, and norms, typically through immersion. Acculturation occurs when two cultures interact, resulting in mutual influence and adaptation of behaviors and beliefs. These processes facilitate cultural integration and adaptation to new ideas while preserving unique identities. Remarkably, they also aid in transitioning firms away from a solely ethnocentric approach.

Values are the dominant component of culture. Researchers of culture often look at the measurement of cultural values, so there are numerous culture models and frameworks that help both scholars and practitioners enhance their understanding of cultural values as these pertain to a company's internationalization efforts. In the sections that follow, we highlight four of these models, which we believe have had the greatest impact on the field of international marketing.

Hofstede's Model of National Culture

The first model is Hofstede's Model of National Culture. Developed by Geert Hofstede in the early 1980s, for years this model identified what would become the most widely cited dimensions of culture in international marketing. Hofstede identified four popular dimensions of national culture: individualism versus collectivism; motivation toward achievement and success; uncertainty avoidance; and power distance. In his model, every country is characterized by a score on each of these dimensions. Over the years, these results have shaped and influenced many decisions taken by international marketing managers.

One of the reasons why the international marketing community long favored these four dimensions is that they were originally identified as the four problem areas that all societies face by U.S. sociologist Alex Inkeles and U.S. psychologist Daniel Levinson in the 1950s. These researchers pointed out that these dimensions (or problem areas as they called them) differ across individuals and societies. The four Hofstede dimensions provided further insights into why these problem areas vary in individuals and between cultures. Over time, other cultural dimensions emerged to strengthen further the insights offered by Hofstede's model. Among these were U.S. sociologist Ronald F. Inglehart's contributions, identifying long- versus short-term orientation and indulgence versus restraint as critical cultural dimensions. Let's have a look at each of the six dimensions and see how they impact companies abroad:

Individualism versus collectivism: In an individualistic society, the focus is on the needs and rights of the individual, while in a collectivist society, the emphasis is placed on the needs and rights of the collective. People in individualistic societies tend to value independence and autonomy, while those in collectivist societies often value interdependence and duty within their group, having been integrated into strong, cohesive in-groups from birth. This dimension has solid implications for marketers as they work through the details of marketing campaigns, including the proper use of language, endorsement from influencers, and traits associated with their company and products.

Motivation toward achievement and success: This dimension, formerly masculinity versus femininity, measures the extent to which individuals in society prefer traits such as achievement, heroism, assertiveness, and material rewards for success, as opposed to traits like cooperation, modesty, caring for others, and quality of life. After its relabeling, this dimension remains critical for businesses to consider, influencing how they market their products and manage their workforce.

Uncertainty avoidance: This dimension expresses the degree to which the members of a nation feel uncomfortable with uncertainty and ambiguity. This dimension again has substantial implications for businesses in foreign markets, as they consider the entrepreneurial environment, the preference for standardization, and the willingness of their partners, customers, and employees to take risks.

Power distance: The extent to which the less powerful members of institutions and organizations within a country expect and accept that power is distributed unequally. Institutions in this context can include families, schools and communities, businesses, and government offices, as they all have some form of power distance. Businesses venturing abroad will be mindful of this dimension as they seek to establish the right corporate culture, decision-making processes, and even the use of authority figures who act on their behalf.

Short- versus long-term orientation: This dimension measures how much a nation relies on its history and traditions while confronting current and future challenges and opportunities. It reflects the degree to which a society values short- over long-term plans and goals. As such, marketers need to consider as they look to market their company and the intrinsic benefits of their products and services in different markets worldwide. For example, companies in a nascent industry may need to work harder to convince a society with a long-term orientation that they are in it for the long haul to provide lasting value.

Indulgence versus restraint: Indulgence tends to allow relatively free gratification of basic human desires related to enjoying life and having fun. On the other hand, restraint reflects a conviction that such gratification needs to be curbed and regulated by strict social norms. Again, this dimension has apparent implications for marketers. For example, if the goods and services you are selling address a short-term, fun, or impulsive demand, this will be more difficult in a society that scores highly on restraint and will, therefore, require more creative messaging and marketing.

The Culture Model

The second model we highlight is the Theory of Basic Values,[11] which was developed by the social psychologist Shalom Schwartz in the 1990s. This model highlights ten types of motivational human values arranged in a circular conceptual framework to demonstrate how values close to each other share some mutual motivational goals, while values on opposite sides conflict.[12] Here is a quick look at the values:

Power: Pursuit of social status, dominance, and control over people and resources.

Achievement: Pursuit of success, demonstrating competence according to social standards.

Hedonism: Pursuit of pleasure, enjoyment, and emotional gratification.

Stimulation: Pursuit of novelty and challenge in life, valuing excitement, and adventure.

Self-direction: Pursuit of independent thought and action.

Universalism: Pursuit of understanding, appreciation, and protection for the welfare of all.

Benevolence: Pursuit of enhancing the welfare of those with whom one is in-group.

Tradition: Pursuit of respect and commitment to the customs and ideas that traditional culture provides.

Conformity: Pursuit of the restraint of actions and impulses likely to harm others and violate social expectations.

Security: Pursuit of safety, harmony, and stability of society, relationships, and the self.

Like Hofstede's Model of National Cultures, the Culture Model aids marketers by offering a framework to comprehend cultural distinctions across countries. For instance, in a nation valuing universalism, a company may emphasize its contributions to social justice or equality when marketing products. Conversely, in a culture valuing achievement, portraying individuals using products or services to pursue success and competence aligns with social norms, catering to the target audience's aspirations.

The GLOBE Framework

The third model is the GLOBE (Global Leadership and Organizational Behavior Effectiveness) framework, which was instigated by the American management scholar Robert House in the 1990s. It would later become a multicountry, multiresearcher study. This study uncovered nine cultural dimensions, seven of which were similar to Hofstede's model: (1) uncertainty avoidance, (2) power distance, (3) future orientation (the degree to which a society values long-term approaches), (4) assertiveness orientation (motivation toward achievement and success), (5) gender egalitarianism, (6) institutional, and (7) societal collectivism (similar to individualism/collectivism). The two cultural dimensions unique to the GLOBE project are performance orientation (degree to which societies emphasize performance and achievement) and humane orientation (the extent to which societies place importance on fairness, altruism, and caring).

In contrast to Hofstede's model, GLOBE researchers also categorized countries into clusters according to their characteristics. These well-known clusters include Anglo, Confucian Asia, Germanic Europe, Latin America, Nordic Europe, Middle East, and Sub-Saharan Africa.[13] GLOBE researchers also introduced six leadership profiles and explained to what extent they are preferred among these various country clusters. Here is a quick look at all nine cultural dimensions of the GLOBE Framework:

> **Uncertainty avoidance:** The extent to which a society, organization, or group relies on social norms, rules, and procedures to alleviate unpredictability around future events. The greater the desire to avoid uncertainty, the more people seek orderliness, consistency, structure, formal procedures, and laws to cover situations in their daily lives.
>
> **Assertiveness:** The degree to which individuals are assertive, confrontational, and aggressive in their relationship with others.
>
> **Gender egalitarianism:** The degree to which a society minimizes gender inequality.
>
> **Performance orientation:** The degree to which a society encourages and rewards group members for performance improvement and excellence.

Humane orientation: The degree to which a society encourages and rewards individuals for being fair, altruistic, generous, caring, and kind to others.

In-group collectivism: The degree to which individuals express pride, loyalty, and cohesiveness in their organizations or families.

Institutional collectivism: The degree to which organizational and societal institutional practices encourage and reward collective distribution of resources and collective action.

Power distance: The degree to which the community accepts and endorses authority, power differences, and status privileges.

Future orientation: The degree to which individuals engage in future-oriented behaviors such as planning, investing in the future, and delaying gratification.

As with the first two models, the GLOBE framework can be an extremely useful tool for businesses and marketers as they expand internationally. Even more so than the first two frameworks, this one also focuses on regional differences, making it easier for marketers, for example, to adopt regional campaigns across countries with similar profiles.

The GLOBE framework can also be very instructive for organizing essential management functions abroad, such as leading, planning, organizing, and controlling. For instance, future orientation and uncertainty avoidance significantly impact business planning. In a culture with low future orientation, the history of the organization is considered, and planning is based on preserving traditions while moving the business forward. In countries with high uncertainty avoidance, planning will be very deliberate and only plans with a shallow risk of failure and high certainty of outcomes will be considered. On the other hand, performance orientation and institutional collectivism affect how firms are organized. Organizations based on teams and group efforts will likely be most effective in countries with high institutional collectivism. More hierarchical structures with clear lines of authority and well-defined responsibilities would likely work best in countries with low institutional collectivism.

Furthermore, organizations can gain insights from the GLOBE framework as they identify which leadership styles would be most suitable for their organization in foreign countries. For instance, power distance and humane orientation are key factors to consider. In low power distance countries, leadership should be more collaborative, and employees are allowed to question rules and procedures that they disagree with. In cultures with a high humane orientation, leaders should strive to be nurturing and empowering, as employees will likely feel motivated by the impact their contributions have on the organization. Finally, assertiveness and power distance can also influence how organizations are managed effectively. In countries with high assertiveness and power distance, authoritarian and directive managers may be more effective than participative managers.

The Culture Map

The final model we look at is the most recent one: Erin Meyer's Culture Map. Meyer compared nations across eight dimensions in a somewhat different approach from the previous three models. Each of these eight scales represents one key area for managers to be aware of, highlighting how cultures vary along a spectrum from one extreme to another.

Communicating: Low context versus high context.

Evaluating: Direct negative feedback versus indirect negative feedback.

Persuading: Principles-first versus applications-first.

Leading: Egalitarian versus hierarchical.

Deciding: Consensual versus top-down.

Trusting: Task-based versus relationship-based.

Disagreeing: Confrontational versus avoids confrontation.

Scheduling: Linear time versus flexible time.

One of the most popular applications and interpretations of Meyer's cultural dimensions is demonstrated in the book she coauthored with Reed Hastings, the CEO of Netflix. In *No Rules, Rules*,[14] both Meyer and Hastings discuss the implications of the eight different dimensions for Netflix's global expansion. Netflix began its internationalization process by opening its streaming service in Canada and a year later in Latin America.

Using Meyer's cultural dimensions, Netflix mapped out its corporate culture and compared it to the national cultures where they were starting operations. Some of the findings were quite surprising yet provided a deep understanding of the company's struggles in each of its foreign offices. For instance, compared to Netflix's home culture, both the Netherlands and Japan fall to the consensual side of the decision-making dimension. This explains the challenges that Netflix employees faced in their Amsterdam and Tokyo offices when individuals became responsible for decision-making.

In another example, the *Leading* dimension revealed that Netflix's corporate culture was more egalitarian than the local Singapore culture. This helped explain why Singaporean employees needed more encouragement to challenge their managers' decisions. On the trust dimension, Netflix was found to be much more task-oriented than most other cultures where it had expanded operations. Unfortunately, this focus on efficiency and spending every second on tasks had a negative impact on productivity in countries such as Brazil, which scores high on relationship-based trust in business.

The Culture Map is especially adept at explaining how corporate culture fits in with national culture, and it has widespread ramifications for executives to understand how foreign operations should be run. The author herself recommends uniform cross-cultural training in areas like diversity and confrontation management, to circumvent and overcome some of the more challenging aspects of national versus corporate culture. The model is perhaps slightly less useful to international marketers for explaining how foreign consumers will react to your company's latest marketing campaigns. Yet, even here, it could help explain why some brand and company messages are more likely to resonate in certain countries than others.

Table 4.2 summarizes the four models and the different dimensions of national cultures under each categorization. It should be noted that there are other classifications that can account for cultural differences across countries as well, such as the commonly cited high versus low context.[15] Individuals in low-context cultures rely on direct verbal communication, while those in high-context cultures rely on participants' nonverbal behaviors and context, such as the participants' background and associations, in addition to verbal communication. Another, more recent

Table 4.2 The evolution of the different culture models and their dimensions of national culture

Culture Model	The Culture Map (by Erin Meyer in the 2010s)	GLOBE Study (by Robert House in the 2000s)	The Culture Model (by Shalom Schwartz in the 1990s)	National Culture Dimensions (by Geert Hofstede in the 1980s)
Dimensions	Communicating Evaluating Persuading Leading: Deciding Trusting Disagreeing Scheduling	Uncertainty avoidance Assertiveness Gender egalitarianism Performance orientation Humane orientation In-group collectivism Institutional collectivism Power distance Future orientation	Embeddedness Hierarchy Mastery Affective autonomy Intellectual autonomy Egalitarian commitment Harmony	Individualism versus collectivism Motivation toward achievement and success Uncertainty avoidance Power distance Long-term orientation Indulgence versus restraint

categorization is cultural tightness versus looseness,[16] which basically captures the strength of societal norms and tolerance of deviant behaviors in a country, with potential impacts on human resource management and marketing practices across countries.

Implications of Cultural Differences on International Marketing Practice

All four of the culture models and classification systems cited earlier provide immense value and guidance to international marketing executives, helping them to effectively support the firm's internationalization efforts. These models are relevant to how the firm is structured, its corporate culture and reporting systems, how it deals with foreign business partners, and, indeed, how it markets its products and services in a foreign market.

The values of a firm largely reflect its national culture, and organizations based in different countries will consequently have different values.[17] Cultural dimensions have implications for leadership and communication styles, building relationships with foreign partners, negotiations, market segmentation, targeting, and advertising. Therefore, when conducting international marketing, understanding the different dimensions of national cultures and how nations vary along these dimensions is critical.

Paying attention to the cultural values of a foreign country is also an invaluable aspect of international expansion planning, both strategic and tactical, and can provide essential guidance on how to manage the day-to-day operations of a foreign operation. Yet, we encourage executives to take national differences with a grain of salt for two reasons. First, no country can be classified entirely in one dimension. Executives need to be aware that these cultural dimensions represent more of a gradient than rigid, exclusive categories. Second, countries in these models are usually evaluated relative to each other. Rather than treating the scores of cultural dimensions as absolutes, they should be used as a guide for international marketing executives to better understand how nations compare to one another. Nevertheless, understanding the culture into which you are entering is critical for success. Indeed, some noteworthy international marketing mishaps have occurred due to a lack of understanding of the foreign culture in which the company now operates.

Let's go back to the Coca-Cola product launch in China, for example, and how the company blundered with a translation mistake. China is a highly masculine society, meaning that people are success-oriented and driven and sacrifice both family and leisure time for work. They tend to set very high standards for themselves and, therefore, also for foreign companies, which likely made Coca-Cola's mistake even more problematic for Chinese consumers. Moreover, China scores lowly in indulgence, meaning that they are prone to cynicism and pessimism, which could have contributed to the negative reception of Coke following the incident. This example reinforces the importance of understanding a multitude of cultural nuances when entering an international market.

Revlon, an American multinational cosmetic, skincare, fragrance, and personal care company, experienced difficulties when it launched a famous perfume called Charlie—featuring camellia flower notes—in Brazil. They did not realize that camellia flowers are used during funerals in Brazilian culture. Brazilian consumers live in a high-context culture, which emphasizes how companies communicate with them, rather than what they say. In addition, trust is a fundamental trait, and making any mistakes in this respect is very damaging for a brand's reputation. As a result, consumers felt offended and perceived Revlon as insensitive to their culture.

On the other hand, Amazon, the e-commerce giant, was aware of the importance of trust and relationships in Brazilian culture. As such, they decided to enter the Brazilian market, beginning with e-books gradually. As they began to gain confidence over the years, they launched other services and finally opened their entire e-commerce store in 2019. Another example is Taco Bell, a division of YUM! Brands that serve Mexican food. Ironically, despite multiple attempts, the company failed to enter the Mexican market. This might be attributed to the cultural gap that exists between Mexico and the United States. Not only do Mexicans have a strong sense of cultural identity, but their society is more collectivist as well, and, as such, they are more easily influenced by others. Little surprise that they were not pleased to find an American fast-food chain trying to sell a food category that they had invented.

Starbucks, the world's largest coffeehouse chain, represents the U.S. second wave of coffee culture. With operations in more than 80 countries, the company has a lot of experience launching their stores worldwide, including Australia. The Australian coffee culture, however, is quite different from the Starbucks model. It began in the 1950s when coffee shops and Italian cafés popped up throughout the country and is centered around quality and experience rather than convenience. Australians appreciate quality beans and value baristas who make drinks with craftsmanship instead of treating the product as a commodity. As a result, Starbucks faced significant resistance after it entered the market in 2000, and the company had to close 61 stores by 2009 due to lack of consumer acceptance. As of 2023, the company still operates 58 stores in Australia, catering mainly to the tourist market. By comparison, Starbucks has nearly 12,000 stores in the United States.

Starbucks's foray into the Turkish market was quite different to its experience down under. Despite a strong coffee culture entrenched in tradition, there were hardly any coffee chains in Turkey prior to Starbucks's arrival, and the company's novel and consistent coffee experience resonated with customers. This allowed it to quickly gain traction and become the second largest Starbucks chain in Europe. By emphasizing the Starbucks experience, it was able to capture the hearts of coffee-lovers and establish itself as an innovative leader in the industry.

Conclusion

This chapter focused on the importance of culture as it influences the marketing strategies, tactics, and even day-to-day operations of an international company. It described the balance between emphasizing and diminishing cultural differences in your global marketing efforts and discussed the implications of various cultural dimensions for international marketers.

Culture is an expansive topic, with countless books and academic articles written on the subject, including its implications for international business and marketing. In a world where many organizations have the privilege of no longer being bound by geography, culture becomes even more critical as international marketers learn new and better ways to adapt their content so that it resonates within the cultural context of their new target audience.

While we highlighted some of the more essential concepts, models, and frameworks related to culture and their implications for international marketing executives, we also provided vivid examples of companies that have either succeeded or failed to bridge the gap between cultural norms and values. We conclude this chapter with some key points, which every marketer should bear in mind.

Culture is a complex subject, yet every aspiring international marketer must become an expert in it. To find the right balance between global integration and local responsiveness in marketing operations, one must first understand cultural differences.

While focusing on cultural differences does not always need to be prioritized, understanding them can make a difference, even in cases where their relevance may not be immediately clear. For instance, in contexts such as business-to-business marketing and day-to-day business practicalities, like legal contracts and trade agreements, adjustments for culture can still be relevant, even though this may not be the priority.

Addressing cross-cultural risks and opportunities for the company needs to be done in unison with consideration of other governmental, institutional, and environmental factors for a more synergistic impact. Often these factors will also be influenced by culture; hence, a comprehensive approach makes sense.

Culture is not a static concept. Instead, cultures change, evolve, and shift because of migration, external influences, and changing demographics. Being aware of cultural differences may not be enough in today's constantly changing global landscape. There are many examples of companies becoming more or less successful over time within specific cultural contexts, which can be an indicator of a shift in culture.

For multinationals, conducting market research and interpreting findings according to the cultural context is not a luxury. It is critical to ongoing business operations, especially for B2C companies. We will address the topic of doing research in-depth in the next chapter. After all, preparation is vital to success.

Bites for Thought

Spotify, the Swedish audio-streaming service provider, was founded in 2006 by Daniel Ek and Martin Lorentzon with a simple goal in mind: offering copyrighted or restricted digital audio content as a freemium service model. It has presence in over 180 countries and has over 200 million subscribers and more than 100 million tracks and 5 million podcast titles.[18] These are some quick numbers that summarize Spotify's international presence today. Wherever you access the Spotify app, the user interface is relatively standard, a minimalistic and easy-to-understand app interface. The only thing that seems to be different, at first sight, is the language. However, one should look beyond the language and understand how Spotify has become, and remains, the most significant contributor to the global music industry, which is highly affected by the culture at different levels.

The key to Spotify's international success is its ability to understand that musical taste goes beyond simply language. For many years, Spotify has offered an "explore" tab, not only allowing people to listen to the top hits of their own country but also enabling exploration across cultures. The company has strategic partnerships with artists, their labels, trending musicians, and podcasters worldwide, which also helps the enterprise reach as many global customers as possible. Moreover, Spotify has also created playlists based on moods, for example, music to relax to, or motivational playlists that change consumer listening behaviors, as they now can be more easily exposed to music they may not have hitherto known existed.

Take Spotify's U.S. launch in 2011, for example. The U.S. market at the time was dominated by Pandora and American radio culture, which is more suited to a *passive listener's* needs. However, Spotify's offering was centered around the *search box*, assuming that the average user was an *active listener* and would search for precisely what they wanted to listen to. To meet the needs of the preexisting user behavior, Spotify built more curation into its streaming services, including the innovative *Discover Weekly* feature. While attending to current habits, being conscientious of the plight of musicians, for example, and pioneering long-term trends in the industry are critical. Spotify's emphasis on curation shows that the founders have a clear vision as to where the global audio-streaming industry is heading further down the line.[19]

Take a moment to search for Spotify ads from India, Brazil, or France and see how they acknowledge each country's specific cultural rituals while it retains a few key, consistent underlying themes—such as an emotional approach to listening to music. Prioritizing emotions in ads helps the company better connect with its target audience worldwide.

Questions
1. *How do you navigate the fine line between adhering to global strategies and accommodating local needs, while respecting cultural nuances?*
2. *Could you propose some models that serve as a roadmap for marketers to decipher and contrast various cultural dimensions?*
3. *When crafting a marketing campaign for a global product launch, how can understanding cultural dimensions assist you in shaping both the overarching strategy and localized operational tactics?*

CHAPTER 5

International Market Research

Netflix

Netflix, a pioneer in the direct-to-consumer (D2C) digital subscription landscape, has established its global footprint through a systematic and data-driven approach. While their customers binged on its shows, they binged on data, becoming experts at generating insights through analytics and quantitative modeling and, in the process, helping connect people from around the world with its digital content. The company has deployed its research-based geographical expansion strategy since 2010. This strategy, in essence, explains how Netflix expanded its presence from 50 to 190 countries, amassing over 230 million paid memberships within a few years. The global growth of Netflix plays a significant role in its success, given that its international streaming revenues now surpass its domestic revenues.[1]

Given the explosive growth in e-commerce, digital services, and subscription models, businesses must understand that consumer shopping habits have evolved. This shift toward a new consumer journey model and decision behavior also has implications for companies with traditional business models. For instance, recent market research by Quirk's, encompassing 22,000 digital services and tangible goods shoppers in 9 countries across 4 continents, can shape the digital journey framework and the go-to-market strategies for companies in the D2C sector, especially in the subscription space. The research findings suggest that consumers navigate through five stages: *trigger, evaluate, engage, stay or go*, and *I'm back*.[2]

Each stage of the digital consumer journey presents distinct market research inquiries that companies must tackle to ensure the success of their offerings across diverse markets. For instance, during the *trigger* and *evaluate* stages, where customer acquisition is paramount, brands should research target audiences, potential touchpoints, and barriers while understanding consumer commitment drivers. In the *stay-or-go* stage, focusing on customer loyalty and retention, brands must balance customer freedom with retention efforts and explore soft exit strategies, such as pausing subscriptions. Lastly, in the *I'm back* stage, understanding the characteristics of *serial rejoiners* and their motivations for returning is crucial for reacquisition strategies, whether through new products, content, or promotions.

Netflix integrates research seamlessly into its teams rather than isolating it into a separate division, suggesting that innovative market research forms the backbone of the enterprise. The company showcases on its corporate website how research informs decision-making, particularly regarding the customer journey in the D2C space and evolving paradigms. Netflix conducts experiments to discern which consumer behaviors are positively impacted by joining, informing effective acquisition strategies. Employing online, longitudinal A/B testing for new product development caters to varying member behaviors, enhancing value and eliminating barriers. Additionally, algorithms are crafted for recommendations, content, and marketing strategies to optimize advertising expenditure and channel mix.[3]

Netflix employs machine learning techniques to support its international growth strategy, leveraging advanced systems to discern country-specific differences and identify resonating innovations. This approach enables Netflix to enter new markets while tailoring unique customer experiences for each country. For example, recognizing that mobile devices are India's primary Internet access point, Netflix introduced a mobile-only membership plan after conducting market-specific research on device usage. Similarly, in emerging economies, where mobile Internet access predominates, Netflix enhances its mobile experience, user interface, and streaming efficiency for cellular networks (Table 5.1).

Table 5.1 *The 3W-1H of market research*

International market research (who—you[!])	Key tasks for IM practitioner (what)	Explain why it is important (why)	Tools and resources (how)
Identify the concrete objectives of your international market research undertaking * Assess the relevancy of your next market research project to different company stakeholders * Determine the various types of research designs and data needs required by your market research project * Decide an action plan based on the market research results and integrate them into company decision-making	Understand the consumer-related drivers, differences, and trends that can help your company expand to international markets * Analyze the competitive context and market dynamics to make an informed decision about how to market in foreign markets * Assess company resources, capabilities, and talent for in-house research versus outsourcing	Research provides the company with competitive intelligence to generate insights about foreign markets, mitigate risks, and market products and services more effectively * Due to cultural differences, different countries tend to overestimate the feedback and reactions that market research aims to control * There is a need to have specific quality control measures and comparability of market research results to ensure correct interpretability	globalEDGE: Your source for Global Business Knowledge * Growth-Share Matrix by Boston Consulting Group * Greenbook: Your Guide for All Things Market Research * International market research information resources by Simon Fraser University * PEW Research Center * Research Foreign Markets by International Trade Administration * Statista—The Statistics Portal for Market Data

Data-Driven Insights

As witnessed in the Netflix case, one of the most critical drivers of success in international business is decision-making based on information, insights, and preparation. Managers must understand differences between countries and cultural disparities, which will influence potential demand for their products and services across different markets. This understanding can significantly reduce exposure to risks and increase the chances of success when venturing abroad. Relying on data, intelligence, and market signals will inform better decision-making and help overcome ethnocentrism.

Market research gives companies the information and insights they need to improve decision-making. Who are our customers? What do they need from our products and services? What is the core value of our offering at home versus abroad? For many internationally active businesses, market research based on rich qualitative and quantitative data, robust analysis methods, and an objective interpretation and communication of findings to derive actionable insights have laid the ground for a more successful marketing practice abroad.

This chapter discusses how international market research (IMR) helps companies expand into foreign markets. We also focus on the opportunities and challenges managers face when conducting research in a new country. We provide a step-by-step research design process to help managers follow a more systematic approach to achieve their research objectives and answer marketing-related questions. Market research has significantly transformed thanks to growing deployment and application of digital technologies. For instance, metaverse platforms now allow marketers to test new marketing ideas quickly, inexpensively, and most of the time accurately, with high confidence. We discuss various data sources and ways of accessing them within the research design process, and we dedicate a separate section to new forms of data, as this aspect of IMR is changing rapidly in line with the exponential growth in digital technologies, thus presenting additional opportunities to executives.

With the high volume, velocity, and veracity of data available in real time, this field is evolving quickly. However, as of 2024, only roughly 20 percent of the generated data are structured and the remaining 80 percent are unstructured data, meaning that the data in this case are unorganized and more challenging to analyze. Firms that figure out how to leverage unstructured data via analytical models and AI technologies for business decision-making have already started to gain a significant advantage over those that do not and will most likely derive more significant economies of scale from automation very soon.[4] Last but certainly not least, we discuss how and why many companies employ Chief Listening

Officers and provide a checklist for managers to measure their confidence levels regarding different aspects of a research project.

What Is International Market Research, and Why Is It Important?

Market research is vital for businesses to help them better connect with customers. A specific extension of market research, IMR, is the systematic design, collection, analysis, and reporting of findings relevant to a specific business decision facing the company in at least one foreign market. In its simplest form, IMR is much like domestic, in-country research, as it tries to find answers to the same or similar questions but in an international context.

Popular research topics include understanding customer needs, preferences, attitudes, and behaviors toward products and services; their perception of competing products in the market; the performance and suitability of marketing tools and tactics such as brands, channels, communications, and prices; and opportunities for new product development and innovation.

Like most other aspects of business, IMR has been tremendously affected by technological advances. Social media platforms, mobile devices, apps, wearable technology, and smart devices constantly produce consumer data and feedback to companies in real time. The era of Big Data and digital technology is transforming how firms access, process, and use data to derive insights. Although much of these data are still unstructured, the amount of usable data available is already massive and expected to increase exponentially in future years.

IMR is like domestic market research; however, there can be more factors, uncertainties, and constraints in a transnational context. So, before discussing these, let's start by examining the three components of IMR, which explain why a company would want to invest time and resources (see Figure 5.1):

1. **Managing risks:** One of the primary goals of International Monetary Fund (IMF) is to anticipate, manage, and alleviate risks associated with doing business internationally. It should come as no surprise that compared to marketing in one's home country,

Figure 5.1 International market research and its components

international marketing entails many more risks, typically categorized into four categories as cross-cultural, political, financial, and
operational.[5] However, in the contemporary business landscape,
which can be volatile, uncertain, complex, and ambiguous, corporations face other novel risks. We have discussed how megatrends
and black swan events can disrupt business as we know it, and good
research can help alleviate some of this uncertainty. Accelerating
technological advances constitute new and heightened concerns, for
instance, cybersecurity, for all businesses utilizing the benefits of the
technological revolution. Global teams use videoconferencing, virtual whiteboards, and file-sharing products to facilitate their work
across borders. The COVID-19 pandemic accelerated remote work
possibilities and led companies to use more technology products
to overcome the challenges of not being physically present in one
place. A natural part of this shift was using more third-party software and vendors, which made company data more vulnerable to
outside breaches, with the obvious ensuing risks of losing sensitive
data and reputational damage. Other contemporary risks include
trade conflicts and tensions like U.S.–China trade wars. Overall,
traditional and novel risks may present unique challenges to companies. Market research is one of the more powerful tools corporations have at their disposal to anticipate and mitigate these risks.

2. **Generating insights:** IMR helps substantiate and guide your business strategy. In international marketing, where most managers start with limited knowledge of the countries or consumer profiles, market research can help steer your company in the right direction. Insight generation usually involves two components. The first component is geared toward a better understanding of your products, brands, and the specific benefits they offer to your existing and potential customers in a target market. For instance, Toyota changed the engine size of its Lexus brand by introducing a smaller version in China due to the Chinese government's higher sales taxes on vehicles with engines greater than 3 liters. The second component is competitive intelligence, which is about understanding the competitors' strategic moves and performance outcomes. It has several goals, such as knowing who your direct and indirect competitors are, discovering strength versus weakness areas where you outperform versus lag behind, finding opportunities you can capitalize on, and risks you need to mitigate. For instance, a global consumer goods giant like Unilever conducts extensive studies on consumer behaviors, local competitors, and emerging trends in the international markets they are considering entering or competing in. One such example is India, where a fragmented distribution network requires adaptation and diverse partnerships, and consumers have distinct preferences compared to Western markets. By partnering with local research firms to understand cultural differences, tailoring marketing messages accordingly, and tracking the activities of key players such as Hindustan Unilever and ITC, Unilever adapted its existing products like Dove soap to suit the Indian market better.

3. **Marketing products and services:** As a result of the insights generated through market research, you may understand the different market segments, which segments to pursue, and how to customize a product for your target market. A successful segmentation–targeting–positioning (STP) strategy can be bolstered by deeper learning of distinctive consumption habits, for example, how you brew coffee, the product benefits that customers prioritize (prestige over price, for instance), as well as the channels that the company should use to reach their target market. An excellent

example of how a company used market research for this purpose was Coca-Cola's successful launch of its Glaceau Vitamin water brand in Britain in the late 2000s. During the prelaunch, the company conducted extensive consumer profiling to define its target audience for the brand. They characterized this rich profiling as young, urban professionals who are open to new ideas, seek simple ways to stay healthy, and find tap water boring, and they married this insight with the right messages through the right outlets in the right consumer, workplace, and retail locations. The project's objective was a successful U.K. launch of Vitamin water by gaining distribution channels in major retail sectors. The company used several data sources and built a customized version of its data-mapping and analysis tool to identify the demographic suitability of towns and prospective sales outlets. As a result, the company enjoyed a very successful rollout of the new brand.[6] P&G's launch of Pampers in China is another example of how, through meaningful market research, a brand can rebound from an initial failure while expanding internationally. There are many more successful (and some not-so-successful) examples of international marketing of products and services, mainly driven by IMR (or lack thereof).

The Challenges to International Market Research

Conducting a successful IMR is not an easy task. The challenges marketers face during the research process are numerous and include, among others:

- Collecting valid, reliable, and timely data.
- Transforming these data into information and information into insights.
- Communicating insights to the decision-makers.
- Crafting the right marketing strategies.
- Designing an impactful marketing campaign.
- Developing a successful new product or service tailored to the target market.

However, being aware of the most common difficulties from the outset can improve your chances of success as explained next:

Being sensitive to the differences between and within countries:
The unknowns and uncertainties in an international context are manifold. Differences in culture, language, religion, infrastructure, politics, money, and even regulatory systems must be considered. These changing variables mean there is no guarantee that something that worked well in one country will work well in another, too. Even research processes such as data collection efforts and insight generation will differ across countries and cultures. Therefore, it is important to be sensitive to these variables and adjust strategies accordingly. Language itself can be a major impediment to effective data collection. Variations in literacy levels, dialects, languages, and the meaning of constructs (i.e., a household might include grandparents, uncles, and aunts in one country but only father, mother, and children in another), as well as differences in response styles (i.e., respondents may give answers that are socially or culturally acceptable), can all impede meaningful data collection. To address these issues, managers should consider involving native speakers in creating and verifying data collection instruments and using translation techniques like back translation or parallel translation.[7]

Another way to overcome this is to employ experts who are well-versed in local customs and cultures when interpreting customer feedback and research projects. Another recommendation is to consider the relative comparability of results across cultures. Market researchers often must address the tradeoff between staying relevant in one market and standardizing the aggregate and comparative results method. Especially as research shifts to online environments and digital platforms, the seemingly invisible boundaries across countries and cultures can lead managers to adopt a *one-size-fits-all* approach in interpreting the customer feedback collected online. To prevent this approach, it is essential to have a thorough understanding of the underlying cultural, attitudinal, and behavioral differences that lead customers to lend their feedback to companies.

P&G's Struggle with Introducing Diapers to China

When P&G first launched Pampers in China during the late 1990s the effort failed. Of course, it did not help that Chinese families had always gotten along just fine with cloth diapers and *kaidangku* (open-crotch pants), which helped children start potty training as early as 6 months. P&G underestimated the importance of these cultural and consumption habits and instead promoted the product benefits highly valued by Western markets, such as convenience, a classic international marketing mistake.

Another failure was relying on a low price point, which the company thought Chinese consumers would find appealing. However, most parents base their buying decisions on what is best for their only child rather than the price. Even though Pampers produced a quality product, revised in 2006 to be softer, more absorbent, and affordable, mothers still didn't see why they should substitute the *kaidangku* for diapers, which they deemed an unnecessary commodity.

Following these early failures, the company—whose purpose is "to improve the lives of consumers around the world"—put its research competency to work. Part of P&G's ethos is that brand leaders visit consumers in their homes to uncover each market's nuances. During their visits to China to better understand parents' nursery habits, employees heard the same thing repeatedly, said Frances Roberts, the global brand franchise leader for Pampers: "*We want more sleep.*"

With the help of the Beijing Children's Hospital's Sleep Research Center, P&G researchers conducted two exhaustive studies between 2005 and 2006, involving 6,800 home visits and more than 1,000 babies across 8 cities in China. Instead of cloth, select babies were tucked into bed with Pampers. P&G reported that, on average, the babies who wore the disposables fell asleep 30 percent faster, slept an extra 30 minutes, and had 50 percent less sleep disruption through the night. The study even linked the extra sleep to improved cognitive development, a compelling point in a society obsessed with academic achievement.

Pampers then launched its famous *Golden Sleep* campaign in 2007. The campaign framed Pampers as a product that could help improve the quality of babies' sleep patterns, allowing parents to sleep better, too. A viral campaign on the Pampers Chinese website asked parents to upload photos of their sleeping babies to drive home the study's sleep message; the response was impressive, with 200,000 photos that P&G used to create a 660 square meter photomontage at a retail store in Shanghai.

Through market research, P&G uncovered a more profound and relevant need (more sleep) for Pampers than price or convenience in the Chinese market. They linked this increased sleep to cognitive development and finally featured mothers' authentic experiences in the Golden Sleep campaign. Deeper consumer understanding, better brand-building, and meaningful innovation paid off for P&G; Pampers not only became the best-selling diaper in China but also helped reframe an entire category of products, creating an enormous growth opportunity and cementing a top-notch reputation for the brand. As discussed in the previous chapter, cultural differences have been a driving force for customizing international marketing strategies and tactics. This is also relevant to market research studies. Many academic and practitioner studies discuss how the different cultural orientations of nations can impact the interpretation of a market research project's results.

Understanding the fast pace of change in consumption trends:
We live in an ever-changing world, with the rate of change moving at a lightning pace. Managers need to be aware that today's research-based insights may become outdated by tomorrow. Moreover, it has become increasingly difficult for companies to keep up with the exponential growth of data types and sources and the various approaches used to analyze them. Businesses must ensure their staff have the necessary skills to manage these rapid changes while investing in ongoing research into trends, preferences, and attitudes instead of settling for one-time studies.

A unique challenge for international marketers is to be aware of how the rate of change varies across regions and countries. Hence, research-driven insights in one part of the world may not apply to another. For instance, in EMs, which constantly evolve in terms of economic infrastructure and openness to trade, global events can quickly alter the business landscape, consumer trends, and product preferences. A good example of regional differences could be seen in the pace of adaptation to e-commerce during the global COVID-19 pandemic. The pandemic accelerated preexisting trends in digital shopping behavior, which resulted in more goods and services being bought online and increased e-commerce's share of global retail trade. In EMs like Brazil and India, the shift toward online shopping was even faster, albeit from a relatively low base.[8] However, in many of the world's least-developed countries, consumers and businesses could not capitalize on pandemic-induced e-commerce opportunities due to infrastructure and economic restraints.

In a recent McKinsey survey, only 60 percent of consumer-good companies in these markets said they were moderately prepared to capture e-commerce opportunities.[9] One implication of the varying pace of change in e-commerce trends is that brands need to customize their offerings and reach target customers according to the context and culture in which they operate and compete. An aggressive e-commerce strategy with a well-developed digital platform for ordering, payment processing, and delivery systems may work well in Europe but not in EMs. The entry of Amazon in China, Brazil, India, and Mexico presented the company with unique challenges and opportunities. These were directly dependent on the development of the infrastructure of each country, and the level of competition in the e-commerce industry. For example, in India, transportation issues posed challenges for Amazon's distribution system. They led to local competitors performing better, as they were more attuned to dealing with these infrastructural challenges. Specifically, local competitor Flipkart of Bangalore outperformed Amazon initially and was later acquired by Walmart, continuing its rivalry with Amazon to this day.[10]

Trends vary across countries, although most can often be traced back to underlying business megatrends, discussed in

Chapter 2. Companies need to be agile and invest in ongoing research to keep abreast of the more dynamic consumer trends, including sustainability, healthier foods, convenience, environmental concerns, diversity, protectionism, and more. Doing so will allow them to respond quickly as different ideas and movements gain or lose traction at various times in other countries.

Prioritizing evidence-based versus intuition-based decision-making: Unfortunately, many marketing managers still rely on common wisdom, simple heuristics, and managerial intuition when making decisions concerning entry and expansion into overseas markets, often ethnocentric, without taking the necessary objective, rigorous, and formal steps.[11]

The marketing discipline has experienced tremendous change over the last 10 to 15 years, enabling managers to access large amounts of data in real time at lower costs than ever before. In theory, this should make it easier to move away from intuition-based decision-making toward evidence-based decision-making. As is apparent by now, adopting a more evidence-based decision-making approach offers many advantages, such as reducing biases and gaining a more comprehensive understanding of the costs and benefits associated with specific marketing decisions.

While an evidence-based approach is advantageous, seasoned managers understand that logistical hurdles in conducting international studies, including vendor availability and infrastructure constraints, may render extensive research impractical. These challenges could significantly inflate costs and delay the market entry strategy and execution. Furthermore, cultural norms or legal barriers like the General Data Protection Regulation, which is a regulation in EU law on data protection and privacy in the European Union and the European Economic Area, may limit research methods. Nonetheless, emerging digital technologies enhance various research strategies, from comprehensive studies to rapid market and competitor analysis. Remember, even a modest amount of research can be more beneficial than none.

The Steps of the International Market Research Process

The market research process typically involves different stages. Below, we explain the steps and the activities involved in each step. In doing so, we adopt an aggregate approach where we summarize the essential elements of the market research process in four steps and then outline the key activities in each stage. We recommend this step-by-step approach to international marketing managers, as it provides a logical roadmap for the whole process. Of course, as with any recommended approach, there can be exceptions.

The first thing managers need to be aware of is that there is typically no one-size-fits-all approach to market research. Depending on the organization's needs, not all research projects need to follow all four steps or all the activities we outlined in each step. For instance, if the research involves only collecting secondary data from government organizations or other market research companies, there is no need to adopt a sampling approach for your research project as the purpose of the sampling is more related to primary data collection.

Sometimes, the steps do not need to be followed in chronological order either; there can be feedback loops as you progress in your research project, which may prompt you to return to an earlier step. For example, due to a roadblock in collecting primary data, you may need to revisit your data collection methods; hence, we put the reverse arrows for each step identified in Figure 5.2.

Furthermore, cultural, infrastructure, economic development, religious belief, or language differences are unique to the international context and might affect a research process. Despite certain caveats and exceptions, we recommend companies follow a systematic approach in their research projects and customize each step according to their needs to reap the benefits of the process.

Step 1: The research need: Research problems, objectives, and cost versus benefits

Imagine that you are at a critical point in your decision-making process. You want to pivot your marketing efforts in a foreign market, but you

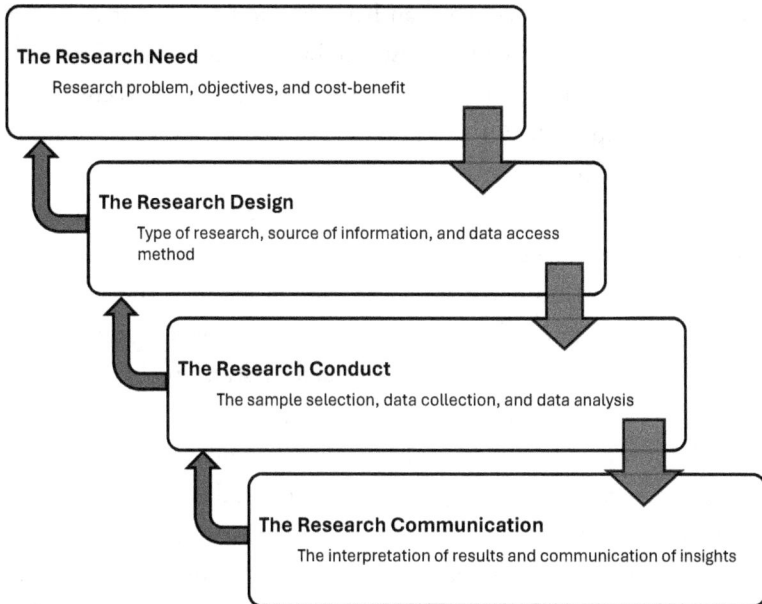

Figure 5.2 *The step-by-step approach to international market research*

do not have adequate information to move forward. Your management philosophy could emphasize the role of market research in this situation. While some managers favor market research over using their intuition, others might think that it is costly, time-consuming, and has other opportunity costs for the firm. Regardless of the approach, we recommend conducting market research to provide valuable input for your decision-making process and accountability for future success.

Before conducting any market research, marketing managers must develop a deep understanding of the company's strategic priorities at home and in its international expansion. Ultimately, this task will be easier in smaller companies with fewer layers of management. Still, even in more prominent companies, the organization's research needs must be evaluated in the context of available resources and business goals. Similarly, managers need to have a firm grasp of the business strategy and direction to assess the areas where market research can provide the highest value to an organization. This can apply to anything from informing business expansion or partner decisions to marketing campaigns or even direct sales targets. Establishing where you can have the most significant impact is especially important, given how costly and time-consuming the research process can be. Furthermore, it is essential to set clear objectives and quantify the expected ROI and benefits any market research will bring to an organization.

Once the needs are established with a positive ROI, a clear, succinct, and easy-to-understand definition of the specific research problem needs to be identified. Since identifying the research problem and objectives will influence the rest of the research process, it may be the most important activity in this first step. If, for instance, the research problem is about measuring the demand for your product in a foreign market, you need to establish the current market share of your competitors' comparable products. Do you only identify current market conditions or look at the potential and changing demographics and underlying consumer trends?

Suppose you have a clear idea about the specific problem you are trying to address. In that case, it will be easier to focus on the underlying causes of the problem, separate the systematic signals related to the problem from the random noise, and formulate the research questions that will address that problem most directly. Clear and measurable research objectives should accompany the research problem. These objectives should be action-oriented, setting out what the researcher hopes to achieve through their research. They should provide a pathway to the research design, and, if appropriate, hypotheses should be proposed to offer predictions about the research outcome. It is particularly important in more experimental projects involving quantitative data.

Considering these activities within the first step, we must also point out that not every decision requires market research. Especially when there is already enough information, additional information is likely to have either low or diminishing marginal returns. Alternatively, a manager with considerable experience in a foreign market may opt out of research and instead rely on tried-and-tested marketing methods. It could also be that time is limited, a speedy decision is more critical than an informed decision, or the costs outweigh the benefits. Market research may not serve the company's objectives in these instances.

Finally, suppose an assessment shows that research is not an investment but rather an expense and the resources it requires can be directed to other purposes (such as advertising or promotions) with the prospect of a higher return. In that case, proceeding with the research project may be unwise. The manager's role in this scenario is to remove as much subjectivity from this decision as possible, clearly laying out the pros and cons of conducting market research to help make an informed decision.

Step 2: The research design: Research design, data, and sources

Once you identify the research problem and objectives, the next step is to create a master plan for your research project, also known as the research design phase. Companies should consider multiple factors when deciding on the type of research to conduct, such as the company's international business orientation, the leadership's attitude toward market research, the kind of industry the company operates in, and the nature of the research problem.

Different research designs may be more appropriate depending on the problem and the context. For example, when introducing a radically innovative product to a new market, exploratory research can provide the background information necessary to make a go or no-go decision. Alternatively, focus groups and in-depth interviews can provide more detailed information about consumer needs and positioning, while quantitative studies can be used to predict demand.

The four basic types of research designs—exploratory, descriptive, predictive, and prescriptive—all have implications for determining the source of information and data and how to access it. Exploratory research is the most unstructured and informal research design. It informs almost any marketing decision, especially if a specific purpose or systematic sampling and data collection plan is not yet in place. Case studies, focus groups, and collecting qualitative and quantitative information from secondary sources online are all exploratory research methods.

The rest of the research designs can be examined from the analytics viewpoint. The three most popular designs are descriptive, predictive, and prescriptive. Descriptive research usually helps to answer the questions of who, what, where, when, and how.[12] Cross-sectional data collected at one point in time through surveys or interviews are common ways to conduct descriptive research. Questions such as the willingness to pay for a new product or asking respondents to rate brands for a particular benefit in a competitive product category are typical examples of descriptive research.

Predictive research takes descriptive research to the next level, answering how and why. Experiments testing causal relationships and longitudinal designs that involve measuring the same unit of analysis over time provide more sophisticated methods to understand the relationships between multiple factors. Popular experimental designs include before-and-after testing, or A/B testing, which can help marketers evaluate different options among target consumers (e.g., Website A or Website B).

Prescriptive research or analytics is a powerful tool that helps companies make informed decisions on their advertising campaigns or new products. It uses techniques such as simulations, neural networks, and what-if scenarios to identify the optimal action based on consumer feedback. For example, Google's self-driving car was developed using prescriptive research. This type of research provides answers to questions such as "What should be done?" and allows companies to make well-informed decisions that will result in the best possible outcome.

Step 3: The research conduct: Data collection and analysis

Once you have concrete research objectives and set a flexible research design, select a sample size and begin collecting the data. Identifying a suitable sample for your research design is essential for inclusivity and representation purposes. The sample size and determining random versus nonrandom sampling are also critical issues that will affect the outcome of your research.

Since it is not typically feasible to reach the entire population to draw inferences, many research designs use samples from a population subset. Sampling techniques such as stratified sampling, cluster sampling, and systematic sampling can be used to ensure the sample is representative.

Stratified sampling divides a population into groups and then includes some members of all the groups. Cluster sampling, on the other hand, involves dividing a population into groups and including all members of some randomly chosen groups. Lastly, systematic sampling involves randomly selecting a starting point and then selecting subsequent population members at a regular and predetermined interval.

Step 4: The research communication: Results and explaining their implications

The final stage of the research process is interpreting the results and communicating their implications. It is important to avoid self-referential criteria and ethnocentrism when interpreting the results to ensure accuracy, objectivity, and ethicality as meanings may vary from culture to culture. Said differently, it is important to avoid making judgments based on one's values and experiences or judging the results of studies conducted in other cultures according to one's cultural biases. By taking an objective and unbiased approach, the implications of the results can be understood in the unique context of each country.

The second activity is communicating these results to the decision-makers. Market research findings are transmitted in a report format, which should be tailored toward the audience. Accuracy, clarity, and actionability are three important aspects of communication. For busy executives, it helps to present the key findings in an easy-to-understand format, such as a graph or summary slide. Similarly, it helps when managers are involved throughout the process and are at least familiar with the research problem and objectives.

Different Types of Data

It is not possible to talk about market research without talking about data. When you hear data, most likely the first thing that pops into your head is numbers. Today, data means much more than that; not all data are created equal. Depending on your company's research objectives, different data types, whether images, texts, audio, or video, will present various opportunities and challenges for your research. Next, we present different and new forms of data available for market research in an international context.

Big Data: Technological advances have given rise to massive quantities of data and information about customers and markets. Such data are obtained from websites, personal electronics, apps, retail activities, sensors, smart devices, and so on. For many of us, these massive amounts of data are associated with "Big Data." However,

Big Data is not only about volume; other characteristics are described as the 4 Vs, referring to volume, veracity, velocity, and variety.[13] Veracity refers to the data quality and the extent it is valuable to analyze and contribute to the overall results. A high-veracity dataset would be from a medical experiment or drug trial test. Velocity refers to the speed with which data are generated. An example of high-velocity data is the stream of tweets on Twitter (rebranded as X) or the real-time internal data generated by a company like Netflix across all the countries it operates. Variety generally refers to the different data sources and is usually classified as structured, semi-structured, and unstructured. For instance, an example of high-variety, structured datasets would be the CCTV audio and video files generated at specific city locations.

One of the reasons why marketing has advanced like no other business discipline in the past 10 to 15 years is the *Big Data* available to marketers. However, it may be perceived as a gift and a curse depending on how you view it. On the one hand, there is now an opportunity to delve deeper into the mindset of consumers and the direction of markets. On the other hand, it can be challenging to always stay on top of all the fast-moving changes in this field, both in the collection and interpretation of data and in the tools now available to researchers, especially if companies lack the necessary skills and talent to manage it.[14]

Marketing analytics, the practice of using software to detect relevant patterns in data to make informed marketing decisions, has arisen as a sub-discipline of marketing due to the emergence of Big Data and digital transformation. Businesses across many industries around the world are utilizing marketing analytics to make data-driven decisions that optimize their marketing spending on the most effective activities. The global market for marketing analytics is predicted to grow by around 15 percent from 2021 to 2026 and segmented based on application, deployment, organization size, end-user industry, and geography. Some application areas include social media, email, search engines, and content marketing.[15]

The digital transformation of marketing practices enables companies to generate and leverage online data to craft more effective advertising campaigns and gain insights into consumer trends. Digital tracking and analytics can answer many market research questions, such as how consumers arrived at a company's website, the conversion rate to sales, the time spent on the website, a consumer's search history, geolocation data, and even detailed consumer profiles. With this data-driven approach, businesses can make more informed decisions tailored to their target audience.

Social media data and intelligence data: Among the different application areas of the global market for marketing analytics, social media marketing is increasing worldwide. The dominance and popularity of social media marketing campaigns can primarily be attributed to the increasing usage of platforms such as Facebook, Twitter (rebranded as X), Instagram, TikTok, and others. Social media has been a game-changer in emerging economies such as India, Indonesia, and Brazil. Whereas data collection and availability presented many challenges to conducting market research in the past, marketers can now ascertain consumers' needs and design appropriate marketing strategies. User-generated data through consumer reviews, ratings, likes, sharing uses of a new product, product pictures, and others can all be tracked by companies through social media monitoring.

Today, many people around the globe freely exchange their viewpoints through social media platforms, regardless of whether they possess expert knowledge. For better or worse, everyone can shape other people's perceptions about products, markets, brands, companies, and so on. One way for companies to leverage this aspect of social media is to identify and engage with influencers (i.e., people with large followings). Another way is to employ web-focused analytics to draw strategic meaning from social media data and channel this information to people within the organization who can use it. Through this mechanism, companies can develop *social intelligence* that is forward-looking, global in scope, and capable of playing out in real time.

A recent McKinsey article identifies four ways in which social media can increase a company's intelligence: (i) identifying data to map people and conversations; (ii) gathering data to engage and track; (iii) analyzing, synthesizing, and structuring its data mining activities; and (iv) providing curated reporting and embedding. When traditional and social intelligence methods work together and adapt to each other over time, they become an invaluable asset for C-level leaders seeking the most robust foundation for their decision-making.[16]

Additionally, social media marketing enables marketing teams to strengthen customer relationships and more effectively assess competition by closely monitoring consumer involvement trends. One cautionary aspect of the use of Big Data and social media data is that with the increasing level of data comes the issue of data privacy, which has been an increasing concern in recent years. Data privacy refers to electronic information security that restricts the secondary use of data according to laws and subject preferences. For instance, in 2018, the EU enacted the General Data Protection Regulation (GDPR), which imposes heavy fines on companies if undeveloped data security systems result in the breach of consumers' personal information due to hacking or similar means. Indeed, due to GDPR, many companies doing business in the EU had to deal with new limits on the amount and type of information they could gather, use, and store about individual consumers without their consent.

Primary versus secondary data: Primary data refer to the data collected firsthand from the direct source. Suppose your company is especially interested in obtaining data for specific company needs. In that case, primary data and research are especially valuable because they are usually collected to solve a particular company's needs and are relevant, unique, and novel. When companies need to make business decisions, develop an action plan, or launch a new product, investment in collecting primary data increases the chances of success. Different types of primary data exist; business problems or specific company needs and resources dictate what type of primary data need to be collected. Some popular primary data types are interviews, surveys, focus groups, observations, and experiments.

While primary research provides several advantages to the researcher, such as having more control over how you collect data and being timely and relevant to the business problem, it can also be very costly and time-consuming. Depending on the respondents' answers can lead to biased and inaccurate results. Secondary data, on the other hand, are the data already available in databases, government sources, international organizations, consulting companies, and market research firms that are publicly available or available for a fee. It is typical for most market research to start with secondary data, such as industry reports and databases, to identify some of the answers to primary research questions. After that, the company may collect its unique data or continue delving deeper into other secondary data sources.

Secondary data can be further categorized as internal or external. Internal data consist of information gathered by a company about various types of business transactions, such as customers, inventory, suppliers, sales numbers, products, and so on. Usually stored as a database or dashboard (depending on the technology level), these databases serve any purpose, from deepening relationships with consumers to identifying prospective customers and suppliers with poor performance. Also, advances in Customer Relationship Management (CRM) systems and technologies have made it possible to mine internal data more effectively and learn from it. External data, on the other hand, are obtained from sources outside of the firm, such as famous marketing research firms (e.g., Nielsen), marketing directories (e.g., AdAge), indices (e.g., American Customer Satisfaction Index), and university centers (e.g., CIBER).

Qualitative and quantitative data: The two types of data collected through market research are typically classified as qualitative and quantitative. Each has several advantages and disadvantages. While collecting large amounts of quantitative data has become more popular due to advances in technology and digital channels, qualitative research methods have not lost their relevance or validity.

Sometimes, numbers can be misleading, and it can be argued that to truly understand the beliefs, habits, and attitudes that make people choose one product or brand over another, it is still necessary to sit down and listen to them. Especially in a cross-cultural context, where meaningful data collection and equivalency are essential, the insights derived from qualitative data can be more impactful for decision-making. Of course, qualitative data are more expensive than quantitative data. A good example of a popular way to collect qualitative data is through focus groups, which require travel and involve hiring moderators, renting facilities, and paying people to participate in the focus groups. Sending teams of researchers into the field to interview people in their homes and workplaces can be even more costly.

Listening to Your Customers

As discussed earlier, technological advances have increased the channels for customers to communicate with companies, and vice versa, in real time, providing new opportunities for managers to listen to their consumers. The Voice of the Customer (VOC) has been a popular technique in market research, involving listening to customers and conducting a critical analysis to provide a more precise customer profile for a product or service. Griffin and Hauser[17] coined the term VOC, which is defined as a complete set of customer wants and needs; expressed in the customer's language; organized in the way the customer thinks, uses, and interacts with the product and service; and prioritized by the customer in terms of both importance and performance.

In the vignette we presented earlier in this chapter, P&G invested in research to understand Chinese mothers' habits, using a VOC approach. Today, with the prevalence of social media channels, marketers can listen to their customers more directly and clearly. The consumer culture that social media has created encourages instant feedback and collaboration with companies. As a result, companies can leverage a VOC approach for better engagement through crowdsourcing contests (e.g., LEGO, Starbucks) and artificial intelligence applications to understand better the consumer decision-making journey (e.g., Walmart is connecting brands with shoppers in the 2021 holiday season[18]) and gamification (e.g., McDonald's unites gamers for Friendsgiving[19] and promotes the line of crispy chicken sandwiches).

With the ever-increasing amount of data, tools, and techniques enabling companies to get closer to their customers, listening to consumers has become more important for large and small companies. In many companies, new roles such as Chief Listening Officers have been created to ensure that customer feedback is adequately considered. Their role is to actively monitor conversations on digital platforms and ensure that relevant intelligence is shared with the appropriate teams within the organization. Additionally, they can let customers know that the company cares about their feedback by responding quickly and clarifying that their opinions matter. Richard Binhammer, communications executive at Dell, explains: "Our Chief Listener is critical to making sure the right people in the organization are aware of what the conversations on the web are saying about us so that relevant people in the business can connect with customers."[20]

A Checklist for International Managers

In Table 5.2, we provide a checklist for researchers to self-assess their confidence in their research process.

Table 5.2 Assessing market research confidence

Use the following statements to evaluate the quality of your market research process	You got this? (1 = least confident to 3 = most confident)		
	1	2	3
We have defined a clear and actionable research objective that all key stakeholders align on.			
Our research design is well-suited to addressing the company's research problems.			
We follow a systematic, step-by-step approach that aligns with our research objectives.			
We have conducted a thorough cost vs. benefit analysis of this research project.			
We ensure that our research is conducted ethically and responsibly.			
We are aware of the limitations inherent in our research design.			

Conclusion

Data, signals, and insights are essential for executing international marketing. Companies can make more informed decisions with the right insights and an evidence-based approach. Studies have repeatedly shown that organizations that leverage market research to make decisions are more successful than those that rely on intuition alone. As the availability of data increases and stakeholders become more aware of the power of research, international marketing research—and, in turn, data-driven and evidence-based approaches to marketing—is likely to continue gaining prominence. With advances in technology, parts of the business research process will likely also become automated.

Technology and burgeoning forms of data are the future of market research, and international research is no exception. As data sources evolve and new methods to analyze them emerge, companies must stay informed to understand markets, consumers, and competitors better. These technologies can make the borders of international marketing less visible while making market research in an international context faster and easier. Mobile devices, social media channels, and online communities are revolutionizing the market research industry and are co-evolving with more traditional methods.

This chapter advocated a step-by-step approach for your company's international research process. However, there is a lot of flexibility; after deciding on the research needs and objectives, the management team can customize each stage of the research process. Taking this approach allows you to see the bigger picture while ensuring that all activities involved in each stage are appropriately focused. Doing so will result in an effective and efficient research process.

A final note: while quantitative data have become more abundant and accessible, companies must incorporate both qualitative and quantitative data to answer their research questions. Quantitative data can be easily gathered and usually exist in large quantities; however, it can be dangerous if used in isolation or manipulated. On the other hand, qualitative data can provide a deeper understanding of the consumer experience and help companies connect with their customers on an emotional level. When used together, these two data types can offer firms comprehensive insights to inform their decisions better.

Bites for Thought

Certain companies opt to conduct market research internally, and many organizations choose to outsource these complex requirements to specialized market research firms. This approach becomes particularly beneficial for international market and consumer research projects, which can drastically increase time commitments and costs and demand unique data collection and analytical techniques. While some market research companies specialize in specific areas, such as field studies or qualitative work, many offer a full menu of services that can be customized based on need.

Take a company like SIS International Research. They provide a comprehensive list of solutions ranging from qualitative research, including ethnography studies and in-home product usability tests, to quantitative market research, including online surveys and advanced analytics based on Big Data. Headquartered in New York, United States, they cover 120 countries and provide services to organizations through their foreign offices and partnerships. Conversely, London, U.K.-based FieldworkHub Ltd. specializes in field studies, conducting online and face-to-face market research in global consumer, B2B, technology, and healthcare sectors. These examples illustrate the various expertise and services available in the market research industry.

As the types, speed, and quantity of data and technologies have evolved, the solutions that market research companies provide to their clients have also changed. The AI-powered market research solutions offered by existing and new companies employ algorithms that process large amounts of data in far less time than traditional research methods to provide strategic research in market opportunity evaluation. Take HumanListening, an Australia-based conversational AI-driven insights platform, for instance. The company runs market research programs with global offices spanning four continents. Using natural language processing and machine learning, their platform enables human-like interactions with consumers to augment the traditional survey approach. It allows consumers to engage in a two-way conversation with a conversational AI companion called Evolved Verbatim Engine.

Market research, particularly on a global scale, rapidly evolves into a tech-intensive, interdisciplinary field. This transformation is geared toward achieving fundamental goals—understanding consumer needs, distinctions, behaviors, and their interaction journeys with products and services more efficiently and robustly. While traditional research disciplines like psychology, statistics, and anthropology continue to play a significant role, integrating data science and AI is increasingly important. Harnessing AI for data collection and analysis enables deeper insights and could offer brands a higher ROI. This blend of traditional and emerging techniques augments the quality of market insights and gives companies a competitive edge in their internationalization efforts.

Questions

1. *What specific goals does your company aim to achieve with the IMR project as part of its global growth strategy?*
2. *How comfortable is your company with leveraging AI-based tools for your market research needs, and what steps have you taken (or plan to take) to build these capabilities?*
3. *If conducting the research internally, how confident is your team in meeting the criteria for effective market research? Alternatively, if outsourcing, what essential attributes are you seeking in a global market research firm for a successful partnership?*

CHAPTER 6

International Brands and Company Reputation

Coca-Cola

"We're at an inflection point," remarked Manolo Arroyo, CMO of the Coca-Cola Company, as he unveiled the company's groundbreaking global brand platform, *Real Magic*. This platform, he emphasized, is not just a tagline but a transformative philosophy that advocates for a more human approach to life, one that embraces our unique perspectives. The inaugural campaign under this platform, *One Coke Away from Each Other*, was a powerful testament to this philosophy, symbolizing unity and bridging the gap between the real and virtual worlds.[1]

In 2016, the Coca-Cola Company launched its *One Brand* strategy, combining its Coca-Cola beverage brands under one global marketing strategy for the first time. This strategy was designed to enhance the company's reputation and create brand recognition with pops of red, minimalistic, clean design, and authenticity at its core. Using universal storytelling to connect consumers worldwide, underscoring its commitment to offering a variety of beverages, the company leveraged its scope and size. It moved away from multiple brand campaigns to one iconic brand campaign encompassing both the product and the brand. Amid the COVID-19 pandemic-related disruptions, the Coca-Cola Company demonstrated its resilience by doubling its core values and emphasizing the importance of togetherness. This strategic move aimed to make the brand more relevant than ever in today's hyperconnected yet divided world. The campaign's message was clear and resonant: The magic of humanity thrives in unexpected moments of connection that elevate the everyday into the extraordinary.

Coca-Cola, one of the world's most valuable and recognizable brands, offers inspiring lessons on building a trustworthy corporate identity, authenticity, and consistent global messaging. The company's success lies in its adaptability and strategic international marketing. Coca-Cola's unified mission *to refresh the world and make a difference* drives its long-term success through globally impactful brands, platforms, and campaigns (Table 6.1).

Table 6.1 The 3W-1H *of branding and reputation*

Branding and reputation (who—you[!])	Key tasks for IM practitioner (what)	Why it is important (why)	Tools and resources (how)
Identify your company's business identity, core competence, and mission * Utilize methods and strategies for global product launches while developing a strong international brand identity and reputation * Discuss the necessary resources and capabilities for successfully managing brand- and reputation-building, globally	Understand and address any home-country biases and cultural challenges to effectively build your brand identity across borders * Ensure your company mission and message are communicated consistently across countries and cultures * Assess the brand architecture regularly to make meaningful additions and dispositions to the existing brand portfolio	Organizations must build strong, resilient brands that resonate with customers' needs and preferences across borders * Companies must evaluate the risks and benefits to their reputation both domestically and internationally when expanding and develop strategies to mitigate risks and maximize benefits * Multinational companies can leverage their position to build partnerships aligned with SDG 17, promoting sustainability, strengthening trust, and advancing global development goals	America's Most Responsible Companies by *Newsweek* * BrandAsset Valuator * BrandIndex by YouGov * Global Brand Database by WIPO * Interbrand Best Global Brands * Kantar BrandZ Most Valuable Global Brands

Company Mission and Reputation

A company's mission serves as a compass guiding its actions and reputation, thereby influencing the effectiveness of marketing efforts. Missions that are clearly articulated and resonate with stakeholders enhance brand acceptance and cultivate trust and loyalty toward the brand. Many well-known companies also have unified missions at the center of their branding and marketing campaigns. Take a look at some of these companies and their respective missions and see if you can recognize the spirit of their mission the next time you see one of their advertisements:

- **Microsoft:** Empower every person and every organization on the planet to achieve more.
- **Unilever:** Make sustainable living commonplace. We work to create a better future every day, with brands and services that help people feel good, look good, and get more out of life.
- **Nestlé:** Unlock the power of food to enhance quality of life for everyone, today and for generations to come.
- **Starbucks:** With every cup, with every conversation, with every community—we nurture the limitless possibilities of human connection.
- **H&M:** Lead the change toward a circular and renewable fashion industry, while being a fair and equal company.
- **Nike:** Bring inspiration and innovation to every athlete in the world. If you have a body, you are an athlete.
- **Google:** Organize the world's information and make it universally accessible and useful.
- **Amazon:** Be Earth's most customer-centric company; build a place where people can find and discover anything they might want to buy online.

Before proceeding any further, take a moment to reflect on your company's identity, business purpose, and mission. Without clear answers to these three questions, the rest of your journey in your home country or abroad will be much more challenging. Integrating the company's mission into your branding, marketing strategies, and campaigns has the added benefit of clearly and concisely communicating your brand purpose. In other words, it allows you to consistently embed a purposeful reason in your communications to the outside world.

Of course, a company's reputation can be damaged or enhanced, and the effects of this can be far-reaching and long-lasting. As the famous saying by Benjamin Franklin goes, "It takes many good deeds to build a good reputation, and only one bad one to lose it." This saying is particularly true in today's digital era, where reputations are shaped by interactions both within and outside company boundaries. For businesses of all sizes, reputation is an invaluable asset that should be carefully nurtured, managed, and protected.

Consider Nestlé, a Swiss multinational food and beverage company with a rich history from 1866. Its mission statement emphasizes enhancing quality of life and contributing to a healthier future. This mission is reflected in initiatives like the Nestlé Nutritional Profiling System, which guides product development based on nutritional criteria. Additionally, the Nestlé Cocoa Plan aims to improve the livelihoods of cocoa farmers and promote sustainable practices.

Research confirms that a good reputation directly and positively impacts sales and customer relations. Additionally, direct marketing expenditures are only effective if your company has earned sufficient "trust" among consumers and customers. Suppose the basic level of trust is low. In that case, marketing efforts can negatively affect consumers and potential business partners, who may ignore your brand and/or category advertising and messages. A diminished reputation also exposes your company to demand-side risks, such as the loss of distribution channels, restrictions on advertising, and regulatory pressure. Additionally, reputation directly relates to a customer's purchasing intentions and willingness to pay a premium, affecting product sales in terms of volume and value at industry and country levels.

The good news is that there is a myriad of ways for a company to influence its reputation positively. However, the bad news for the marketing team is that they may have limited power to affect many factors that are outside their control but directly impact their reputation. These factors include employee satisfaction, product quality, public affairs, or company association with entities of questionable reputations. Consider the case of the Volkswagen Group, a German multinational automotive manufacturer. In 2015, Volkswagen faced a major scandal when it was revealed that the company had installed software in diesel vehicles to cheat emissions tests. This revelation severely damaged Volkswagen's reputation, leading to widespread public outrage and legal repercussions. Despite Volkswagen's extensive marketing efforts, including advertising campaigns emphasizing innovation and environmental friendliness, the damage to the company's reputation was significant and enduring. Consumers lost trust in the brand, leading to declining sales and market share.

Seasoned executives will be aware that almost anything can affect your reputation, from the day-to-day interactions of your sales team to your marketing promotions to the biggest company announcements; everything communicates and can be further amplified, positively and negatively. Nevertheless, having robust policies and guidelines, like anticorruption and employee codes of conduct policies and social media guidelines, can help ensure your company is not blindsided by adverse publicity.

Besides having sound policies and guidelines in place, ensuring internal, cross-functional collaboration and coordination is also very important, as no one wants to be caught napping in the face of a major risk, crisis, or other factors that could negatively impact the company's reputation. Externally, communication and alignment with business partners and other country-level stakeholders can ensure everyone is on the same page regarding the company's external image and main messages. This should be done proactively (e.g., through marketing campaigns and sharing good news) and reactively (e.g., by responding to external crises and events impacting the company).

While a company's reputation extends beyond marketing's direct purview, marketers play a pivotal role in shaping it through brand management and marketing campaigns. By proactively managing the company's image and responding effectively to external events, marketers contribute significantly to building and safeguarding the company's reputation and brand equity.

What Is Brand Architecture?

Brands are one of the most valuable assets of any company. While brands are prominent in many aspects of an enterprise, at their core, they serve three purposes: (i) to define and differentiate a company, product, or service from its competitors in the same category; (ii) to shape customer behavior; and (iii) to create economic and social value. Since companies seldom utilize a single brand for their various products and services, the brand architecture determines the number and nature of brand elements a firm should apply across new and existing products and services. It is a vital component of a firm's marketing strategy.[2] It also provides companies with a strategic roadmap for their international expansion.

There are three main types of brand architecture: branded house (corporate branding), house of brands, and hybrid brands. In corporate branding, the company's name is also the name of its flagship brand. Think Nike, Disney, Coca-Cola, Tesla, Netflix, Starbucks, Virgin, and Amazon. The shares people buy in these companies are also the names on their trucks, products, packages, and buildings. Also referred to as Masterbrand or Branded House, this strategy gives the company extra opportunity for name recognition while also helping to create a strong and unified brand identity.

TESLA's Rocky Journey in China

In late 2021, Tesla opened a large showroom in Xinjian, China, using its official post account on China's popular Twitter-like social media platform Weibo to announce that: "On the last day of 2021, we meet in Xinjiang. In 2022, let us together launch Xinjiang on its electric journey!" Tesla's post was accompanied by pictures from an opening ceremony that included traditional Chinese lion dances and people posing with placards reading *Tesla (heart) Xinjiang.*

Xinjiang has been in the news in recent years because of the limitations on the freedoms of its native Uygur population. Some researchers claim that many Uygurs and members of other minority groups have been detained in camps maintained by the government, something which the Chinese government vehemently denies. China is clearly an important market for Tesla. In addition to its large, wholly owned manufacturing plant in Shanghai, which opened in 2018, the company has showrooms in 30 locations throughout China and has managed to build a popular brand there. By February 2023, the company had sold 33,923 vehicles in China, a fivefold increase from 2 years earlier.

After opening the showroom in Xinjiang, the company experienced significant backlash, damaging its reputation as a green, responsible, and entrepreneurial company. Besides the media coverage, even the White House weighed in. "I can't speak to the specific situation of one company. But, as a general matter, we believe the private sector should oppose the PRC's human rights abuses and genocide in Xinjiang," said Jen Psaki, the White House press secretary in response to Tesla's move.

This is not the first time the company has been in the spotlight for the wrong reasons, but the case shows there is no way of localizing reputational damage. While it may be profitable for companies to cater to the priorities of the market and the local government, as Tesla did in China, this may hurt them in their home market. Whether it affects sales in the long-term remains to be seen.

Conversely, in July of 2021, Swedish fashion retailer H&M reported a 23 percent drop in local currency sales in China for its March-May quarter after it was hit by a consumer boycott for stating publicly that it would not source products from Xinjiang. These two examples show that there is no easy answer for brands navigating increasingly complex and volatile international relations.

However, having the same brand name on the company and its products is not always practical or expedient. By owning multiple brands, companies can diversify their product offerings and target different customer segments while maintaining a unified presence. This strategy is often called the house of brands, where a company owns individual brands in its various product lines. Also called a multibrand company, Unilever, with headquarters in London, is a good example of owning about 400 brands worldwide, including Dove, Lipton, and Ben & Jerry's.

Think about Kering, the French-based multinational corporation in luxury goods, owning Gucci, Yves Saint Laurent, Balenciaga, and more. In this type of brand strategy, consumers may be unaware of the ultimate owner of the brand, and, even if they are aware, they may not care. This is especially true for multibrand consumer goods companies like Procter & Gamble (P&G), a U.S.-based multinational corporation, owning Pampers in baby care, Ariel and Tide in fabric care, and Pantene and Old Spice in hair care. For these large multinationals, the total brand equity (i.e., the value of the commercial perception of the brand name) is tied up in multiple consumer brands and often larger than the brand equity of the corporate brand itself.

The third alternative is the hybrid approach, where the firm realizes that having the same name for the company and the product is not always practical or expedient. Hybrid branding is indeed a combination of the branded-house and house-of-brands approaches. Well-known corporate brands utilize this approach, such as Coca-Cola owning Fanta, Sprite, and Dasani brands; Pepsi owning Frito-Lay, Gatorade, and Tropicana; and Nike marketing also the Converse and Jordan brands directly to consumers. Also, another well-known house of brands, such as Nestlé, utilizes a hybrid approach through the ownership of KitKat, After Eight, and Perrier while also marketing Nestlé-branded products. With the increase in international strategic alliances, mergers, and acquisitions, hybrid approaches and cobranding (i.e., where two or more brands are combined in a product or service offer) have become increasingly popular over the years.

There has been a critical shift in brand management in response to global disruptions and changing dynamics in business environments. Recent research categorizes the shift into two features: (i) from a single to shared ownership of brands and (ii) from a limited geographic reach and impact to a greater geographic reach and a larger impact on societies. First, as increased connectivity and widespread technology have opened the floodgates to information and people worldwide, traditional brand owners have increasingly shared ownership of their brands with more stakeholders to join forces toward creating more meaningful brand experiences. Second, global connectivity has enabled existing brands to reach new markets and take on bigger societal roles, while also allowing for the emergence of new types of branded entities that further expand the branding space. While the first phenomenon has been coined the *blurring of branding boundaries*, the second has been referred to as the *broadening of branding boundaries*.[3]

The earlier discussion pertains mostly to companies that market their products or services directly to consumers. However, many companies market themselves or their products directly to other businesses. In this case, the name of the products or services they market matters even less than the name of the company and its brand equity. Since it is difficult for B2B companies to build brand equity when their target audience is relatively small, it may be beneficial to link the name of the main products directly to the company's name to increase exposure.

Awareness and reputation are all gained over time as you build your track record and earn the trust of your stakeholders. This is true whether a business operates in one market or internationally. For discussion in this chapter, we will refer to brand equity as the total value of your brand. For many companies, this will be the company's name, and, as a default, we will presume it is. Even if it is not, the principles behind sound reputation management and building brand equity are much the same.

For companies venturing abroad, one of the biggest challenges will be building your "brand equity" without a track record or a reputation in the host country. In most cases, brand equity will be nonexistent except for famous brands. This is why many companies choose joint ventures with local partners, leveraging their trustworthiness to the company's benefit. However, even then, building brand equity in a new country requires effort, discipline, and smart alignment in delivering customers what they need, rather than what you think they want. As outlined in previous chapters, conducting comprehensive research beforehand can help companies in this process.

Building Your International Brand

As a company enters international markets, it faces several questions regarding its international brand architecture, such as whether to use powerful domestic brands abroad—for example, Coca-Cola—or develop brands specific to regional and national preferences or use a hybrid approach. No matter which strategy is chosen, rational global brand architecture is integral to the firm's international marketing strategy, as it provides a structure to leverage strong brands into other markets, integrate brands purchased in other markets, and convey the firm's international branding strategy. Managing global brand architectures is essential to balancing domestic, foreign, and global positioning strategies for the company's portfolio brands. Adopting the right brand positioning in a global environment while considering the COO effects, quality perceptions, and brand image is essential for success.

Hence, building your international brand must start with the right processes. At the core of any successful brand lies a combination of its appeal and the uniformity of its implementation. Great brands often have an appealing "edge" to them that builds on the company's mission to occupy a space in the target audience's mind. But before we discuss how to create an edge for a brand, we must first tackle the standard fare—the things that all brands should do, even if it seems somewhat tedious.

Brand Standards

Every company and brand should have a brand standards document, which is easily accessible to all employees and agency partners. This document is an essential reference document and guidebook for internal teams and business partners authorized to use the company's assets in marketing, advertising, and communication channels and on "company-owned" or "company-shared" assets. It outlines the rules for using the company's brand, including logo and other trademarks, helping to ensure that people can recognize the brand through a consistent application. It also helps protect the company's trademarks and intellectual property.

The brand standards document will typically have a detailed illustration of the company's assets, logo (dimensions, company designations, how to use with partners, etc.), brand colors, email signatures, typography, imagery, and other brand communications guidelines, which will vary from company to company. Typically, it is accompanied by legal language and an overview of the company's trademarks. It will also include language about how, when, and where to ask for permission from the marketing department to use the company's logo and trademarks.

Company Story or Narrative

Every company has a unique story to tell; telling this story engagingly and creatively to an audience unfamiliar with your business is an essential step in building brand equity. Your company's story should be slightly innovative and include a narrative of how and why the company was founded. It could also include a description of its products or services and who it is intended for, although this is not always necessary. The story should be centered around the company's mission. It may also include a statement of the organization's values or philosophies, the competitive advantages of the business, or a desired future state—the "vision."

While a vision is often confused with a mission, the two fundamentally differ. A mission statement is a concise description of an organization's purpose and goals, while a vision statement is intended to be both aspirational and inspirational. As such, it doesn't need to be practical in the way mission statements are. A vision can include lofty goals that may never be realized but serve to rally the organization around a greater purpose. For example, a low-cost food manufacturer may envision a world without hunger, even though the chances of this vision coming true are slim. A mission, on the other hand, is attainable and focuses on the core business. A company's mission and vision are typically constant and unchanging, representing the organization's ongoing purpose and focus.

Both your mission and vision are great tools to clearly communicate the company's purpose and direction to its stakeholders, especially to employees, who can benefit from a sense of identity. A company's stakeholders can be broadly classified into primary stakeholders, such as employees, customers, shareholders, and other business partners, as well as secondary stakeholders, like banks, local government, and vendors. As these entities will want to know more about your company, having a clear, concise mission and vision statement will help build your company's brand equity in foreign markets.

Building an Internal Culture Conducive to a Strong Brand

As indicated earlier, having a strong mission statement can serve to create a sense of identity among your employees, which is especially important in foreign markets where people may have been previously unaware that you even existed! To ensure that your employees are empowered to act as your biggest brand ambassadors, considerable effort and time should be spent creating regular communication channels, giving them the resources they need to succeed, and informing them first of any new marketing campaigns. Marketing should also collaborate closely with human resource (HR) to ensure the right policies are in place to protect your reputation.

Among the policies that most companies have for their employees are codes of conduct and others like antibribery and anticorruption policies. These are compliance documents that will go some way toward ensuring that rogue or misbehaving employees do not undermine the reputation your company is trying to build. Social media policies are also especially important in the digital age, as they help to ensure that employees appropriately represent the company.

Social media policy guidance should be clear, concise, and not overly long, as people's behavior online often involves frequent switching between posts and ideas. Additionally, a policy should not discourage employees from posting about their company, as they are often the greatest brand advocates. Some even refer to employees as brand assets, but describing people as assets is usually left to those in the financial profession.

Creating a Differentiated Company Brand

Creating a differentiated brand across time and cultures is a conundrum that has continued to plague managers, both from large and small companies. Part of this comes back to a company's mission, but it also hinges on your brand's competitive edge over its competitors. So, what type of edge are you creating? Research shows that approximately 80 percent of companies with a high level of sustained performance had a well-defined and easily understood differentiation at the core of their operations, exemplified by its brand's "edge." How a company develops an edge, or a differentiation, will depend on their competitive advantage, where it focuses its innovation, the makeup of their portfolio, and their history, expertise, and mission. Here are a few examples of spaces where companies have developed an edge to build their brand:

- **Samsung:** Managing a large portfolio of superior electronics.

- **Disney:** Management system focused on partnerships, M&As, and joint ventures.
- **Airbnb:** Regulatory management expertise, navigating regulations in over 200 countries.
- **Lenovo:** Outstanding supply chain and production capabilities.
- **Amazon:** Unparalleled price, speed, and disruptive value.
- **Google:** Digital innovation.
- **Apple:** Ecosystem of simple, high-quality products and services.
- **Coca-Cola:** Ubiquitous and universal brand.

Note that while every company should create a unique brand, the brand must be built on the unique and relevant features that give it an advantage over its competitors. It should be relevant to consumers in that it has key attributes that they desire, and unique in the sense that the brand's features are tied directly to the product's distinctive performance and/or promise. As such, strong brands are built on the sharp edge of being unique yet relevant. A common mistake many companies make is that they try to differentiate themselves too much, losing sight of what consumers want, understand, and care about. Here, research plays a pivotal role in understanding how your customers and consumers refer to you. The main takeaway here is that you don't need to reinvent the category you play in; you should explain your brand's unique features in an easily understandable way. Here are some examples of a social media policy:

- Promote the company and the brand.
- Speak for yourself, but remember your actions represent those of your company.
- Use appropriate language for a diverse audience.
- Show respect and humility in all communication.
- Identify yourself as working for the company as appropriate.
- Don't release any confidential information.
- Don't pick fights.

- Don't feel obliged to respond to negative comments; if you need guidance on how, when, or with whom to engage, consult the communications and compliance team.
- Have fun!

While most policies and guidelines are created to protect the company and the brand, companies can use several approaches to create an environment where employees are empowered to help build a company's brand equity. First and foremost is exposure to key company messaging. It is customary for sales and customer relations staff to be trained to communicate all the positive aspects of a company and its products and services. Still, other employees should be doing so too!

Here is a list of some of the communication materials and channels that can help increase positive brand loyalty and exposure to key company messaging and engagement:

Internal online channels and tools: Utilizing internal channels, such as intranets and social media, like internal Slack or WhatsApp channels, is a great way to communicate about work-related issues and keep employees informed and connected. Clear guidelines and expectations should accompany these to ensure respectful behavior.

Communication documents: Messaging houses, Q&As, and other documents should be accessible online and in physical locations to ensure employees can access the most up-to-date information.

Physical meetings: Town hall meetings and other events are great for motivating employees to become brand ambassadors and creating a sense of connection and community.

Internal marketing campaigns: Begin a marketing campaign with an internal event to show employees they are valued. Simple things can be effective, such as desk drops for promotional materials.

Social media: This is an effective way of building and maintaining relationships with current and potential customers, but it can also be used internally to build relationships and create a sense of community. Internal social media accounts, such as Facebook groups, can share news, updates, and events to develop a sense of community.

Marketers often overlook the benefits of aligning an organization internally, yet this is essential for achieving a successful company and strong brand equity in foreign markets. Taking the time to align the organization properly will not only benefit the company but also draw potential employees into joining the team, inspired by the passion and enthusiasm of current staff.

Leveraging Celebrity Partnerships to Amplify Your Brand Internationally

When expanding into international markets, celebrity partnerships or endorsements can play a pivotal role in amplifying brand visibility and creating emotional resonance with target audiences. Celebrities often serve as cultural icons and are particularly effective when they embody values and lifestyles that align with a brand's mission. By collaborating with a well-chosen celebrity, companies can rapidly establish trust, foster familiarity, and enhance their credibility in markets where they may otherwise lack a strong foothold.

To maximize the impact of celebrity endorsements, it is essential to do your homework and approach these collaborations with cultural sensitivity. Selecting a celebrity with strong local appeal can help bridge cultural gaps and position the brand as authentic and relatable. For example, a celebrity known for their advocacy of sustainability could enhance the brand's commitment to global goals like the UN's 17 SDGs while also addressing specific regional values. However, this requires a deep understanding of cultural nuances to ensure the partnership feels genuine rather than opportunistic. Misalignment in this area can undermine the brand's reputation and erode consumer trust.

To mitigate potential risks associated with celebrity collaborations, a thorough vetting process is recommended to ensure the chosen partner's values align with the brand's long-term vision. A celebrity's personal actions or controversies can quickly impact the brand's reputation, making proactive planning critical. This includes establishing a robust crisis management plan with strategies for distancing the brand from the celebrity if necessary and implementing clear communication protocols to address public concerns, helping the company maintain control over its narrative.

Equally important is measuring the ROI for these partnerships. Metrics that can be used include increased brand awareness, customer engagement, and sales performance. Beyond short-term gains, companies should assess how celebrity endorsements impact their brand equity over time. Integration with digital platforms is particularly effective in this regard. Many celebrities have extensive social media followings, offering brands a direct line to millions of engaged followers. Collaborations that involve co-created content—like influencer-style posts, campaigns, or even limited-edition products—can significantly boost engagement and ensure sustained impact.

Ultimately, successful celebrity partnerships require a deliberate and thoughtful approach. By aligning collaborations with a company's mission, cultural strategy, and brand standards, businesses can turn these partnerships into powerful tools for expanding global presence. A striking example is the Philippines' girl group BINI, which has partnered with brands like Maybelline, Coca-Cola, and Jollibee.[4] Through these collaborations with BINI, these brands had an opportunity to connect more deeply with the Gen Z market in the host country, significantly elevating their visibility. Examples like this illustrate how culturally attuned partnerships can forge meaningful connections and amplify brand impact.

Challenges to International Branding

International marketers often face several unique challenges when trying to establish a credible brand and build trust among customers and clients in foreign markets. These include counterfeit products, COO effects, and cultural factors. To better understand these issues, let's explore each in more detail.

Counterfeiting

Imagine you paid large sums to build your brand, create awareness, and gain a reputation in a foreign country, only to have others copy your image and/or product. According to the International Anti-Counterfeiting Coalition (IACC), counterfeiting is the fraudulent imitation of a trusted brand or product and is a longstanding threat to international marketing and trade. Whether you are large or small, virtually all international companies use trademarks to help protect their images and brands and help consumers distinguish between products and brands at home and abroad. For bigger brands, these trademarks are well known; think the Rolex crown, the name "Dove" in the Dove brand toiletries, and the golden arches of McDonald's.

Counterfeiting is a major global crime damaging the company's reputation and consumer confidence in the global marketplace and puts consumers at risk of health, safety, and well-being hazards. Popular industries vulnerable to counterfeiting include footwear, fashion accessories, consumer electronics, software, pharmaceuticals, and even business-to-business brands. Counterfeiting harms businesses and puts consumers at risk by using someone else's trademark and/or product likeness without permission to profit from another's brand reputation and awareness.

The global proliferation of counterfeit goods has been accelerated by the globalization of trade, for example, free trade zones, the advances in digital technologies (e.g., 3D printing, e-commerce platforms, lax laws, and regulations) governing the distribution of goods and services, and consumer demand for such goods. The ever-decreasing cost of production and the development of new technologies have enabled counterfeiters to produce quality fakes with high accuracy and at lower costs than ever before. This, in turn, has fueled an increase in demand for false and pirated goods, driving the growth of these markets.

Businesses invest time, money, and resources in protecting their brands and trademarks, and governments, international organizations, and law enforcement agencies fight against counterfeiting, too. Yet counterfeiting prevails and is one of the greatest risks for companies seeking to build their brands and reputations, especially internationally. So, what can businesses do to prevent this from happening?

First and foremost, it pays to take proactive steps to protect your brand and trademarks from counterfeiting. When it comes to identifying and reporting counterfeits and gray market brands, your business can conduct regular monitoring of e-commerce and social media sites using different search engines (e.g., Southeast Asia, South America, Middle East, Africa), to identify the products that use your design rights, copyright, or trademarks and then to get the online marketplace to remove those counterfeit products from their sites.[5] Businesses can also continue to invest in more secure and cutting-edge technologies, such as digital watermarking and blockchain technology, to track and verify the authenticity of products.

Involving consumers in the fight against counterfeit materials is an effective strategy to help protect your brand and build its credibility and reputation. You can educate them about the existence of knock-off goods and urge them to become savvy shoppers by paying attention to the price tag, packaging, and place of purchase. This will help them make informed decisions when buying genuine products and avoid the hidden dangers and costs associated with counterfeiting. To increase the impact of your message, involving third parties who can speak out on your behalf and making sure the message does not come across as self-serving is important.

Lastly, businesses can work with governments, international organizations, and law enforcement agencies to develop collaborative strategies to crack down on counterfeiting activities. By taking these steps, businesses can reduce the risk of counterfeiting and protect their brand and reputation.

Country-of-Origin Effects

COO effects typically refer to the influence a product or service's association with a given country has on consumer perceptions. Various factors, such as the country of manufacture, the country of design, and the location of headquarters, can determine the COO.[6] This external characteristic is a proxy for consumer perceptions of product quality, reliability, and prestige.

COO is particularly influential when consumers possess limited knowledge about a brand or if the country of origin has an established reputation. Studies have demonstrated that COO can create product–country associations or stereotypes that can be advantageous and disadvantageous, for example, Chinese silk, German cars, Colombian coffee, and French fashion. The success of a brand's internationalization efforts is also affected by national branding strategies and a nation's receptiveness to other cultures.

The tension between consumers favoring domestic over foreign brands and vice versa has long been an obstacle to brands' globalization efforts. On the one hand, ethnocentrism and self-reference lead consumers to judge other cultures and foreign products through their own norms and values, likely leading them to favor local companies.

For example, when Disneyland opened Euro Disney in Paris, it received a major backlash from French consumers with strong self-reference and who tend to favor domestic brands over foreign ones. This eventually led to Disneyland changing its name to Disneyland Paris and paying more attention to local consumer sentiment and preferences.

On the other hand, some cultures favor foreign products over domestic ones due to their better quality, prestige, and sophistication.[7] Thus, this tension arising from favoring domestic over foreign brands can often lead to difficulties for global companies attempting to internationalize, as they must straddle both sides while attempting to meet consumer needs.

Alden et al.[8] outlined three distinct types of brand positioning: local consumer culture positioning, foreign consumer culture positioning, and global consumer culture positioning. For example, Budweiser has associated itself with small-town American culture to appeal to ethnocentric consumers. At the same time, Shiseido has used Japanese models in its commercials to appeal to those who prefer foreign brands. Examples of global consumer positioning include brands like Apple and K-pop, which focus on creating shared sets of consumption-related symbols that resonate across cultures.

Certain brands owe their success to successfully integrating into many different countries and cultures worldwide, creating a truly global image that allows them to pursue a global consumer culture positioning easily. Brands such as Coca-Cola, Red Bull, and Phillips can be evaluated independently of their COO image. Despite the recent rise in nationalistic movements and the retreat of globalization in some parts of the world, the digital revolution and the ease of communication through social media have enabled these international brands to continue pursuing a global consumer culture positioning.

The Role of Domestic Culture

International marketers must be keenly aware of the nuances of creating a global brand platform while accounting for the cultural differences between markets. A one-size-fits-all approach is rarely effective, as consumers will interpret and respond differently to branding strategies, product attributes, and messaging based on their distinctive cultural traits. Even successful global brands like McDonald's, Red Bull, Toyota, or Enterprise Rent-a-Car have adopted unique strategies to recognize the cultural differences between markets.

Cultural symbols, norms, and values are particularly influential in the perception and acceptance of a global brand. Language, religion, and symbols are integral to how consumers embrace or reject a global brand. As digital technologies continue to evolve and nationalistic sentiments remain strong across the globe, understanding these cultural elements is essential for international marketers who want to strike the optimal balance between a global brand platform and local marketing.

Concerning these different aspects, international marketing is full of examples and scenarios where the product or the service represented by the "global" brand has to adapt to a domestic culture. Take McDonald's venture into India. Of its 40,000 locations in 120 countries, 500 are in India, serving customers who do not eat beef or pork products depending on their religious beliefs. To cater to the Indian palate, McDonald's revamped their entire menu. Beef patties were replaced with chicken and vegetarian patties. The Big Mac was replaced with the Maharaja Mac, and the Cheeseburger gave way to the potato-based McAloo Tikki. Novel vegetarian items were also added to the menu, and cashiers were segregated between those with and without meat items. This monumental undertaking required a massive investment in R&D, new product development, and the establishment of new local suppliers to provide the required ingredients.[9] Despite this massive adjustment to local culture, McDonald's held onto its core values, such as speed of service and convenience, part of its brand edge or universal messaging, when serving customers.

Language also presents a significant challenge for brands, especially given the increase in communications via different channels thanks to the digital revolution. We are inundated with examples of improper translations, the different perceptions of humor across different cultures, and the often-ignored associations of brand slogans with inappropriate words or phrases in the local language. Many brands have experienced major setbacks in their foreign ventures. To add further complexity to language, brand managers must also consider spoken versus formal language within a society.

As we discussed in the chapter on culture, some cultures tend to be low-context, typically Western cultures such as the United States, Canada, and Western Europe. In these countries, what is said is precisely what is meant. In high-context cultures, typically East Asia, the Middle East, and North Africa, besides what is said verbally, firms should also recognize the importance of the societal standing of the message's source, the tone of voice, body language, and other gestures.

High-context cultures can present a challenge for globalizing brands from low-context cultures. For example, in 2016, BMW introduced its brand-new model in the United Arab Emirates with a commercial that depicted players from a local football team singing the national anthem at the start of a game but breaking off halfway through and rushing out of the stadium into a fleet of waiting BMWs.[10] The implication was that BMW cars were more important than the national anthem, sparking outrage from the local community. This incident taught the company an important lesson in how not to communicate brand values in a collectivistic and high-context culture.

To avoid or overcome the potential challenges posed by different aspects of domestic culture, managers should be mindful of whether to take an adaptive or a standardization approach when building their international brands. In most cases, it will require a combination of strict standardization in some markets and adaptive flexibility in others. Market research is essential in this regard; as discussed in Chapter 5, it can involve various qualitative and quantitative data collection techniques, such as in-depth observations, interviews, focus groups, and web and social media scraping. These data points can inform meaningful international branding strategies and tactics. Companies should also allow local teams more discretion in leading international expansion and local brand-building to understand better and accommodate local cultures.

The role of companies' considering ideas and suggestions from their local teams when making strategic and tactical decisions is critical.[11] Without a system to ensure that the views of local partners, salespeople, vendors, and consultants are heard, the company will miss out on leveraging its expertise and building trust and relationships integral to brand-building in foreign markets.

Above and Beyond: Creating a Sustainable International Brand

"The most powerful way for business to benefit society is not through charitable giving or even good corporate citizenship. But through addressing social issues and connected to the company's industry strategy directly with a business model—through capitalism." (Michael Porter)[12]

First introduced as corporate social responsibility in 1953, the topic of sustainability today includes three broad areas: Environmental, Social, and (Corporate) Governance, which are usually associated with socially responsible business practices. One of the most popular definitions of sustainability can be traced to a 1987 UN conference, which defined sustainable developments as those that "meet present needs without compromising the ability of future generations to meet their needs."

Previously, we examined how the rise of ESG standards and their importance to international business investors and practitioners result from long-term trends. Here, we examine the impact of sustainability initiatives on a company's brand and how they can tangibly improve the operating environment for the firm with customers, government, and other stakeholders.

Environmental

Of the three ESG areas, the "Environment" category has received the most widespread attention and traction around the world. While there is ongoing debate as to whether businesses should be obligated to do more than meet environmental regulations, it is undeniable that implementing sound environmental practices beyond the minimum requirements can be beneficial to international firms. Climate change, extreme weather events, and resource scarcity are major topics in today's news headlines. Therefore, sound environmental practices can serve both as a risk mitigation strategy and as an excellent opportunity for customer/consumer marketing.

On the defensive side, sound environmental practices can help mitigate any risk from environmental pollution, litigation, regulation, or PR nightmares. On the offensive side, businesses can proactively build a brand associated with progressive environmental practices such as sustainable energy sources, water conservation, and electric vehicle fleets. This can not only help protect the environment but also help foster a positive public perception of the brand.

Of course, whether a company can market itself as environmentally sound will depend on the industry and field in which it operates. For instance, is there a link between its core activities, value proposition, and the environment (e.g., natural products, electric vehicles), or is it in a traditionally polluting industry (e.g., extraction industries, airlines)? It is also important to consider how the production or distribution process impacts the environment. Additionally, ancillary industries related to this company may need to be assessed for their environmental footprint. Finally, it is important to consider the latest environmentally friendly technologies and their impact on the long- and short-term bottom line.

The answers to these deliberations will help determine how proactive or reactive a firm should communicate its efforts in the environmental space. In other words, the extent to which a business is defensive, attacking, or even neutral in its approach to the environment will inform its branding and company messaging. Most importantly, from a risk management perspective, it is essential that companies carefully consider their strategies and approaches to improve their environmental-related practices and operations proactively.

Social

In addition to environmental metrics, ESG reporting also encompasses a company's social aspects such as its employee management, corporate culture, representation of genders and racial/ethnic groups, safety and health standards, and its relationship with its stakeholders including customers, employees, and investors. This helps provide a comprehensive understanding of the company's social performance. In recent years, more attention has been placed on diversity, community relations, and sound company culture. The reasoning is that the corporation should reflect society, that is, not be dominated by any subgroup, and give back to the community in which it operates. This can help build trust and goodwill, for example, by creating a workplace culture founded on mutual respect. Therefore, implementing sound social practices is now seen as an essential strategy for many successful brands.

One of the more pressing and difficult components of the social aspect of ESG for international companies is their relative lack of control over their subcontractors and suppliers. Issues such as safety in the workplace, forced labor, and even child labor can become potential issues for international brands due to their indirect association with substandard, inexpensive subcontractors. This may sometimes occur with subcontractors hired by subcontractors, hence further removed from the brand. To mitigate this risk, companies should have a comprehensive supplier code of conduct and compliance policies easily understood and adhered to by all subcontractors and suppliers.

For many of the world's most recognizable brands, addressing public criticism of their suppliers' inadequate working conditions has been a longstanding priority. In the early 2000s, prominent consumer brands like Nike, H&M, and Adidas took action, which continues to this day, by establishing comprehensive monitoring and auditing systems to guarantee that they adhered to their ESG policies.

Governance

The ESG model's last branch examines a company's leadership diversity and its adherence to ethical standards and laws, ownership structures, anticorruption and antibribery policies, as well as compliance with international laws such as the U.S. Foreign Corrupt Practices Act of 1977 and the U.K. Bribery Act. These measures ensure that companies act in the best interests of their shareholders and customers.

Good governance is crucial in identifying, assessing, and managing both legal and reputational risk. Strong governance is arguably even more critical for international companies as they are subject to various social and regulatory environments.

It is important to point out that good governance extends beyond mere compliance; it encompasses robust and ethical business practices that engender trust among all of a company's stakeholders. In fact, companies with excellent governance practices are usually perceived as more secure and better investments and tend to have higher market valuations.

Sustainability and Building Your Brand

Sustainability plays a critical role in shaping a company's reputation and building its brand. It serves as a risk management tool, protects against legal and reputational risks, and enhances a company's image as responsible, innovative, and committed to a sustainable future. By aligning sustainability with their core mission, companies can create a compelling narrative that boosts brand recognition and stakeholder trust. Businesses should assess how their operations create shared values and policies that enhance competitiveness while improving social and economic conditions in the communities they serve. First introduced in 2006 by Michael E. Porter and Mark R. Kramer at Harvard University, the concept of shared value can be defined as policies and operating principles that enhance a company's competitiveness, while advancing the economic and social conditions in the communities in which it operates. Companies that link their strategies to societal progress can unlock new markets, build loyalty, innovate, and improve efficiency. One such example is Patagonia. The brand, known for designing outdoor clothing for activities like climbing and trail running, integrates sustainability into its mission to *Make Positive Impact on the Planet*. Unlike much of the apparel industry, Patagonia is recognized for transparency, rigorous supply chain audits, and prioritizing long-term environmental impact over short-term gains. The company donates a percentage of sales to environmental causes, and, in 2022, its founder Yvon Chouinard transferred 98 percent of Patagonia's stock to the nonprofit Holdfast Collective, dedicating $100 million annually to environmental initiatives. The remaining stock funds the Patagonia Purpose Trust, ensuring the brand's commitment to proving that businesses can balance profit with environmental good.

Deloitte's 2020 *Global Marketing Trends* report highlights that purpose-driven companies grow three times faster than competitors and achieve higher customer and workforce satisfaction. Effective communication of sustainability efforts can include sustainability reports, ESG index features, or marketing campaigns showcasing environmental and social initiatives. Marketers should consider these key questions to ensure alignment with their company's mission, mitigate risks, and set measurable goals for success.[13]

Another area frequently used in marketing efforts is the company's responsible actions toward its stakeholders, particularly in building communities and having a diverse and respected workforce. Authenticity is essential in sustainable marketing. Companies must avoid "greenwashing," which occurs when they highlight limited sustainability efforts while ignoring broader environmental or social impacts. Genuine, comprehensive approaches to sustainability are necessary to build meaningful connections with customers and stakeholders. Before any sustainability or ESG-related marketing campaign, managers should consider asking themselves the following questions:

- Are your company's ESG efforts aligned with your company's mission statement?
- Are there any potential liabilities from your current ESG efforts?
- To what extent have you communicated your ESG efforts to internal and external stakeholders?
- Is your brand well-positioned to link its values and views to topical issues in the ESG space?
- What metrics can you set to measure the success and monitor the performance of your ESG-related marketing campaign?
- How can you effectively use ESG efforts to make a meaningful connection with customers and other stakeholders?

BP's Marketing Tagline—Beyond Petroleum

In July 2000, British Petroleum, then a 91-year-old oil company, embarked on a major rebranding initiative. It had hired Ogilvy & Mather to create a $200 million PR campaign to reposition the company as environmentally friendly. The campaign introduced a new slogan "Beyond Petroleum," along with a modern, green and yellow sunburst[14] logo replacing the traditional 70-year-old shield-style emblem. These changes were designed to underscore BP's commitment to green energy and its substantial investments in solar technology.

BP's efforts were initially praised, with the company drawing accolades from many different groups of stakeholders, including the media. However, skepticism soon grew among environmentalists, industry analysts, and the public. Critics argued that the core business of BP remained heavily rooted in fossil fuels, with renewable energy ventures being a minuscule part of their overall business. The turning point in public perception arguably came after the Deepwater Horizon oil spill in 2010, one of the worst environmental disasters in history. The infamous oil spill from a BP-owned site caused some 5 million barrels of oil to flow directly into the Gulf of Mexico, leading to what many described as the worst environmental disaster in the history of the region. The PR battle for BP was made worse[15] by the emergence of BP chief executive Tony Hayward as the public face of the crisis, as he further inflamed public sentiment against the embattled company, notably by saying, "I'd like my life back." Hayward was ousted from his position within a few months. By the following year, BP's market value had plummeted by nearly a quarter, with the company incurring over $40 billion in cleanup and recovery costs.

Notably for the company, this event contradicted BP's "green" branding and led to further accusations of greenwashing. Critics pointed out that despite BP's PR efforts to appear environmentally friendly, their primary focus and investments remained tied to environmentally harmful practices. These are more than PR liabilities. In 2019, for example, the nonprofit organization ClientEarth sued BP, using its own statistics to challenge its environmental claims. Despite BP's advertising suggesting a strong shift toward renewable energy, the lawsuit highlighted that over 96 percent of its annual investments were still directed toward oil and gas. According to BP's figures, less than 4 percent of its spending was on low-carbon initiatives, starkly contrasting with its public image of fueling solutions to the Climate Crisis.

Today, BP's actions continue to be cited as a classic example of *greenwashing*. Marketing efforts that appear environmentally friendly can backfire dramatically if they do not align with actual practices.

Conclusion

This chapter focuses on creating and managing a positive and valuable brand in the eyes of consumers across international markets. We discuss the key components of building and managing a brand internationally. We also integrate company reputation and how these two concepts are intertwined. We also provide several challenges toward building an international brand identity while maintaining a favorable reputation in the domestic market. Finally, we raise a topic of increasing importance to the key stakeholders of a brand: the strategic initiatives being taken toward creating more sustainable brands.

Building a brand is far more challenging than it may appear at first glance, particularly when attempting to do so in multiple countries and cultures. Creating a logo and deciding what message to communicate are only small parts of the process—to really construct a successful brand, it is essential to understand and properly align the company's mission, value proposition, core offerings, target audiences, and communication strategies.

Powerful brands require both artistry and a scientific understanding of marketing. Consistency in communication and marketing is just one part of the process. To maximize brand equity, the company should ensure that its core purpose aligns with its product, value proposition, and business practices, enabling it to deliver real value to customers. This means that the brand needs to make a real connection with people; trust between customers and the brand is key for strong relationships, successful campaigns, and, ultimately, a powerful brand.

Bites for Thought

Nike is one of the world's most iconic and recognizable brands, dating back to 1964. Originally founded as Blue Ribbon Sports by Bill Bowerman, the company rebranded itself as Nike Inc. in 1978 and went public 2 years later, propelling it to newfound heights. Today, Nike's presence extends to 170 countries, with its signature "swoosh" logo recognized across the world. Boasting revenues of over US$46 billion in the fiscal year of 2022 and ranking 13th in *Forbes*'s The World's Most Valuable Brands List, Nike has become a titan in the athletic shoes and apparel industry, while also being a major manufacturer of sports equipment. Its success has been hard-earned and not without challenges such as the widely publicized 1996 *Life Magazine* reportage on child labor featuring a 12-year-old Pakistani boy sewing a Nike football. This incident sparked uproar about the company's supply chain practices, prompting Nike to implement strict audits and guidelines for its suppliers.[16]

To bolster its brand image, Nike has forged many successful alliances with some of the world's greatest sports superstars, including Michael Jordan, Serena Williams, LeBron James, Cristiano Ronaldo, and Rafael Nadal. While these relationships have been mutually beneficial for the most part, some athletes have occasionally broken the rules or been accused of doping, sexism, and even criminal behavior. In such cases, Nike has had to make difficult decisions regarding whether to stand by their athlete or not—breaking with Neymar and Lance Armstrong, for instance, but standing by Cristiano Ronaldo and Tiger Woods. For the most part, these difficult decisions have largely played out well for the company, allowing it to maintain its status as a leading global brand.

Questions
1. *Name any superstars you know who are endorsed by Nike. Do they have an impeccable image?*
2. *Does your company have the potential to be endorsed by an influential public person? How much benefit would this bring to your brand?*
3. *Do you have a system in place to deal with a crisis that could damage your reputation?*

CHAPTER 7

International Marketing Execution

Getir

Founded in Istanbul in 2015, Getir, a grocery home delivery service, quickly gained a first-mover advantage in the Turkish instant grocery market. However, it was not until the COVID-19 pandemic hit that it experienced explosive growth in the sector across multiple markets, primarily driven by shifting consumer habits and the increased accessibility of digital platforms. At this point, the company seized the moment. *"Getir has been downloaded 7.7 million times in Europe since the beginning of 2021, whereas the downloads for our closest competitors have been hovering around 900K downloads in the European market"*— boasted Nazim Salur, the CEO and cofounder of Getir.[1]

In late 2021, building on its success in Europe, Getir entered the U.S. market, beginning with Chicago and later expanding to cities such as New York and Boston. The Getir app-based grocery delivery service offered unprecedented convenience and speed, providing customers with access to over 1,500 products on-demand that can be delivered to the door in minutes. This innovative approach revolutionized the grocery delivery industry, and its service became a popular choice for customers looking for an efficient and cost-effective shopping experience.[2]

"Our expansion into the United States is well-timed; we've been perfecting our approach in ultrafast delivery since we created the model. Now that we're established and thriving in Europe, it's an optimal time for us to move further afield and introduce ourselves to the U.S. market." (Mr. Salur in an interview before Getir's expansion into the U.S. market)[3]

Getir targeted megacities with large populations, congested traffic, and consumer segments with a clear need for ultrafast grocery delivery by conducting a market potential assessment on a city-by-city basis rather than a country-by-country basis. Furthermore, as the company's international expansion had been largely funded through venture capital, Getir looked to enter key financial centers to gain greater visibility with potential investors. Additionally, when assessing new markets, Getir said it considered consumer purchasing power and habits, local rules and regulations, and infrastructure supporting its digital businesses.[4]

However, Getir's journey from a regional leader to a global player was fraught with challenges that ultimately led to a significant scaling back. In April 2024, Getir announced its exit from the United States, the United Kingdom, Germany, and the Netherlands to refocus on its Turkish base, where it generated over 90 percent of its revenue.[5] This retreat followed earlier exits from Italy, Spain, Portugal, and France in July 2023. The company's valuation plummeted from a peak of $12 billion to around $2 billion.

Getir's aggressive expansion did not account for the nuanced challenges of entering diverse international markets. While the company said it did its homework to guide its strategic expansion, in reality it struggled with local consumer habits, regulatory environments, and competition, showing a clear lack of localized market understanding. Initially, the pandemic-driven demand surge masked underlying issues in Getir's business model. As the world adjusted postpandemic, Getir found its services less in demand, unable to adapt quickly enough to the changed market conditions. The leadership, while ambitious, also appeared to lack the depth of experience required for managing such rapid international growth. This led to decisions that seemed disconnected from operational realities, particularly in logistics and supply chain management, crucial for their business model (Table 7.1).[6]

Table 7.1 The 3W-1H of international marketing execution

Marketing execution (Who—you[!])	Key tasks for IM practitioner (what)	Explain why it is important (why)	Tools and resources (how)
Align strategic with executional elements of your business model * Assess and implement the right pricing, communication, and value chain elements * Consider the triple bottom line (People-Planet-Profit) in your international marketing execution	Assess the impact of environmental factors, consumer habits and attitudes, and cultural traits on the level of standardization versus adaptation in your product offerings in international markets * Ensure a solid multistep communication campaign and leverage the ever-growing technology and digital platforms to execute and measure the effectiveness of your campaigns * Predict, assess, and manage the potential disruptions to global supply chains	The tension between globalization and national protectionism has influenced companies' international market offerings * Digitalization and technological transformation have revolutionized the way the international marketers connect with consumers worldwide * One of the major risk areas in international business is the disruptions in the global supply and value chains; hence, managing them has become imperative * Companies now have a bigger responsibility to reflect the true costs of ownership in their pricing models	• BrandAsset Valuator * • Environmental Performance Index by Yale University * • ESG Rating by Morningstar * • Sustainalytics * • Interbrand Global Brands * • International Trade Administration: Services for U.S. Exporters * • International Organization for Standardization (ISO) * • U.S. Bureau of Economic Analysis (BEA)

International Marketing Execution

While Getir's initial model was groundbreaking, its failure to execute, pivot to changing market conditions, and replicate its model in global markets highlights the challenges that can arise during rapid international expansion. Many of the company's issues were discussed in different sections of this guidebook. For instance, in Chapter 2, we discussed how long-term trends, such as changing technologies like artificial intelligence, machine learning, and focus on user experience, can shape a company's expansion strategy and contribute to its success. While understanding and adapting to these trends is a pivotal task for international marketers in an ever-evolving global landscape, perhaps the biggest factor in the success of the international ventures is the ability of companies to execute effectively. In other words, you can have the best-laid-out plans and strategies, but ultimately your ability to react to and adapt to local markets, trends, and competitive pressures will mark the difference between success and failure. In the section that follows, we will review the basic tenets of execution as it relates to international marketing success, including the types of products and services you offer, pricing, advertising, and the difference a well-oiled supply chain can make.

A Revisit to the Key Executional Elements

Products and Services

International marketing managers often grapple with the challenge of creating globally appealing products while maintaining a local touch to ensure successful international expansion. When companies venture into foreign markets to sell their goods and services, they quickly understand the balancing act between standardization and adaptation. This balance is crucial in various aspects, such as the main benefits sought from the product or service, the appearance and design aspects, and potential enhancements tailored to specific foreign markets, such as perks, warranties, delivery terms, or customer support.[7]

The debate between standardization and adaptation is therefore central for international marketers, mainly concerning where and how much to adapt. Global product development and global branding lie at the core of this standardization-versus-adaptation debate. Both play a pivotal role in securing the benefits expected from establishing a presence in various foreign markets. The objective of global product development extends beyond merely creating a standardized product with global appeal. It also involves infusing the necessary flexibility and adaptability into products to meet regional tastes and preferences.

Why Home Depot Failed in China

Consumers in the U.S. market know that the Home Depot is a staple for *home-doers to get more done.* With its iconic bright orange façade, successful do-it-yourself (DIY) model, and robust sales, one might assume that the 44-year-old company, as the largest home improvement retailer in the United States, would easily replicate its domestic strategy abroad. However, a less-than-perfect understanding of local market culture and needs led to a strategy that failed to resonate with Chinese consumers.

Following the housing market changes after the liberalization of the 1990s, China experienced a surge in construction and home improvement demands. Inspired by early entrants like Sweden's IKEA and the United Kingdom's B&Q, Home Depot ventured into the Chinese market in 2006. They did so by acquiring Home Way, a local home improvement retailer, aiming to cater to burgeoning market demands. Yet, within a short span, a contrasting scenario emerged: while IKEA envisioned doubling its store count, Home Depot was contemplating an exit. By 2012, Home Depot had indeed left the Chinese market. Fast forward to the 2020s, and IKEA maintains a robust presence in China, even making its largest-ever investment there into e-commerce and digitalization. This begs the question: What did IKEA get right and Home Depot get wrong?[8] In short, Home Depot's brief venture into the Chinese market faltered due to an inadequate international marketing and business strategy, which overlooked essential local consumer preferences, lifestyles, and sentiments toward manual labor.

Home Depot's preference for stores in suburban locations, mirroring their U.S. strategy, didn't align with the Chinese trend of gravitating toward urban centers with rising affluence. Moreover, product offerings and pricing failed to resonate with local consumers. With many Chinese living in smaller apartments and condos in the city, there was little room to store the large equipment typical of Home

Depot's inventory. Pricing also became a barrier, with many of the products perceived as overpriced, especially considering that many of these goods, manufactured in China, were available at local stores at lower and often negotiable rates.

Adding to these challenges was a cultural disconnect. The DIY ethos, celebrated in the United States, holds a different connotation in China. There, DIY often implies a lack of affluence; the thinking being, *if you could afford it, you'd hire someone.* In a society that values highly upward mobility and the Do-It-For-Me approach over manual labor, Home Depot faced an inherent bias against DIY. This preference, combined with an abundance of affordable labor and homes often requiring significant renovations, meant that Chinese consumers preferred hiring professionals over doing it themselves. Ultimately, these unique factors combined to render Home Depot's offering incompatible with the Chinese market's needs and preferences, resulting in a swift exit.[9]

Similarly, global branding requires not just a consistent core marketing message that can seamlessly transfer across countries with requisite modifications. Most of the time, global branding is not just about a single brand but involves a portfolio of brands and entails a robust understanding of the brand strength, stature, and consistency across international markets. Take Red Bull,[10] for instance, an Austrian energy drinks company. Red Bull sells its products in more than 170 countries and cleverly modifies its energy drink, originally developed with inspiration from a Thai drink, to consumer tastes in the Western hemisphere. While Red Bull presents its brand image similarly worldwide (as a trendy energy-boosting drink, focusing on young professionals and adults), they are also successful in adapting to various regions, countries, and cultures through localization efforts. This effort goes beyond the product, as they are also a top media company, sponsoring local events, extreme sports, as well as local athletes. Red Bull adeptly localizes its brand through platforms like Instagram. For each country, they maintain a distinct Instagram page featuring content from local brand ambassadors. This infuses a touch of local culture and perspective for viewers. For instance, the Japanese account showcased videos from a Japanese box car race, while the

Swiss page highlighted sled racing. By promoting brand content rooted in local events, Red Bull skillfully circumvents language and translation challenges, ensuring authenticity. Beyond Instagram, Red Bull leverages print[11] and various digital platforms to tailor their sales and marketing strategies to each region.[12]

In recent years, major global economies have also transitioned from manufacturing-centric to service-oriented offerings, largely propelled by technological advancements (see Figure 7.1). The worldwide growth in

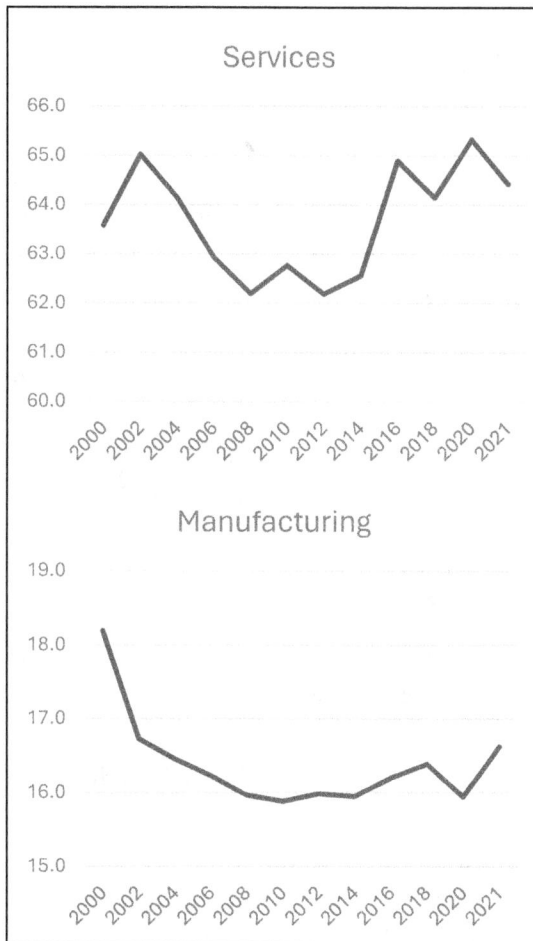

Figure 7.1 Manufacturing and services value added as a percentage of world GDP

Source: Data from World Bank Open Data. accessed April 3, 2024. https://data.worldbank.org/.

the services sector has outstripped that of product trade. Digitally deliverable services, especially in computing, business, and finance, have been at the forefront of international service trade, particularly during the COVID-19 pandemic. Many service providers have quickly become global since digitally deliverable services do not always require a local presence, and distances do not matter in foreign expansion. As digitalization has opened new horizons for global services, a company's presence needs to be maintained through a variety of channels, including a multilingual website, actively managed social media accounts, and various e-commerce platforms, which have become the mainstream channels to access customers and conduct international business.

This shift toward services impacts companies that focus on products, as consumers expect better pre- and postsale support services and engagement with companies selling the products. Offering products and services on an international scale and tailoring them to fit local contexts present challenges that go beyond marketing and communications. These include navigating tariff barriers, ensuring compliance with international product standards (e.g., ISO 9001 and ISO 14001), undergoing testing or approval procedures, navigating supply chains, and grappling with the intricacies of local bureaucracies. As highlighted earlier in this book, counterfeit products are another concern, as are safeguarding intellectual property rights—through copyrights, patents, and trademarks.

To succeed in international marketing, the strategic execution following product development is crucial. Said differently, knowing when to launch a product and/or service in a foreign market is key to success. This decision should be guided by three key considerations: the competitive landscape, the advantages of a "first-to-market" strategy, and the product's alignment with the target market's needs. Based on this assessment, marketers generally have three options to launch the product and/or service in foreign markets, each with drawbacks and advantages.

Simultaneous launch involves introducing a product and/or services globally simultaneously. While it creates a global buzz and enjoys economies of scale, it also carries higher risks. Any product issues are magnified across all regions, and coordinating a global launch can be logistically challenging. A sequential launch means debuting a product in one region before others. This allows companies to adjust based on feedback and learnings from the initial launch, optimizing for each region. However, it does give competitors time to observe and potentially respond or preempt the product in subsequent markets. A hybrid launch combines both strategies. A product and/or service might debut in several key markets simultaneously, followed by phased rollouts elsewhere. This strikes a balance, harnessing the buzz from simultaneous launches while allowing for adjustments based on early feedback. However, it demands precise planning and resource management.

Pricing

Pricing plays a pivotal role in international marketing execution. More than just a competitive instrument, it holds strategic significance. While pricing primarily aims to drive demand for your products or services, it also serves various other functions. It can segment markets, signal quality or exclusivity, mirror demand and supply, and even align with your company's triple bottom line. In fact, many marketing executives rank pricing expertise just behind product and service development in terms of its importance to any rollout.[13]

Pricing is a crucial executional element, directly affecting both the customer's cost of ownership and the company's revenue. Still, it must harmonize with other execution elements. Price setting typically considers factors like costs, customer demand, and competition, but it also requires understanding cultural variances, distribution-channel lengths, currency rates, and government regulations.[14]

Generally, companies choose between two approaches to pricing in domestic and international markets: skimming or penetration. Skimming involves initially setting higher prices to target premium segments, while penetration means setting lower prices to quickly capture a large market share. IKEA,[15] for example, discovered that adopting penetration pricing in China led to a significant sales volume increase, a higher market share, and deterred competitors.

However, establishing appropriate prices is just the first step toward sustainable profitability in global markets. Besides setting accurate prices, providing comprehensive and precise quotations, deciding on sales terms,[16] and selecting payment methods can also significantly affect your profitability.

In global markets, pricing strategies can fall into three categories: standardized, differentiated, or coordinated. Standardized pricing, also known as universal pricing, means setting a single price for all markets, based on average costs such as fixed, variable, and export-related costs. This strategy may be suitable for industries with little differentiation potential.

However, markets differ in costs, customer demands, competitive landscapes, and regulations, so a one-size-fits-all pricing strategy may not always be effective.[17] Therefore, differentiated pricing, where each market has its unique pricing structure, might be more appropriate. This approach considers market-specific factors such as competitor prices, certification costs, and local regulations.

In today's era of increased economic integration, digital business models, and global markets, coordinated pricing is also gaining significance. This approach strives to strike a balance between global price control and local market adaptability. It involves harmonizing prices across different markets while allowing for some local flexibility to accommodate market-specific conditions. Regardless of the approach chosen, success hinges on thorough local market research. Understanding competitors' prices, compliance costs, product modification expenses, and after-sales service costs is crucial for ensuring profitable international expansion.

When it comes to sustainable products, companies have a big responsibility to ensure that their pricing reflects the true product cost. International marketers should factor in the entire customer cost journey, from purchasing to using and disposal, when setting their strategies.[18] Customers often make choices with limited information, which can be even more limited when considering foreign products or brands. Sometimes, they need to switch from conventional to sustainable products, which can come with costs like learning and perceived risks. Despite sustainable products often having higher prices, marketers need to communicate the full value, emphasizing the extended product lifespan or other benefits. The goal is also to lower any additional perceived or real costs associated with sustainable purchases, such as search costs or transportation fees.

How a sustainable innovation is introduced, adopted, and priced varies across markets, from developed to developing and emerging economies. In more developed markets, due to legal requirements, institutional forces, international agreements (e.g., UN's 17 SDGs, the Paris Climate Accords), and societal pressures, sustainable innovations and practices tend to be more readily embraced and implemented at a lower cost.

Advertising and Communication Campaigns

Executing successful international promotion, advertising, and communication campaigns has become increasingly complex. The landscape of this aspect of international marketing execution has undergone a seismic shift in recent years, as global connectivity improved, communications channels proliferated, and markets became more accessible for both consumers and marketers. This change, influenced by Western expertise and customs as well as new global platforms, has redefined how marketing and communication occur in emerging and developing markets and has made coordination and collaboration between international marketers and their local partners more critical.

A framework is proposed for developing an international promotion or advertising campaign to help overcome some of the new and traditional challenges associated with executing international campaigns, such as understanding the subtleties of local cultures, values, norms, language use, religious contexts, and demographic variables.[19]

> **Selecting the right target audience:** An international marketer operating in multiple markets naturally faces not only a larger number of audiences but also a greater variety in audiences in terms of their responses to an offering. With the rapid surge in culturally relevant and sustainable options for consumers, international marketers are increasingly directing their focus toward audiences that exhibit a keen interest in brands that prioritize not only economic but also cultural and environmental impact.
>
> **Setting campaign objectives:** To execute an impactful advertising campaign, it's essential to have clear, objective, and quantifiable goals. These objectives can be mapped out on global, regional, or country-specific levels. While aligning with the directives from

the global headquarters, it's crucial to incorporate local insights to ensure that objectives are both relevant and achievable. Effective execution and evaluation of local campaigns hinge on tapping into local expertise. For example, Netflix's strategy of producing localized original content for its overseas expansion has not only garnered a significant foreign audience but also smoothed its entry into new markets.

Budget development: Every successful campaign hinges on a well-planned budget. While the vision and objectives are paramount, they cannot be realized without allocating the necessary financial resources. When approaching international markets, it's prudent to set advertising and campaign budgets on a country-by-country basis. Using the objective-and-task method can be particularly beneficial in this context. This method involves defining specific objectives for each market, determining the tasks needed to achieve those objectives, and then estimating the costs associated with each task. This ensures that resources are allocated in a manner that's tailored to the unique needs and opportunities of each market. Remember, a one-size-fits-all budget may not account for the nuances of individual markets. Being adaptable and flexible in financial planning can often be the key to a campaign's success.

Developing a media and message strategy: The marketing landscape has dramatically evolved with a diverse media mix and increasing digitization, with businesses now venturing into the realms of the metaverse and virtual reality to captivate their audience. This evolution demands a meticulous approach from international marketers to prioritize, coordinate, and implement their media strategies effectively. Global advertising is thus increasingly complex. To add to the complexity, local regulations means that not all media channels are accessible everywhere, and certain products, like tobacco, pharmaceuticals, or alcohol, might face advertising restrictions due to local regulations. Nonetheless, there are unparalleled opportunities to amplify your global reach through strategies like search engine optimization (SEO), creative use of AI, pinpointed online ads, and engaging interactions on social media. On the cutting edge, brands are now harnessing NFTs, virtual reality, and the metaverse for unique, immersive consumer engagements. Take Nike, for instance. They acquired RTFKT (pronounced as artifact), which leverages blockchain and augmented reality to create digital sneakers and other artifacts for the metaverse. This move aligns with Nike's vision at the crossroads of sports, artistry, gaming, and culture.[20] Many brands are still navigating the waters of virtual reality, testing its potential for deepening consumer engagement. While some see it merely as another platform to advance their global marketing aims, others recognize its multidimensional richness, believing it might even reshape their core mission. As with all marketing elements, diving into the metaverse without a well-thought-out, long-term strategy can backfire.

Executing the campaign: International marketing campaigns are inherently complex, demanding a mix of resources and collaborators that can often surpass what is required for domestic initiatives. When mapping out an international campaign, international marketers will need to coordinate and collaborate with advertising agencies, media buying companies, macro and micro influencers, and local marketing services firms, among others. The structure of the campaign's execution will also inevitably vary, depending on the company's strategic approach. Some organizations prefer a centralized model where decision-making authority is concentrated in the company's global headquarters. This ensures a consistent brand message and tight control over the campaign's direction, assets, and budget. It can be especially beneficial for brands that prioritize uniformity in their global image. On the other hand, a decentralized approach delegates more power to foreign affiliates, allowing for tailored marketing strategies that are deeply embedded in local nuances.[21] This approach can be advantageous in markets where local customs, preferences, and regulations demand a unique touch that a central office might overlook. Ultimately, the chosen execution structure should align with the brand's overarching goals, the specific challenges of each market, and the resources available to the marketing team.

Measuring the success and follow-up: What should follow a multistep execution of a communication, advertising, or promotional campaign is proper measurement. These measures can range from financial measures such as sales, market share, and profitability, to attitudinal measures like awareness and recall, as well as behavioral metrics such as conversion, purchase intent. Finally, other promotional follow-up elements in the world of international marketing can include international trade shows, PR, direct selling, and sponsoring sporting and other events.

The X-Factor in International Marketing Success— Creativity in Execution

As we've seen throughout this book, international marketing revolves around data-driven decision-making, segmentation analysis, market potential metrics, and the like. On the other hand, the art of international marketing lies in understanding cultural nuances, adapting messages to resonate with local sentiments, and designing campaigns that capture the essence of diverse audiences. In other words, the creative aspects of the campaign. Here are a few examples of creative execution resonating with local audiences worldwide.

KitKat in Japan: KitKat creatively embraced Japanese culture by playing on the phonetic similarity between KitKat and the Japanese phrase *Kitto Katsu*, which translates as "you will surely win." They introduced localized flavors like Matcha Green Tea, Sake, and Wasabi. The brand capitalized on this good fortune by conducting a variety of campaigns to emphasize this link. In 2009, Nestlé even partnered with Japan Post to allow people to write messages and mail the chocolate bars from 20,000 post offices. The special packages included a space to write a message of encouragement and affix a stamp. These promotional packages were sold out within a month. The campaign won the Media Grand Prix in 2010's Cannes Lions International Advertising Festival.

Heineken's "Ken" Ambush and The Barbie Movie: In the summer of 2023, Mattel premiered a Barbie film that didn't just captivate audiences but shattered box office records globally. While Mattel had its patents and trademarks securely locked away, making them untouchable for other companies, it couldn't fence off the buzz and energy the movie generated. Heineken, the beer giant, saw a golden opportunity and got cheeky. Without infringing any copyrights, they launched an ambush marketing campaign that was as witty as it was bold. On billboards, the tail end of their iconic green Heineken logo was magnified to highlight just one word: "ken." And below? A sly tagline—"Come on … Let's go party!" The Internet loved it. The billboard images surged across social media, with fans and even casual observers admiring Heineken's audacity and clever play on words. The campaign was not just a hit; it was a master class in leveraging cultural moments for brand visibility.

HSBC's "The World's Local Bank" Campaign: Travelers in the 2010s were invariably greeted by HSBC's standout campaign, "The World's Local Bank," as they made their way through international airports. Through clever visuals, HSBC highlighted its international prowess while simultaneously showcasing its intimate knowledge of local customs and perceptions. The campaign's distinctiveness was in its presentation: Each ad showcased a single image with contrasting interpretations, emphasizing how a particular object or scene could hold varying significance across cultures. For instance, a memorable ad featured hands adorned with henna. The ad simply read: "Bride in Delhi or Rebel on 8th street?" emphasizing that for Western viewers it could be perceived as a trendy tattoo, while in cultures like India it is linked to significant celebrations. Such campaigns not only reinforced HSBC's image as a global bank but, more significantly, as a bank that deeply values and understands the intricacies of local traditions and viewpoints.

Global Supply and Value Chains

A successful marketing campaign is deeply intertwined with a well-orchestrated supply and value chain. Although the intricacies of supply chains might not typically fall within the purview of international marketing managers, it is pivotal to understand—at the very least—the underlying complexities these chains present in today's globalized world.

Supply chains are multifaceted networks that encompass a series of value-added activities and involve various partners, including suppliers, manufacturers, and distributors, all aiming to produce and deliver goods and services to the ultimate consumer. Broadly, a supply chain can be segmented into key components:

- Sourcing: This involves either manufacturing or procuring raw materials.
- Inbound logistics: This encompasses the transportation of raw materials to manufacturing sites.
- Manufacturing: The phase where raw materials undergo transformation to become final products.
- Outbound logistics: Here, finished products move from manufacturing facilities to the marketplace, reaching wholesalers or retailers who then ensure these products find their way to the end-consumers, be they businesses or individuals.[22]

In today's globalized business landscape, companies are increasingly distributing their operations from product design and component manufacturing to assembly and marketing across various regions, giving rise to global value chains. Consequently, consumers often end up with a product that is the culmination of inputs from multiple countries, aptly termed *Made in the World.* Yet, a potential pitfall emerges when the full commercial value of a product is attributed solely to the final country involved in its production. This can skew perceptions of the product's origins and result in misguided decision-making. A solution lies in harmonizing different statistical frameworks and national accounting systems. By doing so, international collaborations inherent in these globalized supply chains can be accurately captured, promoting more informed discussions among decision-makers across borders.[23]

Driven by rapid digitalization and the disruptions from the pandemic, global value chains are evolving rapidly. They now extend beyond conventional manufacturing routines to encapsulate services and intangible assets. This reshaping is notably more consumer-focused and is influenced by dominant megatrends. This shift presents a novel learning trajectory for globally operating businesses. For instance, there is now an amplified emphasis on user experience. This experience begins long before a product is acquired and extends well beyond its purchase. Moreover, enterprises must prioritize transparency, sustainability, and responsiveness to geopolitical shifts. Addressing the rise in protectionist stances and staying attuned to external shifts, as well as adapting to changing consumer tastes, have become integral to a company's supply chain strategy.

The effective management of supply and value chains is critical. They are not only sources of tremendous value for businesses expanding abroad but are also areas susceptible to significant risk. According to a study by PwC done in 2023, supply chain risks are considered among the top three concerns for CEOs, alongside cybersecurity and climate change risks. Specifically, 43 percent of the CEOs surveyed in PwC's 26th annual global CEO survey view supply chain disruptions as a substantial influence on their industry's short-term profitability.[24]

The risks related to supply chains can be categorized into two primary groups. The first category encompasses challenges such as raw material shortages, escalating energy costs, geopolitical upheavals, and labor supply decline. This category has witnessed a surge due to the recent pandemic, increasing inflation, and trends toward national protectionism. The second category concerns the sustainability impact of delivering goods and services to consumers.[25] Interestingly, high-performing supply chains often generate more adverse environmental and societal impacts than a company's operations alone.

Understanding and managing these two categories of risk can play a significant role in the success of an international marketing campaign. However, despite the looming risks in global supply chains, surprisingly, only a minority of companies delve deeper than their immediate suppliers to tackle these challenges collaboratively. For example, a recent survey on how businesses address the climate impact of their supply chains found that only 25 percent of companies that report on greenhouse gas emissions say they engage their suppliers in efforts to reduce emissions.[26]

A leading risk management tactic involves leveraging cutting-edge technologies and analytics. These tools often involve interconnected dashboards brimming with valuable data. They help pinpoint crucial business metrics, enabling companies to address budding challenges preemptively. Supporting this notion, a PwC survey of 1,601 firms highlighted that investments in sophisticated supply chain capabilities yield tangible benefits. These include cost reduction, revenue augmentation, enhanced sustainability, optimized asset utilization, superior risk mitigation, and timely customer deliveries.[27]

Another risk management strategy intertwines a company's overarching sustainability objectives with those of its supply chain. Moving away from the traditional linear *take–make–use–dispose* business model, many brands are embracing a circular economy approach. This strategy extends the lifecycle of products and encourages resource reuse. Integrating practices such as donating, second-hand trading, repairing, refurbishing, recycling, upcycling, and using regenerative materials transforms product innovation. While this shift may help reduce the environmental impact of companies and stave off shareholder pressure, it also comes with significant supply chain and implementation challenges. For instance, many of the largest global fashion brands signed the UN Fashion Industry Charter for Climate Action in 2018, which expects them to manage climate-related emissions throughout the supply chain. However, a recent report on Fashion Supply Chain Emissions shows they have not performed in line to keep global warming below 1.5 degrees Celsius, illustrating that for many companies, this is perhaps easier said than done and requires additional efforts.[28]

Hence, even as consumers demand reasonably priced goods and services that are sustainably made, companies often struggle to implement business models—at scale—that are truly sustainable. The following case study delves deeper into the executional challenges that fashion companies face while trying to implement their ambitious sustainability goals.

Haute Couture Meets Hard Reality: The Struggle for Sustainable Supply Chains

Stella McCartney, one of the leading designers in the fashion industry, has been a firm advocate for sustainability since launching her brand in 2001. For example, she collaborated with the environmental organization Parley for Oceans to create products from ocean plastic debris, such as the Adidas Ultraboost X sneakers. In her 2019 Agents of Change campaign, she highlighted the fight against global warming with upcycled bags and dresses. McCartney also launched the Stella x Greenpeace collection in 2021 to support Greenpeace's campaign against deforestation in the Amazon. These are only a few examples of the designer's efforts to transform an industry labeled as the second most polluting in the world by the United Nations Conference on Trade and Development (UNCTAD).

While Stella McCartney is considered something of a trailblazer, she is not alone in trying to make the industry more sustainable. Many brands are following suit, often at the behest of public pressure. Yet, the uncomfortable truth is that luxury fashion faces numerous complex sustainability issues, including overproduction, the fate of unsold products, and the lifecycle of luxury goods. For example, a common practice among luxury brands is to incinerate unsold merchandise to preserve their brand value, despite criticism over the environmental damage this inflicts. In 2021, American luxury brand Coach faced considerable backlash due to allegations of destroying unsold handbags. In response, the company's global head of sustainability clarified that they were actively working to abandon this practice, acknowledging it as a prevalent issue not just for Coach but also for the wider fashion industry.

High fashion is still figuring out the executional elements of a more sustainable future. For instance, how should a Victoria handbag by Hermès, made from mushroom roots (mycelium), be priced compared to one made from recycled leather? Gabriela Hearst, designer for Chloé, believes that sustainability and social justice go hand in hand. She showcased her sustainable and inclusive spring/summer 2022 collection along the Seine, with onlookers seated on cushions made from Chloé fabric scraps. Spectators on a bridge above could also view the show. Leftovers were donated to a Paris NGO that provides food to the needy.

But how will high fashion's pivot to sustainability resonate with its luxury-loving clientele, who often value exclusivity and status? And what about supply chain challenges arising from increased use of leftover fabric or innovative recycled materials? Designers can now buy remnants from top brands like Dior and Louis Vuitton at reduced prices. Prada is incorporating econyl, a recycled nylon, into its lines and aims to stop using virgin nylon this year. While over 100 major fashion brands have pledged to reduce their climate emissions by 2030 under the UN Fashion Industry Charter for Climate Action, many will struggle to stay on track.

Environment–Strategy–Execution Alignment

Once you have a well-crafted international market expansion strategy in place, including thorough segmentation and targeting of markets and comprehensive market research to understand the landscape deeply, the subsequent phase is implementing an execution plan. This plan should encompass a cohesive set of tactics, ensuring the delivery of products and services at the appropriate price and place and communicated in a manner that resonates with the local market.

While understanding the potential market and customizing your marketing strategy accordingly can be hard work, its effectiveness heavily relies on efficient execution. If your strategy is realistic and clear, and in line with your company's core competence, high-level business objectives, and environmental context, it can serve as an anchor for the correct executional decisions and efficient implementation in international markets as illustrated in Figure 7.2.

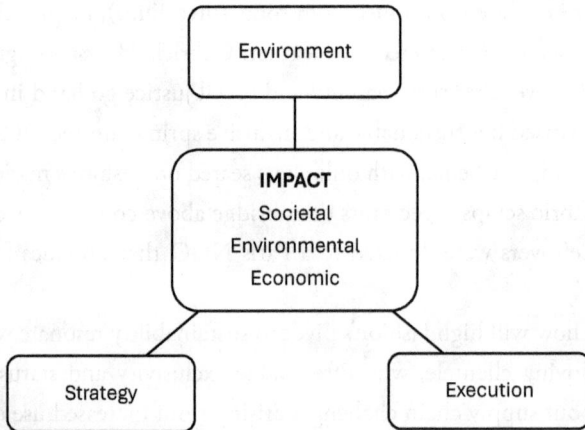

Figure 7.2 Environment–strategy–execution alignment for a more impactful international marketing

Misalignment

We began this chapter by looking at how Getir ultimately failed in its international expansion because of a lack of focus on execution and an inability to pivot due to changing market conditions. Both research and industry practices have consistently shown that execution trumps strategy. Misalignment between the two is likely to lead to an unsuccessful international venture. Surprisingly, companies falter in implementing their strategies more frequently than many would prefer to acknowledge. These challenges can be generally grouped together under the umbrella of strategy–execution misalignment. But what causes such lapses in execution? Potential pitfalls include a lack of strategy, too much focus on short-term executional tactics, or even an overly ambitious or complex strategy. Here are some of the more common causes of misalignment.

- **Overemphasis on strategy:** In some organizations, there is a disproportionate focus on strategy, often at the expense of execution. While strategizing is vital, it is the execution that brings a plan to life.
- **Absence of a clear strategy:** Conversely, some companies focus on short-term wins, and their shortsighted execution that focuses on immediate gains reflects a lack of foresight and long-term vision.
- **Ambiguous or overreaching strategies:** Strategies that diverge from a company's core values or objectives, or that are overly ambitious, can lack credibility. As a result, they might not inspire confidence, making successful execution challenging.
- **Communication gaps:** Even the best strategies can falter if they aren't effectively communicated. Clear and consistent communication ensures that everyone is on the same page and aligned with the company's mission and vision.
- **Lack of discipline:** At times, a sound strategy is in place, but the organization falls short in its execution due to a lack of discipline or focus.
- **Diverse skill sets for strategy and execution:** Crafting a strategy and implementing it require different skill sets. Recognizing

this distinction is crucial. To succeed globally, companies must ensure they have the right talent, both at the headquarters and in international locations, who are adept at strategizing and executing.

When one company thrives and other falters in the same foreign market despite offering similar products, several factors come into play. Among these are a company's failure to conduct thorough market research before venturing abroad, overestimating their product's value, often due to past successes in their home market, and a tendency to overlook the intricacies of local culture, values, and lifestyles. However, a more over-arching concern is how companies approach these unfamiliar, often volatile ventures. In efforts to manage uncertainty associated with foreign markets, they often compartmentalize the process, leading to a siloed and disjointed approach. This can also result in a disconnect between strategy, context, and execution, frequently a root cause of a company's international market failure.

A misalignment can also lead to other challenges in international marketing execution.[29] These include miscalculation of risks and lack of flexibility and accountability. International expansion, by its very nature, demands significant resources such as time, capital, or human effort. Moreover, companies operating across multiple countries grapple with a kaleidoscope of ever-evolving conditions. The stakes are invariably high; the repercussions of failure can weigh heavily both in financial terms and reputational damage. Entering unfamiliar markets exposes companies to the *liability of foreignness*, a phenomenon where differences in institutional frameworks, cultural nuances, and competitive dynamics can be disadvantageous to foreign companies. Crucially, elements outside a firm's control can influence outcomes. A successful international strategy hinges on a careful balance: It must be sensitive to local needs while leveraging global technologies and methodologies. This means that decision-making cannot be the sole preservation of either the headquarters or the local teams.

A final and recurrent pitfall is the tendency to underestimate local contexts. Companies flourishing in their domestic market might be tempted to apply a templated approach overseas, neglecting the distinct needs and subtleties of the new market. An inadequate initial research phase can exacerbate this, leading to skewed risk assessments and, ultimately, flawed execution.

Conclusion

Marketing executives are, not surprisingly, at the forefront of their company's expansion into international markets. As discussed in the previous chapters, they are typically responsible for developing an international expansion strategy, conducting market research, determining where and how to enter the foreign market, and then crafting an execution plan to cultivate demand for the company's offerings.

This chapter has focused on the last but certainly not the least step in this process. The key to successful execution in global marketing isn't only about devising a robust strategy or conducting thorough market research; it hinges on the multifaceted and nuanced execution of these strategies. Businesses need to garner a comprehensive understanding of their global industry's structure, dynamics, and trends to drive competitiveness and secure long-term profitability. Once your company assesses these global factors, you can move to a more localized analysis and customization. While following this approach, we recommend that companies take the necessary measures to ease the challenges and avoid the common mistakes[30] mentioned in the previous section:

- Identify the blind spots in your execution so that you can develop strategies to minimize their impact or avoid them altogether.
- In advance, conduct market research both at the global and individual country levels. Build dashboards for real-time feedback to realize and anticipate (where possible) the pain areas sooner. This can also increase your focus on timing and taking the right measures at the right time to save your company.
- Align your execution with the strategy and the environment for a more disciplined, coordinated, and consistent international expansion and a more positive impact on the environment and society at large.

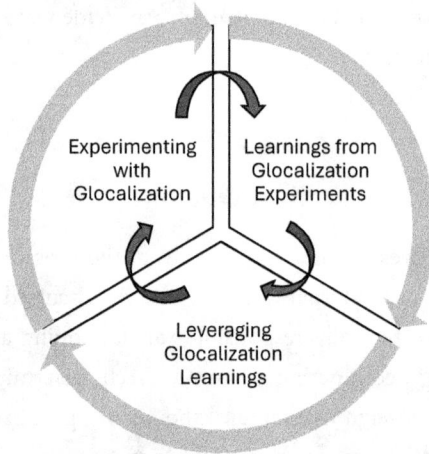

Figure 7.3 The different phases of glocalization in international marketing execution

- Balance top-down against bottom-up. Address the disconnect (if any) between headquarters and local partners to cultivate demand in foreign markets collaboratively. The flexibility provided within a framework to local talent can be very rewarding.
- Balance globalization with localization, that is, glocalization efforts through an experimenting, learning, and leveraging framework, as can be seen in Figure 7.3.

Bites for Thought

The LEGO Group, a Danish toy manufacturer, is blazing a trail in eco-friendly toy production. Starting with the LEGO Ideas Treehouse in 2018, they have begun using sugarcane for some pieces, 185 out of its 3,036 components, to be exact. This sustainable sugarcane can be regenerated in an eco-friendly cycle. LEGO sees this as the beginning of a significant environmental journey.

Plastic has dominated the children's toy industry since the twentieth century due to its affordability and adaptability. However, with increasing emphasis on ESG standards, plastics are losing favor. LEGO's shift to more sustainable materials points to their commitment to a circular economy, emphasizing recycling and reducing single-use plastics. "At the LEGO Group we want to make a positive impact on the world around us, and are working hard to make great play products for children using sustainable materials," said Tim Brooks, vice president of environmental responsibility at the LEGO Group.

Since announcing its goal to use environmentally friendly and recycled materials for most of its products and packaging by 2030, the company has made impressive strides. Evidence of this commitment is showcased in their new campus at the company's headquarters in Billund, Denmark. Constructed using nearly 5 tons of recycled toys, this expansive facility can accommodate 2,000 employees and boasts outdoor furniture entirely derived from repurposed toys.

The LEGO website now prominently features a dedicated sustainability page, highlighting its initiatives focused on Children, Environment, People, and Reporting. As part of its commitment to sustainability, LEGO introduced LEGO Replay, available in the United States and Canada. This initiative encourages LEGO enthusiasts to donate bricks they no longer use, aligning with the company's ambitious goal to achieve Zero Waste to Landfill by 2025. Further emphasizing their commitment to the environment, LEGO collaborates with the World Wildlife Fund for Nature's (WWF) Climate Savers program. Additionally, they have invested approximately $1 billion in offshore wind farms in Germany and the United Kingdom, ensuring their energy consumption is offset by 100 percent by renewable sources.

Questions

1. *Given the global reach and popularity of LEGO products, how does the company adapt its sustainability initiatives, like LEGO Replay, to fit different cultural, legal, and logistical contexts in international markets?*

2. *Does your company have a sustainability program and the means to consistently maintain the program in line with your business plan, marketing strategy, and execution elements?*

3. *How might the trends of circular economy and initiatives such as product take-backs, donations, and repairs affect the relationships with key stakeholders in a company's international supply chain?*

CHAPTER 8

International Digital Marketing

Instagram

In 2009, 27-year-old Stanford University graduate Kevin Systrom was searching for his next big idea. Having already worked at Google and Odeo (a company that later transformed into Twitter and now X), he began experimenting with a prototype web app called Burbn. The app allowed users to check in, post their plans, and share photos about fine whiskey and Bourbon. In 2010, Systrom attracted $500,000 in venture capital, marking a turning point for his fledgling project.

The seed funding enabled Systrom to assemble a team to support his venture. One of the first to join was 25-year-old Mike Krieger, a former Stanford acquaintance. They analyzed top photography apps and noticed the absence of social media–sharing capabilities. Consequently, they aimed to merge the filter features of photography apps with popular social media elements, simplifying Burbn down to its photo, commenting, and like buttons. After 8 weeks of testing, Burbn was rebranded as Instagram, a blend of *instant* and *telegram*.

Instagram launched on October 6, 2010, amassing 25,000 users in just 1 day. By December, the user base exceeded a million. In under 2 years, it grew to nearly 30 million users and was acquired by Facebook (now Meta) for $1 billion. By 2018, when Systrom resigned as CEO, Instagram had become one of the world's largest and most influential social media platforms, boasting a valuation of $100 billion and reaching 1 billion daily active users. By late 2022, this number had surged to almost 2 billion, and Meta was generating around $4 billion in monthly advertising revenue from Instagram.

Today, Instagram is a globally leading social media platform, with North America lagging Asia, Europe, and South America in daily users. India represents the largest single market. The platform's meteoric rise has made it indispensable for marketers seeking direct communication and customer engagement. Instagram's appeal is further enhanced by its ability to target specific customer profiles and interact with segments more likely to purchase products.

Due to multiple factors, Instagram has become a critical tool for companies doing business internationally. First, it has access to a global audience. By expanding across various countries and demographics and allowing businesses to reach a diverse international audience, Instagram allows companies to target specific markets and connect with potential customers worldwide. The second factor is its localized content. On Instagram, brands can tailor their content to make their products and services appealing to specific international markets. Their third asset is visual storytelling. Instagram is primarily a visual platform, making it ideal for storytelling through videos and images, which transcends language allowing companies to engage their customers through powerful visuals and storytelling. In addition to these capabilities, Instagram's hashtag system enables companies to target specific keywords related to their international marketing campaigns. Through influencer marketing and targeted ads, brands gain focused exposure to their desired audience in international markets.

The meteoric rise of Instagram underscores a broader trend in the digital age: the pivotal role of social media platforms in shaping global marketing strategies. Beyond Instagram, platforms like Facebook, Twitter (rebranded as X), TikTok, and LinkedIn have also revolutionized how brands engage with international audiences, offering unique tools for targeting, engagement, and analytics. These platforms enable marketers to craft compelling, culturally nuanced campaigns that resonate across borders. As we explore further in this chapter, understanding the dynamics of various digital marketing platforms is crucial for any brand looking to significantly impact the global stage (Table 8.1).

Table 8.1 The 3W-1H of international digital marketing

International digital marketing (who—you[!])	Key tasks for IM practitioner (what)	Explain why it is important (why)	Tools and resources (how)
Understand the components of an effective digital marketing strategy for your company's unique products and services in a specific international market * Tailor your approach to individual markets and understand what types of tools and insights can raise the effectiveness of digital campaigns * Learn how to optimize and measure your efforts for better ongoing results	Evaluate your own company's digital tools and assets to assess your readiness to expand these to international markets * Create a buyer persona and digital platform strategy and content for the targeted personas * Ensure that your online content and digital campaigns are locally relevant and appropriate * Monitor and evaluate campaigns continuously	Understanding the target market, key online habits, and digital platforms in different countries is critical to ensuring that your marketing campaign has a chance to succeed * Adapting digital marketing content to the local language, culture, and customs is essential for connecting with and targeting international audiences * Regularly tracking and measuring the success of digital marketing efforts allows marketers to optimize campaigns, make data-driven decisions, and allocate resources effectively in each market	• Cybersecurity Framework by NIST * • Email tools like Intuit Mailchimp * • Facebook IQ by Meta * • Geotargeting by Meta * • Google Analytics * • LLM tools like ChatGPT, Gemini, Bing CoPilot, Claude * • Make My Persona by Hubspot * • SEO Tools for Digital Marketers

The Digital Transformation

As discussed in Chapter 2, the rise in technology is also known as the Fifth Industrial Revolution. Characterized by technological innovations and digitalization, it is one of the significant megatrends of the 21st century. Indeed, marketing is one of the disciplines most deeply impacted by digital transformation, both from the consumer and firm sides. This chapter examines the fast-moving world of digital and social media marketing. As the Instagram example demonstrates, companies now possess unparalleled opportunities to engage and target potential clients, customers, and the public. It is a world that has come into being over the past 25 years. Today, digital marketing provides marketers with seemingly limitless possibilities to build their brands, enhance their reputations, and drive sales.

The world of digital marketing contains many different tools with larger flexibility than traditional marketing. This flexibility permits firms to tailor their strategies to different markets, effectively expanding their reach and growing their business internationally. Instagram is just one among many social media platforms, Nevertheless, its high reach almost uniquely enables companies to advertise their products and services to relevant audiences worldwide as part of their digital marketing strategy and campaigns.

Depending on the stage of their internationalization and their goals, companies can leverage digital marketing in various ways to facilitate their international expansion. Some of those popular ways include: (i) creating localized websites with translated content and region- or country-specific offerings for a seamless user experience; (ii) developing valuable and relevant content marketing through blog posts, videos, infographics, and more, that resonate with target audiences in different countries; and (iii) running SEO strategies, email and mobile marketing, and pay-per-click advertising campaigns to generate better leads.

The digital transformation is not complete yet. In fact, it is accelerating even as we write this book. Hence, it is neither possible nor within our capability to equip managers like you with every possible trend and tool. Every tool serves a different purpose. Only you can identify the correct one depending on the role of digital marketing in your company's international expansion strategy. Therefore, we aim to pursue a more general outlook and provide you with some of the fundamentals of digital marketing for strategic-level thinking and what they mean for your company. With this goal in mind, we will explore the multifaceted world of digital marketing, which prominently includes effective utilization of SEO, influencer marketing, social media marketing, email direct marketing, online advertising, and more.

What Is Digital Marketing?

A simple definition of digital marketing is any marketing method conducted online through an electronic device. In digital marketing, a business might leverage websites, search engines, blogs, social media, video, email, and similar channels to reach customers. McKinsey offers a more comprehensive definition of the operations required to conduct digital marketing, referring to the many processes and parts of the business now engaged in it. Digital marketing operations involve the application of capabilities, processes, structures, and technologies to cost-effectively exploit and scale the interactivity, targeting, personalization, and optimization of digital channels. As such, they argue that marketing operations have a critical role in driving bottom-line growth, especially for companies selling their products and services directly to consumers. Done well, successful digital marketing directly enables the speed, agility, iterative development, experimentation, and responsiveness that successful companies need to react to and shape the marketplace.[1] In other words, digital marketing is now key to any firm's success. Not long ago, large multinational companies primarily relied on global marketing campaigns to operate across borders. However, today's norm is a more localized and targeted approach, made possible by social media and digital capabilities. Many of these innovative tools have emerged from the widespread use of email as the primary means of business communication and search engines as the go-to resource for finding any desired information. However, the most significant opportunity for international marketers may reside in the rapid expansion of social media. Social media gives companies a unique chance to engage directly with clients and consumers in local markets. Accomplishing this is no simple feat. Social media is as straightforward as it is intricate, and marketers striving to harness its vast potential for driving business growth must master the fundamentals and engage experts to help spearhead local digital marketing initiatives. The complex nature of social media lies especially in how boundaries between borders and languages have become increasingly blurred in today's interconnected world. As discussed in the previous chapter, a company's actions in one country can easily influence other countries, potentially positively or negatively impacting its reputation. Social media is a driving force behind this phenomenon, making it challenging for international brands to remain confined to single markets, as local issues often transcend their geographical origins.[2]

Social media holds numerous advantages over traditional media forms (e.g., print, radio, television) and is proving to be a transformative force in shaping the future of international marketing. The primary reason is its interactive nature, which enables users to view, follow, and engage with content that genuinely resonates with them. Additionally, social media enables marketers to collaborate more often with influencers and capitalize on word-of-mouth (WOM) marketing. Individuals are far more likely to be influenced by recommendations from friends or acquaintances with whom they interact. This concept is not new; since the early days of human civilization, WOM has significantly influenced purchasing behavior among traders in bazaars and throughout international commerce.[3]

Social media generates enormous user-generated content in text, voice, and video. We began this chapter by looking at Instagram, owned by Meta, the fourth most popular social network globally, reaching 2 billion monthly active users. Market leader Facebook was the first social network to surpass 1 billion registered accounts and currently sits at more than 3 billion monthly active users as illustrated in Figure 8.1. Meta owns four of the biggest social media platforms, all with 1 billion monthly active users each: Facebook (its core platform), WhatsApp, Messenger, and Instagram. YouTube is the second most popular social network after Facebook, with 2.5 billion active monthly users as of 2024. More than 500 hours of video content are uploaded every minute on YouTube. Localized versions of YouTube exist in over 100 countries worldwide, across 80 languages, making it an ideal platform for marketers. With technological advances, savvy marketers can use the latest tools to track and follow consumers and clients likely to be interested in their industry, products, and services.

Laying the Groundwork for an International Digital Marketing Strategy

Now that we have established the enormous scale and opportunity offered by social media and the potential for digital marketing to help drive

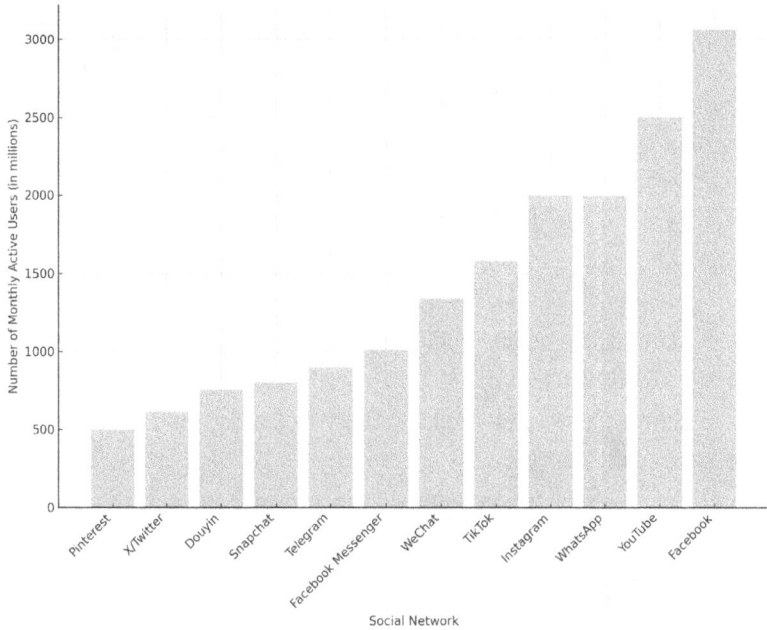

Figure 8.1 *Most popular social media networks worldwide*

Source: We Are Social, & DataReportal, & Meltwater. April 24, 2024. "Most Popular Social Networks Worldwide as of April 2024, Ranked by the Number of Monthly Active Users (In Millions)." Data retrieved from Statista. Accessed January 2025. https://www-statista-com .unh.idm.oclc.org/statistics/272014/global-social-networks-ranked-by-number-of-users/.

business success, let us examine what this looks like in practice. In the next two sections, we will look at what businesses can and should do to lay the groundwork for a successful digital marketing campaign and then examine some of the tools companies have at their disposal, like content marketing and SEO. Recognizing the value of a digital marketing strategy is just the first step; actually, implementing a digital marketing strategy requires careful and methodical planning. Whether you are doing e-commerce or reaching out to consumers and asking them to buy your products and services in a physical location, you will need a plan.

The first step in the planning process is understanding your core audience, in the same way as you would try to understand your audience for any other marketing campaign. Before this, of course, an internal discussion should take place to discuss which audience you really need to reach to drive business results. One can assume that this is the end-customer of your product, but this is not necessarily the case for all businesses. In some more restrictive countries and cultures, it may be that your core audience is the regulators of your products or services, or influencers accepted by governing authorities. For companies operating in a business-to-business environment, your core audience may be limited to buyers and suppliers operating in one specific region.

Yet, whatever your core audience, understanding the socioeconomic environment in which they live and how they engage with others is key to the ultimate success of your digital marketing campaign. Here, it would be best to consider traditional beliefs, values, lifestyles, behaviors, and overall culture. As we indicated in the IMR, having good data on your core target audience will help you tailor your ultimate message. It will also help prevent you from potentially embarrassing or controversial situations stemming from a misunderstanding of cultural norms.

In line with understanding your audience comes understanding the culture in which you intend to conduct a digital marketing campaign. As an international marketer, you will know that no two markets are the same. Moreover, none of them are static; not only are the markets different, but conditions within those markets can also change, sometimes rapidly. That's why you must customize your approach depending on your target audience and the situation. Said differently, your plans must be flexible enough to adapt your tactics in real time. How do you, for instance, react to the news that your competitor is introducing a new product that performs better than yours in some key respects and has just launched a local marketing campaign or the arrival of regulation that limits the use of a key ingredient? These are all things that need to be managed daily; the more engagement and flexibility you show, the higher your chances of success.

As with traditional marketing, understanding your client or customer is key to success. Luckily, one of the distinct advantages of our increased access to data is that you can easily create a "target persona." Here, an excellent digital strategy should go hand in hand with a traditional market research strategy, using the tools discussed earlier in the book. Hence, a target persona should cover all the relevant demographics, including gender, age, location, education, and income, as well as psychographics, including values, beliefs, goals, problems, and solutions. Some tools, mainly on social media, now allow you to target potential clients and customers based on their psychological profiles. Therefore, knowing your audiences' psychographics—their default personality, values, opinions, attitudes, interests, and lifestyles, will further help. Information like this will help you throughout a digital marketing campaign, no matter what your chosen medium, and will also inform your content strategy. This will help if your international marketing budget is limited, as you can create specific, targeted, and cost-effective campaigns focusing only on those you aim to reach, with a message that resonates.

Not all digital campaigns require a detailed persona or dataset. Sometimes, you may not know the level, education, or gender of your target audience. Still, you know you want to target an audience working in a specific industry sector in a specific country or region. The good news is that we can now also gather data as we go. Many software tools and digital media agencies can help you monitor, learn, and adjust your international digital media campaign in real time. Conducting a thorough competitor analysis is essential for crafting an international digital marketing strategy. Gathering data on key competitors aids in understanding the target market, encompassing factors such as market size, potential, trajectory, economic climate, and prospective customers. Typically, you want to analyze your main competitors' products, investors, brands, their years of operation, and their relative size. You could also analyze their primary and secondary audience, marketing spend, pricing, and customer reviews. All these will further help you understand what works and what doesn't in the new market.

The Executional Elements of Your Company's Digital Strategy

A good digital marketing plan should be scalable, multifaceted, and not overly reliant on one tactic. Having a strategy that uses different media increases the likelihood of success. When one channel does not resonate with your target audience, another likely will. When text does not work, maybe a well-placed photo or a series of videos will. Avoid creating a plan that relies on one social media channel, like Facebook or even LinkedIn, or anchored around one influencer, a certain event, or competing products. You should also be prepared to conduct plenty of real-time A/B testing, but more on that later. In this section, we will have a look at the different components of an international digital marketing strategy, including implementing an international SEO strategy, creating great content (at the basis of everything!), and other tactics such as geotargeting/geofencing, email campaigns, and the use of influencers.

Search Engine Optimization

SEO is a set of practices designed to improve the appearance and positioning of webpages in organic search results. Simply put, it means improving your site to increase visibility when people search for products or services related to your product/service category or company. International SEO, on the other hand, builds on this concept and deals with offering optimized content for multiple languages and multiple locations. Search engines pull information about your company and products primarily from your website. Since most people search for your products or services when they are actively looking to engage with your company (i.e., organic search) or product category, how you appear and rank in their local language is extremely important for international marketers. SEO in the international arena is considerably more complicated than targeting a single market, mainly because of language issues. Still, it is important to note that even search engines will differ from country to country. For example, while Google is the most widely used search engine globally, accounting for roughly 90 percent of all global online searches, the most popular search engine in China is Baidu.[4]

To control how its search engines rank and display information, Google maintains a complex and proprietary algorithm that can be difficult for novices to understand. Hence, for most marketers, learning the ins and outs of technical SEO is a subject better left to specialists and technical experts. Nevertheless, plenty of free and useful tools are available to marketers wishing to become more familiar with the subject. Popular websites like Yoast.com or moz.com offer a host of online learning videos, tutorials, and "plug-ins" that you can attach to your website to help them rank better. Of course, there are a few things that every international marketer should be aware of. First, when targeting a country, you need to translate the content of your website into the local language. However, this is not as straightforward as it seems for several reasons as follows:

Translation: Good local content should not be "automatically" translated, as there will be many errors and unintended phrases. As such, we suggest engaging a local, native language speaker to iron out the nuances and account for cultural differences in translated content. There are many examples of literal translations that mean one thing in one language but are potentially offensive in another.

Duplication: Targeting your website for an audience in different languages and localized for different countries can lead to a lot of duplicate or near duplicate content. This can negatively affect your SEO strategy and how you appear on different searches. You can avoid this issue with *hreflang*, an HTML code that can help your international SEO strategy. Search engines use *hreflang* to understand websites' lingual and geographical targeting and use the information to show the right URL in search results, depending on user language and region preference. There are three basic scenarios that can be covered with *hreflang*: (i) same country, different languages; (ii) different countries, different languages; and (iii) different countries, same language.

Web domain name: To successfully target your audience in a local language, you need to consider which pages you want them to land on. There are several options as to what domain structure to use. Do you need to get the ccTLD (i.e., country code Top Level Domain) like company.fr for France, or can you create a subdirectory for your site, like company.com/fr or a subdomain like fr.company.com? What about countries that have multiple languages? Sometimes, creating an entirely new website can have distinct advantages, as it allows you to offer an experience tailored specifically to your audience in the foreign market.

Considering these factors, a simple website translation to a local language is surprisingly complex. How you handle this situation will depend on your company's structure, size of your business, marketing budget, and prioritization of your target market. As we write this book, several SEO tools are starting to integrate AI capabilities rapidly. This technology is expected to dramatically change how SEO keywords and online searches for information will work in the future. AI algorithms can analyze many more factors, like a person's search history, location, and behavior, to provide customized results. For companies, this means that their content will need to be increasingly tailored and optimized to specific audiences rather than generic ones.

Content Creation

Ranking high on organic searches is one benefit to creating content specifically for a local market, but not the only benefit. Among all the tactics a marketer can deploy in a foreign market, creating unique, fresh, and relevant content for your audience is perhaps one of the most powerful tools a marketer can deploy. Many have argued that the quest for people's attention is one of the most challenging aspects of a marketer's job. With the rise of social media, in addition to longer-established media like television, newspapers, and radio, it is estimated that people are subjected to 6,000 to 10,000 advertisements daily, the vast majority of which go unnoticed. With people exposed to so many impressions from advertisers and would be sellers of goods and products, how can your company stand out? Put simply, you distinguish yourself from the competition by getting your message out through great content. Using multiple content media and strategies in your international digital marketing helps to reach a wider audience.[5]

Let's explore what we mean by great content. First, many businesses' most common mistake is creating content about what they want to tell or share but not necessarily content that people want to hear, watch, or listen to. Of course, some content about your company and products will be information about you and only about you. Yet, every marketer should start the content creation process by trying to bridge the story they want to talk about their company, product, service, or industry, to what people are interested in. In other words, approach it from their perspective, not your own. As the old saying goes, good marketing content makes you look good; great marketing content makes the buyer feel great, perhaps through humor, a fascinating insight, or a self-affirming message or other means. Counterintuitively, great content is, therefore, less about you than it is about your target audience. How do you go about creating great content that people want to consume? Here are some examples of where this may apply or in what medium/tools you can use to tell your story:

- A clean and compelling story on your own website, including an engaging narrative around your vision (broader than you), mission, people, and core values.
- Newsworthy company announcements, amplified by press releases, exclusives for journalists, and social media.
- Blogs by senior leadership and company experts on interesting and insightful stories for publishing on your website or other online publications.
- Curated photos, videos, reels, tweets, and other posts for social media.
- Shared content with local industry partners—how you are working on something collaboratively.
- Paid content where external influencers and stakeholders promote your industry, company, service, or product, either directly or indirectly.

The Holy Grail for marketers is to have others disseminate your message and content, benefiting your company by extension. Traditionally, companies have paid for this type of exposure, either through hired spokespersons who speak on behalf of their products or, more recently, through harnessing online influencers who make money from brands looking to spread their message. Influencer marketing is a form of social media marketing that involves product placements and endorsements from online creators. In today's competitive marketing landscape, brands are collaborating with influencers, as partnerships with well-known creators can open the door to large potential audiences.[6] This type of paid content creation by third parties on your behalf is a great way for companies to reach audiences in any foreign target country. Identify an influencer who is well-liked by your target audience and work with them to create content that promotes your company. In return for a relatively modest outlay, companies benefit by associating themselves with credible online person-alities with large followings. Marketers of consumer goods often use this approach, as they are often more expensive and time-consuming and will likely need the help of local intermediaries and agencies. Figure 8.2 shows that the global influencer marketing market size has more than tripled since 2019.

User-generated content can also be a key strategy for different digital marketing campaigns. This unpaid (or paid for with free products/services) content written or produced by locals will help you build your brand and gain trust. While setting up campaigns that solicit content from third par-ties, thoughtful consideration will have to be given to ensuring your brand and company are portrayed as you would like. Given the cost, time, and possibilities associated with creating great content, the first step for every would-be digital marketer is to familiarize themselves with the business

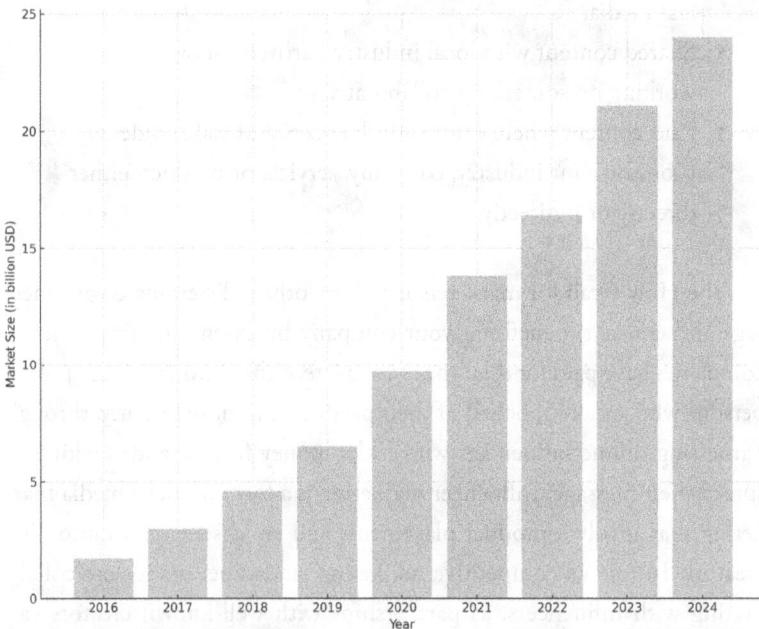

Figure 8.2 The market size (in billion U.S. dollars) for influencer marketing worldwide

Source: Influencer Marketing Hub. February 1, 2024. "Influencer Marketing Market Size Worldwide from 2016 to 2024 (in billion U.S. dollars)." Data retrieved from Statista. Accessed January 16, 2025. https://www-statista-com.unh.idm.oclc.org/statistics/1092819/global-influencer-market-size/.

and growth plans of the company in foreign markets. Once you know what you want to achieve from a business perspective (e.g., achieve a certain percentage of market share, gain certain number of customers, realize certain amount in savings, or new supply chain partners), the question for every marketer to understand is—which group of stakeholders you need to target to achieve these objectives? As mentioned earlier, this sounds straightforward, but it is a step often overlooked in favor of a broad consumer strategy. Sometimes, you may need to promote the entire industry, working with associations to grow the overall market. Other times, you will need a content strategy that appeals to government officials or regulators. Mostly, you will want to cater to the buyer persona you identified and create content according to their interests. Once you have identified the core audience to help grow your business and the content, they are likely to be interested in, you are ready to consider the type of messaging and channel or medium you want to use to disseminate the message. Let's look at one of the most direct and effective ways marketers reach their core target audience next.

Direct Outreach (Email/InMail)

Imagine you are new to a foreign market and need to find a way to communicate with, market, and sell to a new audience that will help your business. You can do so in myriad ways, but one of the most effective for companies doing business directly with larger customers (e.g., business-to-business) is direct email marketing. This tool is especially effective for small- and medium-sized businesses with limited budgets. However, again, it is not as simple as it seems. First, you will need to collect email addresses in the new market and create a list of contacts. You can use many strategies to collect addresses, but among the most popular is getting people's information in exchange for great content. These customized pop-up email opt-ins guarantee that you get people's permission to contact them directly. You can also start growing your audience through direct incentives in exchange for an email address, offering potential customers a direct reward through a discount, exclusive membership, or similar. Whatever your strategy is to collect emails, offering some reward or incentive is usually a good idea.

Once you have collected enough emails, it is relatively easy and cost-effective to communicate with this audience using targeted, curated messages that resonate with them. Ensure you categorize your customers according to what you think these categories of customers may want from you. Traditionally, this is easier to do than with other marketing campaigns, reflecting the importance of email marketing.[7]

Take note that privacy laws, such as GDPR compliance, make using unsolicited emails somewhat more complicated than it used to be. Increasingly, digital marketers operating internationally need to deal with stringent privacy laws, prohibiting companies from sending out unsolicited emails and messages and keeping data about potential clients and customers on their servers. The GDPR is an EU data protection and privacy regulation. Adopted in 2018, the legally binding regulation prohibits companies from soliciting clients unwillingly and provides guardrails on using and storing personal data. The resulting fines can be steep for any company doing business in the EU and found noncomplying. Some of the largest fines have been handed down to Meta and Google, which draw revenue from targeted advertising, but many others have also been fined. For example, in 2021, Vodafone Spain was fined €8.15 million for targeting customers with unsolicited marketing activities, including calls, emails, and SMS without proper consent.[8]

InMail on LinkedIn: An Effective Tool for Direct Messages to Business Prospects

LinkedIn is the world's largest professional network, with over 850 million users as of early 2022. For marketers wishing to reach out to potential buyers, suppliers, and industry professionals, it is one of the best practical tools on the market, especially for business-to-business marketing. Like email, one of its paid *InMail* features allows users to contact other professionals directly on LinkedIn.[9]

LinkedIn InMail's main advantages over regular cold messages or connection requests are higher response rates and the ability to follow up. Some of the best practices to increase response rates are: (i) choosing prospects wisely, such as according to their industries; (ii) creating an optimized profile to build trust and credibility in the eyes of the prospects as they likely jump on your LinkedIn profile; (iii) creating compelling and enticing subject lines as it is shown that subject lines that have a personal touch and call to action are likely to have open rates as high as 90 percent; (iv) personalizing messages by including your prospect's profile; common interests or vulnerabilities; (v) starting a conversation instead of trying to get straight to the point or sell something; (vi) choosing conciseness and brevity, as more than 50 percent of InMails are read on a mobile phone and messages with 400 characters or less perform much better in terms of conversion than longer ones.

InMail is commonly used by companies for various purposes, such as recruitment to reach out to potential job candidates; business development to offer a more direct approach to building relationships, sales, and marketing to highlight the value of products and services and engage leads; and networking and supporting customers. Here is a simple and successful example of an InMail sent by a social media marketing executive to a training video producer. The key components to the success of this message were that it was personalized by calling the recipient by his first name, explains how his contact information is acquired, and, finally, that it specifically addressed the recipient's needs based on the profile information, immediately connecting him to the solution.

Hi Kevin,

I came across your profile in the Social Media Marketing group and wanted to reach out. I'm connecting with professionals like you who are leveraging video for corporate training.

At KLB, we specialize in making training videos more effective—our transcription services enhance accessibility, searchability, and usability, helping organizations get the most out of their content.

Would you be open to a quick chat? I'd be happy to offer a free consultation to assess your current video strategy and share actionable insights. If there's someone else on your team who handles this, let me know—I'll reach out to them directly.

Looking forward to connecting!

Karen Johnson

Enhancing Customer Experience

Digital marketing platform sites are rife with jargon such as sales funnel and customer journey. Simply put, the customer journey consists of actions your customers take before and after purchasing. By understanding the different actions your customers take before and after a conversion, you can start brainstorming new marketing tactics to improve the customer experience and keep them returning for more.[10] The purchase funnel, or purchasing funnel, is similar to the customer journey in that it illustrates the theoretical customer journey toward purchasing a good or service. The origin of the sales funnel far predates the digital revolution. In fact, in 1898, E. St. Elmo Lewis developed a model that mapped a theoretical customer journey from when a brand or product attracted consumer attention to the point of action or purchase. St. Elmo Lewis' idea is often referred to as the AIDA model, an acronym that stands for Awareness, Interest, Desire, and Action. This staged process is summarized as follows:

1. **Awareness:** When a prospective customer becomes aware that a seller offers a product, solution, or service that will meet their needs, they are in the awareness stage. Today, this can happen through advertising, tradeshows, direct email/mail, viral campaigns, social media, webinars, and more. This is where lead generation takes place.

2. **Interest:** When a prospect expresses interest in a service, they go through an evaluation process in which they seek more information, compare the offerings of various competitors, and become more educated about the factors surrounding the offering. Marketers can use tools like SEO, content, emails, newsletters, and more to ensure interest is directed to their company.

3. **Desire:** Getting a prospect to decide boils down to giving them all the information they need, answering any questions holding them back from taking action, and convincing them that the action they are about to take is right. In the digital world, this can occur when a product is placed in a shopping cart on an e-commerce site, in a survey, or after a product demonstration.

4. **Action:** The final stage of the sales funnel is action. This is the point at which the prospective customer completes the process by becoming an active customer. As an additional stage to the action component, converting a one-time customer into a repeat customer is possible.

Digital marketing has greatly increased the possibilities for marketers to optimize the sales funnel using modern tools like optimized websites, great content, email campaigns, and others. Building on this concept, international digital marketers can choose more sophisticated sales funnels with content in the local language and focus on optimizing the customer experience. Marketing technologists are critical in navigating the ecosystem of thousands of marketing technology providers to create solutions that deliver the most effective customer experiences. These providers effectively act as a bridge between the customer experience and marketing operations and choosing one that is the right fit and has the right capabilities for your target market. Delivering these omnichannel customer experiences requires marketing technology that can automate processes, personalize interactions, and coordinate actions across potential clients and geographies.[11]

Geographic Targeting

Geotargeting and geofencing are commonly used to reach target audiences in foreign countries. While they sound similar, they serve different purposes and applications in international digital marketing. Geotargeting is a technique for delivering advertising or marketing messages to users based on their geographic location. This can be done by identifying a user's IP address, GPS data, or Wi-Fi connections. For example, if a company wants to promote a product only to customers in a specific country or region, they can use geotargeting to restrict the ad's visibility to those users, making this technique particularly useful to international marketing practitioners. On the other hand, geofencing is a specific technique that involves creating a virtual boundary around a physical location. This can be done using GPS, Wi-Fi, or cellular data. Once a user enters or exits this boundary, they can be targeted with specific messages or advertisements across various online channels. For example, a business could create a Facebook ad displayed to users within a certain area, encouraging them to come and visit.

By combining these techniques, businesses can keep users engaged with their brand as they move between physical and digital spaces. Both geotargeting and geofencing begin by using location-based data to identify potential customers, and they subsequently rely on cookies to follow users across different media channels. Cookies are small data stored on users' devices that track their online activity and preferences. As users engage with personalized content or ads, cookies enable marketers to gather information about their behavior, allowing for further customization and retargeting across various platforms. This combination of location data and cookies helps marketers create a more effective, tailored marketing experience for their audience.

Social Media

As mentioned at the beginning of this chapter, the possibilities for marketers to conduct cost-effective and targeted social media campaigns in foreign markets are almost endless. Many companies have succeeded in creating momentum in both domestic and global markets by leveraging social technologies to energize and embrace existing and potential customers on social media.[12] A solid social media strategy can support your company's presence and expansion in international markets by shaping views and public opinion and creating value. Sheth (2020) defines a three-pronged value statement: Social media can help equip companies in international markets.

First, it provides access value by informing customers in foreign markets about the availability of products and services, offering quicker and easier access to them. Second, it provides an activation value as various brands have initiated market entry and launched new products on digital platforms and social media sites before introducing them into traditional retail channels in foreign markets. Third, it provides an awareness value as social media platforms allow companies to tap into potential customer networks and amplify the WOM effect through engagement and behavioral targeting. In fact, personalized experiences for existing and new customers can often be achieved effortlessly through social media, enabling companies to target customers with specific promotions according to their respective lifecycles.[13]

Another major impact of social media platforms is the spectacular growth of transnational virtual communities.[14] A virtual community is a social network of individuals who connect through specific social media, potentially crossing geographical and political boundaries to pursue mutual interests or goals. Virtual communities resemble real-life communities because they both provide support, information, friendship, and acceptance between strangers. Given these characteristics, these communities offer great opportunities for marketers to interact with their target audience directly. For example, a company selling cold-weather clothing could engage directly with a community of outdoor climbing enthusiasts.

For companies entering foreign markets using social media, another key tool they have at their disposal is A/B testing. A/B testing is a shorthand for a simple randomized controlled experiment, in which two samples (A and B) of a single vector-variable are compared. These values are similar except for one variation that might affect a user's behavior. A/B tests are widely considered the simplest form of controlled experiment and can be used effectively to test the efficacy of social media posts. They can also be used to test digital ad campaigns, videos, emails, and other digital content. Today, many different commercial tools allow you to optimize your international social media campaigns by following the data and directly tie these back to your marketing goals.

Emerging Technologies and Their Implications in Global Digital Marketing

In the fast-moving world of digital marketing, nothing is constant except for the continuous stream of new innovations. With marketers ranking "experimenting with new marketing strategies and tactics" as their second highest priority, it makes sense that tomorrow's digital trends should be on today's radar screens. Digital trends defining the next web, such as AI, Virtual and Augmented Reality (VR/AR), cryptocurrency, Non-Fungible Tokens (NFTs), the metaverse, and Web3, are at the top of the experimentation list. For example, 51 percent of marketers reported already having a strategy for Web3. And the top elements of Web3 strategies are focused on virtual products, VR/AR, and cryptocurrencies. These innovations are reshaping marketing strategies, setting new benchmarks for customer engagement, and redefining data management on a global scale.[15]

AI's impact is particularly profound in transforming how marketers understand and interact with their local and global audiences. Through advanced data analytics, AI enables marketers to analyze vast amounts of consumer data, leading to more personalized and targeted marketing campaigns. AI-driven algorithms can predict consumer behavior, optimize pricing strategies, and even automate customer service interactions, offering a level of personalization and efficiency previously unattainable. Take Starbucks' "Deep Brew" AI program enhancing the customer experience, for instance. It assists in personalizing offers and recommendations to customers. It also significantly improves operational efficiencies and marketing efforts by allowing marketers to innovate and experiment. They can leverage machine learning technologies to customize the drive-thru experience for customers and automate inventory management and preventive maintenance through their IoT-connected machines.[16]

In VR/AR, IKEA's AR app, "IKEA Place," allows customers to visualize furniture in their own spaces before purchasing. This technology transcends geographical barriers, offering an immersive experience to customers worldwide. Another example is Sephora's Virtual Artist App, which uses AR to let users try on makeup virtually, merging the digital and physical shopping experiences seamlessly.[17] Blockchain technology also has significant marketing applications worldwide. Established through a collaboration of LVMH, Mercedes-Benz, OTB, Prada Group, and Cartier, the Aura Blockchain Consortium's mission is to create the technological standard for the luxury industry and enhance the customer experience. This enhances consumer trust, especially in e-commerce, where product authenticity is often questioned (Table 8.2).[18]

As the latest edition of the State of Marketing Report by Salesforce indicates, emerging technologies create change and opportunities for marketers who identify their priority and challenge areas both around the effective and efficient use of the right tools and technologies. As digital tools and services continue to evolve and offer better and faster solutions,

Table 8.2 Top opportunities and headwinds of AI uses in marketing

Top marketing AI use cases	Top marketing priorities	Top marketing headwinds
Automate customer interactions	Enhancing the use of tools and technologies	Ineffective use of tools and technologies
Automate data integration and processes	Experimenting with new marketing strategies and tactics	Measuring marketing ROI/ attribution
Personalize the customer journey across channels and resolve customer identity	Modernizing company's kit for tools and technologies	Balancing personalization with intruding into customer comfort zones

Source: The State of Marketing Report, Eighth edition.[19]

marketers will be pressed to embrace change and leverage the latest tools that allow the best real-time engagement, feedback, and performance for their global digital marketing strategies.

Measuring Performance

How well you measure performance will determine how your company competes and succeeds in a digital-first world. Hence, international marketers should always document the implementation of an international marketing plan and measure the performance in real time. Before implementation, they must agree on key performance indicators (KPIs) and evaluate whether the business is meeting its overall objectives. The money spent on online ads, content, social media, email campaigns, and other digital efforts should have real, measurable results that can be directly (or sometimes indirectly) linked to the campaign. While there are more commonly employed marketing performance metrics such as ROI, customer acquisition cost, customer lifetime value (CLV), customer satisfaction, and brand awareness, understanding the success of digital marketing efforts generally requires tracking other KPIs. Here are some essential KPIs and key metrics that most marketing organizations are now tracking in the digital realm, often in real time.[20]

- **Impressions:** The number of times your ad or organic content is displayed or viewed—regardless of whether it garners clicks. While this KPI doesn't reflect how many customers engage with your content, it helps boost brand awareness.

- **Search engine rankings:** To ensure you reach a large online audience, your website needs to appear at the top of search engine results pages. Its rankings directly influence your brand's visibility and accessibility to potential customers in the awareness stage.

- **Click-through rate:** A critical KPI for assessing online advertising campaigns and search engine results. It is calculated by dividing the number of clicks your ad or link receives by its impressions and then multiplying that number by 100 to get a percentage.

- **Cost per click:** A KPI that considers the amount you pay each time a user clicks on your paid advertisement. It is calculated by dividing the total cost of your ad by its number of completed clicks.

- **Conversion rate:** The percentage of visitors to your website or digital platform who take a desired action, such as purchasing, signing up for your newsletter, or filling out a contact form. It is calculated by dividing the number of conversions by the total number of visitors and multiplying that by 100.

- **Customer acquisition cost:** A marketing KPI that calculates the total expense incurred to acquire a new customer. It is calculated by dividing the sum of all marketing and sales expenses over a specific period by the number of new customers acquired during that period.

- **Return on investment:** A KPI that can provide crucial insight into marketing initiatives' anticipated and actual results.

Common Pitfalls

The good news about tracking everything in real time is that you can adjust your strategy midstream. The bad news is that you can't hide the failure of a digital campaign to deliver business results. Searching for one single reason for why a campaign has failed can be an elusive and difficult task, but, with the help of key metrics, one can get as close to the reason for the failure of a campaign as possible. Here are some of the more common reasons for failure:

- **Lack of planning:** As Sun Tzu famously said in *The Art of War*, "*strategy without tactics is the slowest route to victory. Tactics without strategy is the noise before defeat.*" Failing to have a clear strategy in line with business objectives or rushing to implement tactics without a clear strategy is a recipe for failure and probably the number one reason why many digital marketing campaigns fail.

- **Lack of flexibility:** The customer is always right, and failing to listen to their real-time feedback, either collected through testing, comments, or other means, is the modern-day equivalent of being tone-deaf. Reading the room is as pertinent online as it is in real life, and international marketers need to be able to adjust in real time to on-the-ground conditions based on the feedback they receive.

- **Insufficient investment:** Some digital marketing strategies fail because the company hasn't invested enough money to make the strategy work. If you are not spending money on content or social media buys, and your competitor is, your chances of success decrease significantly. The good news is that the more time you spend marketing and advertising, the more you will learn about your audience, your competition, and even your own company, products, and services. This will allow you to spend your resources wisely.

- **Incorrect channels/targeting:** Go where your customer is. Learn where your customers will likely engage with you as part of the strategic planning process. Similarly, you may be on the right channel, but your marketing isn't working because your targeting is too broad. For example, if you are looking to engage more of a targeted B2B campaign, you may prefer a very targeted LinkedIn campaign over an Instagram campaign that targets a discrete demographic. Similarly, you may be wasting your time if you are optimizing your website for incorrect keywords that no one is searching for in a particular market.

- **Failure to optimize the customer experience:** If your marketing language is too focused on you, rather than what the customer wants or if you are making it difficult for your customers to buy your products in a reasonable timeframe, chances are that something is off in your buying process. Making it easy for people to find you in terms that they understand and delivering a smooth sales process is key to success in any market. We live in a world where people expect instant solutions, and you must keep this in mind when designing your customer experience process.
- **Lack of cultural insights:** Even though the world has become smaller, cultural nuances still matter greatly, especially in the fast-changing world of consumer goods and social media.
- **Impatience:** The push for immediate solutions is not limited to a business's clients and customers. Sometimes, the internal pressure to deliver instant results can be overwhelming. Establishing a brand in a new market can take months, if not years, of investment. Sometimes, marketing doesn't work simply because you gave up too quickly!

Governance

Successful entry into foreign markets depends on using the correct marketing operations and, by extension, the correct digital marketing strategy, given how ubiquitous our online activities have become. Getting the appropriate support from senior management is integral in this respect. The enterprise environment can be complex, especially in foreign markets, with multiple business groups, stakeholders, and new technologies that can make decision-making challenging. Companies need to focus on developing governance structures to guide marketing technology's evaluation, selection, and management.

As discussed earlier, emerging technologies are rapidly transforming the way marketers experiment with new strategies and tactics, and such practices are not without challenges. The digital divide is stark, creating a significant development divide. For instance, advanced technologies like AI and VR/AR are more prevalent in advanced economies with robust digital infrastructures, while their adoption may be slower in EMs. This significant difference in diffusion rates has a range of implications for any country's production and use of digital technologies, from digital jobs, digital services exports, and app development to Internet use, affordability, quality, and more. These factors significantly influence a company's internationalization efforts in terms of expansion strategies and pursuing specific marketing strategies and tactics in certain countries.[21]

Moreover, as these technologies evolve they face diverse regulatory landscapes. For instance, AI-driven marketing strategies must navigate varying privacy laws across countries. The European Union's latest additions to GDPR, for example, impose strict guidelines on how consumer data can be mined, which directly impacts AI marketing strategies.[22] As the marketing function has become a function enabled and supercharged by new technology, there is a real need for digital marketers to work together with IT professionals and nontechnical marketers to craft better campaigns, programs, and customer experiences that effectively leverage software and data. McKinsey argues that there are five different enterprise capabilities to support companies' digital marketing efforts, with governance and processes at the core. The comprehensive approach, or Big 5, described by McKinsey, implies that marketing should work closely with the IT function to assess KPIs, customer insights, customer experience, and IT infrastructure. Working jointly, the two functions can move beyond data to a more holistic and nuanced approach that puts the customer at the center. Marketers tend to have a deeper understanding of consumer relationships and instinctively know that establishing emotional connections transcends the quantifiable realms of data. Hence, their interpretative insights are pivotal in crafting and implementing successful digital marketing strategies.[23]

Conclusion

As we have argued throughout this book, expanding into new markets presents companies with immense opportunities, allowing them to grow their global customer base, generate additional revenue streams, and seek new opportunities. A well-executed digital marketing strategy can be instrumental in a company's entry into new markets, provided you employ the right combination of strategic planning and tactical execution. This process is, however, no easy task, requiring careful planning, adequate budgeting, flexibility, and a deep understanding of the complex and ever-changing world of digital marketing.

The rapid evolution of digital marketing is propelled by technological advancements, shifting user behavior, and expanding Internet access, which adds further complexity to the challenge of implementing effective digital marketing strategies. Navigating the intricate digital landscape, encompassing multiple devices, platforms, and channels, often necessitates external agency support and strong backing from company leadership.

The challenges are amplified for international marketers, who must accommodate diverse cultural, linguistic, and regulatory environments and adapt to varying online behavior across cultures. Moreover, compliance with different data privacy laws in each region adds another layer of complexity. Despite these challenges, mastering digital marketing is crucial for businesses seeking international expansion. When executed skillfully, digital marketing can significantly boost a company's foreign expansion and growth by enabling it to engage with a diverse global target audience while simultaneously building its global brand.

Ultimately, integrating digitalization and emerging technologies significantly influences global digital marketing strategies. As these technologies continue to evolve, they will offer innovative opportunities for global customer engagement and challenge marketers to adapt to diverse technological and regulatory environments. In conclusion, a successful international digital marketing strategy harmoniously blends localization efforts with global brand coherence and focuses on driving value amidst disruptive change while allowing businesses to thrive in the international marketplace.

Bites for Thought

One of Canada's fastest-growing AI Solutions and Services businesses (the company name is kept anonymous per the contributor's request) has experienced significant growth over the past 2 years by combining its applied AI consulting services with a data science skills and experience training program. Initially prompted by a request from a Canadian provincial government agency, this training program aimed to enhance workforce skills and develop local talent in the tech industry. To the company's surprise, the training program quickly gained traction. Within 2 years, over 300 graduates from 90 partner firms completed the program, which combined real-world data science projects with hard and soft skills development. An impressive 95 percent of the graduates secured employment after the program, with many joining the firms they had collaborated with during their training.

Encouraged by this success, the company leadership team explored the potential for expanding their business model into the United States and South America. They discovered a gap in the market, as no direct competition for their unique model existed. Furthermore, only one U.S. university offered a similar program, despite the company's proven track record over a 3-year period in the commercial sector. The company decided to establish key academic hubs in the United States, aligning them with regional industries or partners. They first created a test hub in the Northeast to pilot the program. This hub would not only serve as a template for additional centers across the United States but also act as a "home office" to franchise the offering to universities nationwide, enabling them to participate in this innovative "learn to earn" program.

The company's commercial approach to training and skill development, grounded in real-world experiences, holds great potential for improving talent pipelines in advanced analytics, data science, and machine learning. These areas are in high demand in today's rapidly advancing digital world. Although it is still too early to evaluate the company's growth strategy fully, they have successfully established commercial hubs in New England, Texas, Chicago, and California, catering to various industry sectors. With additional investments and a unique three-part business model, the company has achieved lift-off across North America.

Questions
1. *What do you think about XYZ's approach to leading its market entry to the United States with a training hub program?*
2. *Do your potential and existing customers require training to use your products and/or services? If so, how can this training be integrated into your international expansion efforts?*
3. *How crucial is training in the latest technology for your firm's ability to conduct effective international digital marketing campaigns?*

CHAPTER 9

Looking Ahead

Burger King

A few years ago, Burger King's U.K. division initiated a Twitter thread that reverberated across the social media landscape. On International Women's Day, it tweeted, "Women belong in the kitchen."[1] It was intended, of course, to be provocative, aiming to seize attention and stimulate discourse. The company followed up the initial tweet with two more tweets, one that said, "If they want to, of course," explaining that "only 20% of chefs are women. We're on a mission to change the gender ratio in the restaurant industry by empowering female employees with the opportunity to pursue a culinary career." The third and final tweet announced a new scholarship program to help women get a degree in culinary arts to help reduce the gender gap in the restaurant sector.

How did the campaign fare? Poorly, to say the least. Many Twitter users only saw the first tweet and reacted angrily to the seemingly sexist tweet. Even many of those who saw all three tweets commented that using a sexist trope to get attention was in poor taste and, at the very least, the company could have combined the first two tweets. The campaign caught the attention of mainstream media, who wrote about the backlash against Burger King on social media. Upon seeing the reaction, Burger King deleted the original tweet, saying, "It was brought to our attention that there were abusive comments in the thread, and we don't want to leave the space open for that." By then, it had been retweeted more than 160,000 times and received over half-a-million likes.

This case highlights a crucial lesson. The peculiarities of each social media platform, including their algorithms and display mechanics, warrant nuanced consideration. The sequence of tweets in this case, seemingly structured to progressively reveal the brand's inclusive intent, was potentially hampered by Twitter's (or X's) algorithmic tendencies that segmented the tweets. What most social media platforms have in common is that feedback and interaction with the audience are almost instantaneous, and companies should be prepared to engage, react, and adapt their campaigns in real time.

Second, cultural awareness is not optional any longer. A phrase or play on clever or humorous words in one culture could be outright offensive in another. Given the global reach of social media, brands need to exercise more cultural sensitivity than ever. In a world where geographical boundaries are blurred by digital communication, the need for heightened cultural acumen within branding and marketing campaigns becomes paramount. To borrow from a familiar saying, in our digitally interconnected era, what happens in Vegas no longer stays in Vegas, and immediately shared with the world.

Furthermore, the case also underscores the transformation of audience behavior and engagement within the digital ecosystem. The modern consumer, navigating an ever-expanding content landscape, often engages with fragments rather than consuming complete messages. This emerging pattern demands an evolution in marketing strategies, catering to abbreviated attention spans and piecemeal content consumption. In sum, the Burger King campaign's trajectory exemplifies a convergence of lessons for ever-evolving international marketing: the impact of social media's unique mechanisms, cultural empathy, and the imperative to tailor content for swift, partial engagement within a digitally driven consumer landscape.

Courting Controversy to Build Your Brand

The Burger King International Women's Day tweets serve as a powerful reminder of the subtleties and intricacies involved in international marketing and brand-building. It underscores the need to weave impactful messages that are also culturally sensitive, considering the nuances of various social media and communication platforms. Many brands may be tempted to think that any attention is good attention. With the competition for media, savvy brands and company CEOs seem to be making controversial statements to get media attention. You could argue that Elon Musk—at the time of writing, the world's richest person—has built a more prominent brand name for himself than even his own companies (Twitter, SpaceX, and Tesla), each of which has massive brand equity.

Adopting a strategy that thrives on controversy and seeks attention through divisive issues is fraught with potential pitfalls. For one, it may leave opportunities for competitors to attract customers who disagree on issues that were used to gain attention. In the Burger King example earlier, this was called out directly by people in different countries in real time. Without the "short-cut" of being controversial or having a major newsworthy announcement that captures the public's attention, navigating through the relentless barrage of commercial messages to make a mark and stand out is undeniably challenging, especially internationally. So, if you are looking to court controversy and amplify your brand's visibility, while minimizing potential risks, here are some strategic steps your organization can consider:

1. **Utilize focus groups and test audiences:** Before launching a major campaign, especially one addressing sensitive topics, it is prudent to involve diverse focus groups in identifying potential pitfalls. This ensures that messaging is rigorously assessed from various cultural, gender, and sociological perspectives. Postassessment, you can gauge your tolerance for potentially upsetting any of these groups and develop preemptive responses.

2. **Engage advocacy and stakeholder groups:** Connecting with NGOs, advocacy groups, or organizations that focus on issues related to your campaign and/or your product/service ahead of a launch can be invaluable. Prior engagement can provide meaningful insights, and it is important to identify potential partnerships and allies that would bolster the campaign's authenticity.

3. **Leverage brand ambassadors and influencers:** Instead of relying solely on your brand's voice, enlisting respected and well-known people to champion your cause and brand's initiative can add

to exposure and credibility, and ensure your message is received positively.

4. **Prepare reactive messaging and Q&A:** Having a backup plan is always a good idea. If your campaign faces backlash or is open to misinterpretation, swift, empathetic, and transparent communication strategies are essential for addressing concerns. This approach helps in damage control and preserves trust.

5. **Prioritize internal engagement:** Ensure that internal teams, especially outward-facing functions like communications and client relations, are aligned with your campaign's intent. Your organization needs to provide the necessary training for handling inquiries or criticisms professionally, appropriately, and empathetically.

In international marketing, once a company chooses to court controversy to gain attention, it is crucial to remain resolute in its stance. Wavering or attempting to appease all sides often dilutes the brand message and may result in mistrust. Attempting to cater to all sides in a multifaceted international context can be perceived as being insincere or lacking in cultural understanding. Hence, whether you issue an apology or stand by your decision unapologetically, it is essential to provide a clear position and articulate how this aligns with the brand's mission, core values, and proposition. Before doing so, consider how this position would impact your image, brand equity, and, ultimately, your sales, and keep in mind that a cautious approach may not work as well here.

Transformative Trends

The move toward embracing controversy underscores the increasing challenge for brands to stand out in a world inundated with advertising and marketing messages. While the exact number of daily exposures to such messages remains uncertain, it is undeniable that only a handful of them genuinely capture our attention. So, what strategies can astute international marketers like you employ to elevate your brand's visibility and foster meaningful engagements? A critical first step is staying attuned to emerging trends and positioning your brand and company at the forefront of industry changes. Below, we explore transformative trends poised to impact international marketing and reshape the communications ecosystem. Their current influence is merely the tip of the iceberg; as they continue to evolve, they hold the potential to redefine how marketers conduct research, develop strategies, and forge more profound, more meaningful connections with consumers and other stakeholders:

- **Data, data, and more data:** The influx of data is truly transformative. While we discussed data's impact at length earlier in this guidebook, it bears repeating, especially as more useful data become available to marketers. Never have we had such extensive access to multidimensional data. From macroscopic cross-national datasets to microscopic granular insights, there is an expansive list of options to explore, for example:
  - *Cross-national data:* These datasets provide a broad perspective, offering insights into global market trends, economic indicators, and cultural variations. For example, analyzing cross-national data can help a company identify EMs with growing consumer demand.
  - *Panel or longitudinal data:* This type of data track changes over time, allowing marketers to spot evolving consumer preferences and behaviors. For instance, a company can use longitudinal data to adapt its marketing strategies to changing customer trends.
  - *Granular demographic data (e.g., region, country, city, household, individual):* Granular demographic data provide a deep understanding of consumer segments, helping companies tailor their products and messages to specific audiences. For instance, a company can advertise to households with specific income levels or preferences.
  - *Behavioral data:* These are data that reveal how consumers interact with products and services. For example, analyzing behavioral data can help a company refine its user experience based on how customers navigate its website or app.

Savvy companies equipped with this treasure trove have the potential to unlock new insights and learnings to support their international expansion. It helps them understand market dynamics at macro levels and devise strategies that cater to specific consumer segments, similar to having a bird's eye view and a microscope simultaneously. A noteworthy example of a brand that harnessed data to its advantage is Netflix. As mentioned earlier, they did not do it blindly when Netflix wanted to break into international markets. Using granular viewing data, they tailored their content to each region, resulting in hits like "Money Heist" in Spain and "Sacred Games" in India. On the flipside, however, when companies like Home Depot entered China without a deep, data-driven understanding of local consumer preferences, they faced significant challenges in establishing their brand in the Chinese market.

- **AI and human instincts—the dynamic duo:** AI and machine learning have undeniably revolutionized market analysis and the ability to craft best-in-class marketing campaigns. These new AI tools offer unprecedented scale and speed, enabling marketers to process vast amounts of data and make data-driven decisions at a pace never before possible. Yet, while AI and machine learning are revolutionizing marketing, human interpretation and guidance remain indispensable. For the foreseeable future, seasoned marketing professionals have an opportunity to integrate their knowledge and experience with sophisticated algorithms. Combining machine intelligence with human insight makes for a formidable team, blending scale with sensibility and experience. For example, Spotify's algorithms are masterful in suggesting new tracks to users, but their human-curated playlists, like "RapCaviar," give them that necessary human touch. Without the latter, AI might never have recognized the cultural importance and nuance of certain tracks. As we advance, as the use of advanced AI systems and machine learning becomes more prevalent, the value of anything uniquely human is set to increase. These qualities—like creativity, intuition, empathy, and unpredictability—are difficult, if not impossible, for AI to replicate.

Marketers should emphasize these skills during the planning phase of a marketing campaign and during its execution. In our increasingly digital world, a growing premium is placed on nondigital experiences. Consider, for example, the resurgence in the popularity of vinyl records in a world of digital music or handwritten letters in an age of instant messaging. Similarly, while an AI-driven chatbots may provide instant answers, only a customer service representative can respond to a query with genuine compassion, authenticity, and understanding, which algorithms struggle to replicate. In conclusion, AI empowers marketers with data-driven insights and efficiency, while human instincts contribute creativity, empathy, and authenticity. As AI advances, the distinctively human aspects of marketing are expected to become even more valuable, underlining the enduring importance of the human touch in a digital age.

- **Speed, the new normal:** In today's VUCA world, things are moving fast, really fast. Marketers find themselves in a perpetual race to generate rapid insights that align with the swiftly shifting preferences of consumers and the ever-evolving competitive landscape. Staying ahead of the curve demands agility without compromising on quality. This holds particularly true for consumer products and extends to trends in service offerings. For example, when the pop-it (i.e., a children's toy) trend took off, quick-moving companies immediately capitalized on it, producing them in millions and selling them for healthy margins. Zara, a Spanish fashion outlet, is a great example of a fast-fashion model that capitalizes on rapidly changing fashion trends. They move from design to store shelves in a matter of weeks, ensuring they are always on trend, although sustainability questions may affect this commercial model. In healthcare services, marketing entire countries for their ability to provide quality and affordable healthcare has become a trend of late, and first movers in this space have gained a big advantage. A prime illustration of this trend can be found at Istanbul's state-of-the-art airport, one of the world's largest. You can frequently spot travelers recovering from what are usually elective surgeries, a testament to the success of Turkey's healthcare marketing campaigns. The VUCA world demands that international marketers embrace speed as the new normal. Adapting to changing consumer dynamics and market trends is imperative to stay competitive and relevant. Companies that can navigate this accelerated landscape while maintaining quality and relevance will be the true winners in international marketing.

- **Social media—listening and two-way engagement:** Social media has transcended its role and evolved from a mere communication tool to a vital channel for maintaining engagement with your most devoted supporters. By keeping a finger on the pulse of real-time conversations, brands can adapt, innovate, engage, and communicate and stay relevant. In today's commercial landscape, active engagement and listening across various social platforms are essential for success. However, it is not just about being present on social media but also about standing out meaningfully. For example, the fast-food outlet Wendy's Twitter (rebranded as X) account is often praised for its real-time engagement and cheeky humor. It emphasizes how tuning into social media nuances can create a winning brand personality. Another noteworthy example is Airbnb's use of social media to engage with global audiences. Airbnb leverages user-generated content and personal stories on platforms like Instagram to showcase unique accommodations and experiences worldwide. On the other end, brands that misuse memes or try too hard can come off as inauthentic, leading to ridicule, as we read in the opening case study in this chapter, where a brand's inauthentic engagement on social media backfired. In international marketing, social media serves as a bridge between brands and their global customer base. Companies can create a loyal and engaged international customer community by actively listening to customer feedback, addressing concerns, and fostering genuine two-way conversations.

- **Alignment of brand and company values:** Digitally empowered and well-informed consumers have plenty of choices and information at their fingertips. While traditional factors like price, quality, and convenience remain central to purchasing intent, plenty of research has shown that people are naturally drawn toward companies and brands that share their values. Whether these values are cultural, based on ESG considerations, a dedication to innovation, or other factors, this alignment of values drives long-term brand loyalty, rendering the price of a product less important than it otherwise would be. A myriad of examples underscores the significance of this alignment. Take, for instance, Apple, a company whose customers remain remarkably loyal, contributing to its status as one of the world's most valuable companies. The profound connection between Apple's values and customer base extends beyond mere product functionality. It is rooted in a shared ethos, a belief in innovation, and a commitment to pushing boundaries, which resonates deeply with its customers. The alignment of a company's products and values within marketing campaigns serves a multifaceted purpose. Not only does it attract and retain the finest talent, it also engages influential brand ambassadors. This alignment distinguishes a company from its peers in a saturated market, establishing a unique brand identity that appeals to consumers seeking deeper connections with the brands they support. As consumers seek authenticity and shared values in the brands they patronize, companies prioritizing alignment with their target audiences will continue to reap the benefits of long-term loyalty, advocacy, and a distinguished market presence.
- **New market research trends:** Several factors are changing the way market research is conducted:
  - *New digital research tools:* Today's digital research tools have the power to do many things, from mining user-generated content for insights to tracking long-term trends. These tools offer a more nuanced understanding of market dynamics, allowing marketers to gain many new insights—like analyzing

competitors or testing out a hypothetical campaign. For international marketers willing to experiment and maximize the potential of these tools, this trend represents a golden opportunity. A good example is the trend toward new digital survey tools. With the shift from online to mobile-first methodologies, surveys are now more like casual conversations with your customers. They are accessible, versatile, and cost-efficient and reach people in their comfort zones. Many brands use mobile surveys in select markets to gauge interest in potential new products or services. This direct line to customer preferences frequently leads to innovations and to emphasis on profitable and popular products and services. In short, this continuous stream of real-time feedback helps brands identify opportunities, fix problems, and enhance experiences.

○ ***Emphasize diversity—the global mosaic:*** What constitutes a "representative sample" today differs vastly from the past. The emphasis on inclusivity ensures that samples reflect the diverse world we inhabit, providing a holistic understanding of markets. This starts with research but has real-world implications. For example, H&M faced a backlash from an ad that many perceived as racially insensitive. A more diverse and representative sample during their ad-testing phase could have highlighted potential issues before the campaign went live. In contrast, Dove's "Real Beauty" campaign resonated globally because they took care to ensure diverse representation in their advertisements.

○ ***In-house research—the DIY trend:*** The DIY trend in market research points toward a decreased reliance on external agencies. As brands bring research functions in-house, they offer greater control, alignment, and swifter decision-making. Driven partly by a rise in real-time intelligence tools, this trend is likely to be here to stay. Using data generated by your products and services can be a real source of competitive strength. Unilever's acquisition of Dollar Shave Club is a good example of a company recognizing the value of in-house insights.

Instead of relying solely on external data about the rise of subscription services, Unilever brought this expertise in-house, giving them a competitive edge and real-time data into consumer behavior.

The Evergreen Trends

In contrast to the ever-shifting sands of transformative trends, evergreen trends in international marketing are pillars of stability and enduring relevance. These fundamental strategies have proven their worth over time, continuously providing a solid foundation for organizations and brands aiming to achieve lasting success in global markets. While the digital age and cultural shifts bring new challenges and opportunities, the core principles of evergreen trends—such as the role of cultural differences, prioritizing long-term strategy over short-term tactics, and customer-centric approach—remain crucial. Below, we delve into these trends and discuss how they influence consumer behavior and drive effective marketing across diverse international landscapes.

- **Understanding and celebrating culture:** Understanding and respecting cultural nuances isn't merely a trend; it is an enduring imperative for international marketers. In fact, you could argue that it is at the very bedrock of successful international marketing. As we've read time and again throughout this guidebook, many brands learn this lesson the hard way. A true understanding of culture demands more than surface-level knowledge; it requires immersing oneself in the fabric of local customs, traditions, and values. It is about experiencing culture firsthand and deriving profound insights from local perspectives. The timeless saying goes, "When in Rome, do as the Romans do." Brands that embrace this wisdom thrive and set themselves apart from their competition. They don't just acknowledge the differences; they celebrate them. This celebration is evident in their marketing strategies and tactics, tailored to resonate with the unique characteristics of the target audience. Take McDonald's, for instance, which exemplifies cultural adaptability. In different countries, McDonald's menus feature items tailored to local tastes, such as the McFlurry with green tea in Japan or the McAloo Tikki burger in India. This commitment to cultural alignment has earned McDonald's a global brand presence and power.

- **Having a long-term strategy:** Another evergreen trend is the continued need to focus on a long-term company strategy. While many of the trends mentioned earlier underscore the immediate effects of research, technology, and marketing on financial results and market success, the value of forward-looking strategies cannot be overstated. As such, international marketers must strike a balance between catering to the pressing needs of today and anticipating the shifts of tomorrow. In other words, while there is a rush for what is trending today, we must not lose sight of what lies around the corner. Think of it as listening to today's hit songs while keeping an ear out for emerging trends in music. While BlackBerry was busy capitalizing on its existing market dominance in the 2000s, it missed the touchscreen trend. They might have better navigated the changing tech landscape if they balanced the present with an eye to the future. Kodak, despite inventing the digital camera, failed to pivot away from film quickly enough. They focused too heavily on their current cash cow, failing to see the long-term shift toward digital photography.

- **Embedding marketing into the business:** Today's international marketers and market researchers are not isolated entities. They play pivotal roles in setting the company strategy, enhancing organizational resilience, creating demand, and mitigating risk, ensuring that businesses not only thrive but also deal with unforeseen challenges. More than just meeting growth targets, marketers are increasingly expected to provide a compass for the ship, helping ensure smooth sailing through turbulent waters. For example, when Toyota faced massive recalls due to faulty accelerators, their loss of market share went beyond the immediate numbers. However, by gauging public sentiment and trust, they formulated a recovery strategy that addressed the mechanical issue and helped rebuild brand trust. LEGO's turnaround story involved them seeking feedback from core enthusiasts. Beyond sales figures, they wanted to understand the emotional reasons for people's love of LEGO. This helped them realign their brand value proposition with their audiences' passion.

Final Thoughts

As we close this book on international marketing, it goes without saying that the global marketplace is an ever-evolving landscape of cultures, trends, and technological innovations. Navigating today's VUCA world demands a lot from the modern-day marketer; not just a toolkit of strategies, it requires adaptability, resilience, empathy, collaboration, and a genuine commitment to understanding the diverse tapestries of markets worldwide. The nature of "international" reminds us that we are dealing with not just faceless consumers but with individuals and cultures with rich histories, beliefs, passions, and aspirations.

New technology and interconnectedness offer so many opportunities for the marketer, but they also, and perhaps more profoundly, imply a loss of control that must be utilized wisely. Information flows in real time, and brand stories and experiences can be shaped and influenced by anyone, anywhere in the world, with a digital device. As such, modern-day international marketers must be storytellers, listeners, and business strategists. It is a dance between leading the narrative, guiding it, and allowing it to be coauthored by audiences worldwide; hence, it implies some loss of control.

Lastly, the new economy prioritizes those working collaboratively across cultures and organizations, bridging cultural and institutional boundaries to find common ground and shared objectives. This uniquely human skill of collaboration and bringing together diverse perspectives and expertise helps marketers succeed in today's dynamic and complex global business environment. Practically, collaboration can result in insights into local market dynamics, consumer inclinations, and regulatory environments, allowing opportunities to pool resources, research, and developmental or promotional expenses. As such, collaboration is frequently indispensable.

We hope this guidebook offers useful guidance and advice on this journey, helping you navigate this dynamic VUCA world. Remember! Authenticity, adaptability, and understanding of local cultures are your most important assets in international marketing.

Notes and Bibliography

Chapter 1

1. James Rogers, "For Budweiser, Qatar World Cup Has Been a Tale of Tough Logistics and Quick Thinking," *MarketWatch*, December 14, 2022, https://www.marketwatch.com/story/for-budweiser-qatar-world-cup-has-been-a-tale-of-tough-logistics-and-quick-thinking-11670880004.
2. Sarah Lyall, "Pouring Through a Crisis: How Budweiser Salvaged Its World Cup," *New York Times*, December 11, 2022, https://www.nytimes.com/2022/12/11/sports/world-cup/budweiser-world-cup.html.
3. James Rogers, "Budweiser Announces Details of World Cup Victory Celebrations in Argentina," *MarketWatch*, December 19, 2022, https://www.marketwatch.com/story/budweiser-announces-details-of-world-cup-victory-celebrations-in-argentina-11671466563.
4. Louis Brennan, "How Netflix Expanded to 190 Countries in 7 Years," *Harvard Business Review*, October 12, 2018, https://hbr.org/2018/10/how-netflix-expanded-to-190-countries-in-7-years.

Chapter 2

1. DHL, "Trends in Logistics: Shaping the Way We Work and Live," accessed April 11, 2025, https://www.dhl.com/global-en/delivered/global-trade/trends-in-logistics.html.
2. DHL, "Trends in Logistics: Shaping the Way We Work and Live," accessed April 11, 2025, https://www.dhl.com/global-en/delivered/global-trade/trends-in-logistics.html
3. Everstream Analytics, "Leading Supply Chain Risk Analytics Companies, Resilience360 and Riskpulse, Combine and Rebrand as Everstream Analytics," March 2, 2021, accessed March 25, 2024, https://www.everstream.ai/media/everstream-analytics-launch/.
4. Deloitte, "How 5 Megatrends Will Disrupt Your Supply Chain Planning," accessed March 25, 2024, https://www2.deloitte.com/uk/en/pages/consulting/articles/five-mega-trends-distrupt-supply-chain-planning.html.
5. Tesla, "2020 Impact Report," accessed March 25, 2024, https://www.tesla.com/impact-report/2020.
6. Rebecca Elliot, "What if Tesla Is…Just a Car Company?" *Wall Street Journal*, January 13, 2023, accessed March 25, 2024, https://www.wsj.com/articles/tesla-stock-elon-musk-electric-vehicle-11673623093.

7. C. Mui, "How Kodak Failed," *Forbes Magazine*, July 14, 2020, accessed December 6, 2024, https://www.forbes.com/sites/chunkamui/2012/01/18/how-kodak-failed/?sh=5b9a0ce96f27.

8. Jonathan Salem Baskin, "The Internet Didn't Kill Blockbuster, The Company Did It to Itself," *Forbes Magazine*, November 18, 2013, accessed March 25, 2024, https://www.forbes.com/sites/jonathansalembaskin/2013/11/08/the-internet-didnt-kill-blockbuster-the-company-did-it-to-itself/.

9. J. Naisbitt and P. Aburdene, *Megatrends 2000* (Sidgwick and Jackson, 1990), 5–10.

10. J. Linthorst and A. de Waal, "Megatrends and Disruptors and Their Postulated Impact on Organizations," *Sustainability* 12, no. 20 (2020): 8740.

11. Sydney Business Insights, "Megatrends for the Future of Business," accessed March 25, 2024, https://sbi.sydney.edu.au/megatrends/our-megatrends/.

12. S. Banker, Megatrends Reshaping Supply Chain Management. *Forbes*, February 1, 2021, accessed March 25, 2024, https://www.forbes.com/sites/stevebanker/2021/02/01/megatrends-reshaping-supply-chain-management/?sh=183869764d61.

13. PwC UK ,"Megatrends—What is a Megatrend and Why Do They Matter?" posted April 2, 2014, 4 min., 53 sec., accessed March 25, 2024, https://www.youtube.com/watch?v=foP3nZRM6GU.

14. S. Ghoshal and C. A. Bartlett, "The Multinational Corporation as an Interorganizational Net-work," *Academy of Management Review* 15, no. 4 (1990): 603–26.

15. S. T. Cavusgil, "Megatrends and International Business," in *Megatrends in International Business. The Academy of International Business*, ed. S. Batas, O. Kuivalainen, and R. R. Sinkovics (Palgrave Macmillan, 2022).

16. R. Amarnath, "Five Data Analytics Trends on Tap for 2023," *Forbes Magazine*, January 11, 2023, accessed December 6, 2024, https://www.forbes.com/councils/forbestechcouncil/2023/01/11/five-data-analytics-trends-on-tap-for-2023/.

17. IPCC, "Special Report on Climate Change and Land," Chapter 3: Desertification, accessed March 25, 2024, https://www.ipcc.ch/srccl/.

18. Staff Author, "Public Company of the Year—Beyond Meat," *Los Angeles Business Journal*, November 2, 2021, accessed March 25, 2024, https://labusinessjournal.com/advertorials/public-company-year-beyond-meat/.

19. Google Sustainability, "24/7 by 2030: Realizing a Carbon-Free Future," accessed March 25, 2024, https://sustainability.google/reports/247-carbon-free-energy/.

20. Cavusgil, "Megatrends and International Business."

21. World Bank, "Urban Development," accessed December 6, 2024, https://www.worldbank.org/en/topic/urbandevelopment/overview.

22. *Ibid.*
23. E. Dugarova and N. Gülasan, "Six Megatrends That Could Alter the Course of Sustainable Development," *The Guardian*, 2017, p. 18, accessed April 9, 2025, https://www.theguardian.com/global-development -professionals-network/2017/apr/14/six-megatrends-that-could-alter-the -course-of-sustainable-development.
24. "Smart City Hub," accessed March 25, 2024, https://smartcityhub.com/.
25. Oxfam International, "Richest 1% Bag Nearly Twice as Much Wealth as the Rest of the World Put Together Over the Past Two Years," January 26, 2023, accessed March 25, 2024, https://www.oxfam.org/en/press-releases /richest-1-bag-nearly-twice-much-wealth-rest-world-put-together-over-past -two-years.
26. Statista, "Number of Smartphone Network Subscriptions Worldwide from 2016 to 2022, with Forecasts from 2023 to 2028," accessed March 25, 2024, https://www.statista.com/statistics/330695/number-of -smartphone-users-worldwide/.
27. The CMO Survey, "Fall 2023," accessed March 25, 2024, https:// cmosurvey.org/wp-content/uploads/2024/03/The_CMO_Survey-Highlights_and_Insights_Report-Fall_2023-20240328-142725.pdf.
28. Benetton Group, "Benetton Group Is Among the Top Companies in the Greenpeace Rankings Also in 2015," accessed December 6, 2024, https:// www.benettongroup.com/en/media-press/press-releases-and-statements /benetton-group-is-among-the-top-companies-in-the-greenpeace-rankings -also-in-2015/.

Chapter 3

1. M. Mithat Uner, Burak Cetin, and S. Tamer Cavusgil, "On the Internationalization of Turkish Hospital Chains: A Dynamic Capabilities Perspective," *International Business Review*, June 2020, https://doi.org/10.1016 /j.ibusrev.2020.101693.
2. D. M. Brock, "Building Global Capabilities: A Study of Globalizing Professional Service Firms," *Service Industries Journal* 32, no. 10 (2012): 1593–607; S. T. Cavusgil, G. Knight, and J. Riesenberger, *International Business: The New Realities*, 5th ed. (Pearson Higher Education, 2020).
3. McKinsey & Company, "Marketing's Moment Is Now: The C-Suite Partnership to Deliver on Growth," June 20, 2022, accessed March 26, 2024, https:// www.mckinsey.com/capabilities/growth-marketing-and-sales/our-insights /marketings-moment-is-now-the-c-suite-partnership-to-deliver-on-growth.
4. S. T. Cavusgil, G. Knight, J. Riesenberger, and A. Yaprak, *Conducting Market Research for International Business* (Business Expert Press, 2009), 15–34.

5. M. R. Czinkota, I. A. Ronkainen, and S. Gupta, *International Business* (Cambridge University Press, 2021), 200–35.

6. S. Gupta, "Volkswagen in India," *Bangalore: Indian Institute of Management* (Harvard Business School Publishing, 2013).

7. S. T. Cavusgil, G. Knight, and J. Riesenberger, *International Business: The New Realities* (Pearson, 2020), 334–61.

8. Czinkota et al., *International Business*, 200–35.

9. A. Ozturk, E. Joiner, and S. T. Cavusgil, "Delineating Foreign Market Potential: A Tool for International Market Selection," *Thunderbird International Business Review* 57, no. 2 (2015): 119–41.

10. Cavusgil et al., *Conducting Market Research for International Business*, 15–34.

11. B. Schlegelmilch, *Global Marketing Strategy: An Executive Digest* (Springer, 2022), 63–80.

12. M. R. Czinkota, I. A. Ronkainen, and A. Cui, *International Marketing* (Cengage Learning, 2023), 179–202.

13. D. Lascu, *International Marketing* (Textbook Media Press, 2022), 260–83.

Chapter 4

1. Tim Adams, "K-Everything: The Rise and Rise of Korean Culture," *Guardian*, September 4, 2022, accessed April 5, 2024, https://www.theguardian.com/world/2022/sep/04/korea-culture-k-pop-music-film-tv-hallyu-v-and-a.

2. *BTS: Blood, Sweat & Tears* (VIZ Media LLC, 2020).

3. Mark Savage, "BTS Were the Top-Selling Act in the World Last Year,' *BBC*, February 24, 2022, accessed April 5, 2024, https://www.bbc.com/news/entertainment-arts-60505910.

4. Untitled, "Our Big Mac Index Shows How Burger Prices are Changing," *Economist*, January 25, 2024, accessed April 5, 2024, https://www.economist.com/big-mac-index.

5. Geert Hofstede, Gert Jan Hofstede, and Michael Minkov, *Cultures and Organizations: Software of the Mind* (McGraw-Hill, 2005), 3–26.

6. Susan C. Schneider and Arnoud De Meyer, Interpreting and Responding to Strategic Issues: The Impact of National Culture," *Strategic Management Journal* 12, no. 4 (1991): 307–20.

7. Michael Zakkour, "China's Golden Week—A Good Time to Make Sure You Don't 'Bite the Wax Tadpole'," *Forbes*, October 2, 2014, accessed April 5, 2024, https://www.forbes.com/sites/michaelzakkour/2014/10/02/chinas-national-day-golden-week-a-good-time-to-make-sure-you-dont-bite-the-wax-tadpole/?sh=2b418c560f46.

8. Joe Escobedo, "The Biggest Winners and Losers of Ramadan Marketing," *Forbes,* June 11, 2017, accessed April 5, 2024, https://www.forbes.com /sites/joeescobedo/2017/06/11/ramadan-marketing/?sh=2f347b8f2d55.

9. Jean-Claude Usunier, Hester Van Herk, and Julie Anne Lee. *International and Cross-Cultural Business Research* (Sage, 2017), 30–56.

10. T. A. Shimp and S. Sharma, "Consumer Ethnocentrism: Construction and Validation of the CETSCALE," *Journal of Marketing Research* 24, no. 3 (1987): 280–9.

11. Schalom H. Schwarz, "An Overview of the Schwartz Theory of Basic Values," December, 2012, *Online Readings in Psychology and Culture,* accessed April 5, 2024, https://scholarworks.gvsu.edu/orpc/vol2/iss1/11/.

12. Alvise Persegato, "Practical Applications of Schwartz's Theory of Basic Human Values," July 13, 2023, accessed April 5, 2024, https://medium .com/@alvise.nudge/practical-applications-of-schwartzs-theory-of-basic -human-values-332da0879d19#:~:text=Schwartz's%20Theory%20 of%20Basic%20Human%20Values%20offers%20a%20universal%20 model,tradition%2C%20conformity%2C%20and%20security.

13. F. C. Brodbeck, P. J. Hanges, M. W. Dickson, V. Gupta, and P. W. Dorfman, "Comparative Influence of Industry and Societal Culture on Organizational Cultural Practices," in *Leadership, Culture, and Organizations: The GLOBE Study of 62 Societies,* ed. R. J. House, P. J. Hanges, M. Javidan, P. Dorfman, and V. Gupta (Sage Publications, Inc., 2004), 654–68.

14. Reed Hastings and Erin Meyer, *No Rules Rules: Netflix and the Culture of Reinvention* (Penguin Press, 2020).

15. Edward T. Hall, *Beyond Culture* (Anchor Books, 1976), 105–17.

16. Michele J. Gelfand, Jana L. Raver, Lisa Nishii, et al., "Differences between Tight and Loose Cultures: A 33-Nation Study," *Science* 332, no. 6033 (2011): 1100–4.

17. Jean-Francois Hennart and Ming Zeng. "Cross-Cultural Differences and Joint Venture Longevity," *Journal of International Business Studies* 33 (2002): 699–716.

18. Spotify, "Equity and Impact Report 2021," accessed April 5, 2024, https:// www.lifeatspotify.com/reports/Spotify-Equity-Impact-Report-2021.pdf.

19. Spotify, "Culture Next," accessed April 5, 2024, https://culturenext2022. byspotify.com/en-US.

Chapter 5

1. Louis Brennan, "How Netflix Expanded to 190 Countries in 7 Years," *Harvard Business Review,* October 12, 2018, accessed April 9, 2024, https://hbr.org/2018/10/how-netflix-expanded-to-190-countries-in-7-years.

2. Mike Mabey, Brady Silva, Julia Murphy, and Laurie Gaby, "Navigating Digital Direct-to-Consumer and Subscription Consumer Journeys,' *Quirks Media*, May 1, 2023, accessed April 9, 2024, https://www.quirks.com /articles/navigating-digital-direct-to-consumer-and-subscription-consumer -journeys.

3. Netflix Research, accessed April 9, 2024, https://research.netflix.com/.

4. Untitled, "What Percentage of Data is Unstructured? 3 Must-Know Statistics," *Edge Delta*, March 6, 2024, accessed April 9, 2024, https://edgedelta .com/company/blog/what-percentage-of-data-is-unstructured.

5. S. Tamer Cavusgil, Gary Knight, John Riesenberger, and Attila Yaprak, *Conducting Market Research for International Business* (Business Expert Press, 2009), 3–13.

6. Serendipity 2, "Customer Insight, Store Location Strategy, Shopper Insight, Sales Territory Planning, Sales Activation Campaign," accessed April 9, 2024, https://serendipity2.com/project/vitamin-water/.

7. Agnieszka Chidlow, Emmanuella Plakoyiannaki, and Catherine Welch, "Translation in Cross-Language International Business Research: Beyond Equivalence," *Journal of International Business Studies* 45 (2014): 562–82.

8. McKinsey & Company, "The Next Normal Arrives: Trends That Will Define 2021—And Beyond," January 4, 2021, accessed April 9, 2024, https://www.mckinsey.com/featured-insights/leadership/the-next-normal -arrives-trends-that-will-define-2021-and-beyond.

9. Arun Arora, Hamza Khan, Sajal Kohli, and Caroline Tufft, "DTC E-Commerce: How Consumer Brands Can Get It Right," *McKinsey & Company*, November 30, 2020, accessed April 9, 2024, https://www .mckinsey.com/capabilities/growth-marketing-and-sales/our-insights /dtc-e-commerce-how-consumer-brands-can-get-it-right.

10. Rosemary Marandi, "Flipkart Beats Amazon in India's Record $8.3bn Festive Sales," *Nikkei Asia*, November 30, 2020, accessed April 9, 2024, https://asia.nikkei.com/Business/Retail/Flipkart-beats-Amazon-in-India -s-record-8.3bn-festive-sales.

11. M. R. Czinkota, I. A. Ronkainen, and S. Gupta, *International Business* (Cambridge University Press, 2021), 168–99.

12. Alvin C. Burns and Anne Veeck, eds. "Research Design," in *Marketing Research*, 9th ed. (Pearson, 2020).

13. Enterprise Big Data Framework, "The Four V's of Big Data," accessed July 2, 2024, https://www.bigdataframework.org/the-four-vs-of-big-data/.

14. Greenbook, "2023, GRIT Business & Innovation Report," accessed April 9, 2024, https://www.greenbook.org/grit/grit-business-and-innovation -edition.

15. Untitled, "Global Marketing Analytics Markets, 2021–2026 with 2020 as the Base Year," *Business Wire*, July 27, 2021, accessed April 9, 2024, https://www.businesswire.com/news/home/20210727005770/en/Global -Marketing-Analytics-Markets-2021-2026-with-2020-as-the-Base-Year ---ResearchAndMarkets.com.

16. Martin Harrysson, Estelle Metayer, and Hugo Sarrazin, "How 'Social Intelligence' Can Guide Decisions," *McKinsey*, accessed April 9, 2024, https:// www.mckinsey.com/~/media/mckinsey/dotcom/client_service/BTO/PDF /MOBT29_22-29_SocialIntelligence_R5.ashx.

17. Abbie Griffin and John R. Hauser, "The Voice of the Customer," *Marketing Science* 12, no. 1 (1993): 1–27.

18. Walmart, "Unleashing a Season of Joy: How Walmart Is Connecting Brands with Shoppers in New Ways This Holiday," accessed April 9, 2024, https:// corporate.walmart.com/news/2021/10/29/unleashing-a-season-of-joy-how -walmart-is-connecting-brands-with-shoppers-in-new-ways-this-holiday.

19. Peter Adams, "McDonald's Powers Up 'Friendsgaming' Livestream with FaZe Clan to Unite Gamers," *Marketing Dive*, November 2, 2021, accessed April 9, 2024, https://www.marketingdive.com/news/mcdonalds-powers -up-friendsgaming-livestream-with-faze-clan-to-unite-gam/609295/.

20. Andy Beal, "Why You Need a Chief Listening Officer," The Original Online Reputation Expert™, accessed April 9, 2024, https://www.andybeal .com/why-you-need-a-chief-listening-officer/.

Chapter 6

1. 85. The Coca-Cola Company, "Coca-Cola Launches 'Real Magic' Brand Platform, Including Refreshed Visual Identity and Global Campaign," September 19, 2021, accessed April 11, 2024, https://www.coca-colacompany .com/media-center/coca-cola-launches-real-magic-brand-platform-including -refreshed-visual-identity-and-global-campaign.

2. Tim Oliver Brexendorf and Kevin Lane Keller, "Leveraging the Corporate Brand: The Importance of Corporate Brand Innovativeness and Brand Architecture," *European Journal of Marketing* 51, no. 9/10 (2017): 1530–51.

3. Vanitha Swaminathan, Alina Sorescu, Jan-Benedict E. M. Steenkamp, Thomas Clayton Gibson O'Guinn, and Bernd Schmitt, "Branding in a Hyperconnected World: Refocusing Theories and Rethinking Boundaries," *Journal of Marketing* 84, no. 2 (2020): 24–46.

4. "BINI (group)," *Wikipedia*, Wikimedia Foundation, accessed December 2, 2024, https://en.wikipedia.org/wiki/Bini_(group).

5. Eliot Champion, "How to Identify and Subvert Counterfeiters in E-Commerce Marketplaces," *WTR*, September 29, 2023, accessed April 11, 2024, https://www.worldtrademarkreview.com/guide/anti-counterfeiting -and-online-brand-enforcement/2023/article/how-identify-and-subvert -counterfeiters-in-e-commerce-marketplaces.

6. Thomas Aichner, "Country-of-Origin Marketing: A List of Typical Strategies with Examples," *Journal of Brand Management* 21 (2014): 81–93; Jos Hornikx, Frank van Meurs, Jauke van den Heuvel, and Anne Janssen, "How Brands Highlight Country of Origin in Magazine Advertising: A Content Analysis," *Journal of Global Marketing* 33, no. 1 (2020): 34–45.

7. Claudiu V. Dimofte, Johny K. Johansson, and Ilkka A. Ronkainen, "Cognitive and Affective Reactions of US Consumers to Global Brands,' *Journal of International Marketing* 16, no. 4 (2008): 113–35.

8. Dana L. Alden, Jan-Benedict E. M. Steenkamp, and Rajeev Batra, "Brand Positioning Through Advertising in Asia, North America, and Europe: The Role of Global Consumer Culture," *Journal of Marketing* 63, no. 1 (1999): 75–87.

9. Shilpa Kannan, "How McDonald's Conquered India,' *BBC*, November 19, 2014, accessed April 11, 2024, https://www.bbc.com/news/business -30115555.

10. Dominic Dudley, "BMW Pulls Ad after Falling Foul of Local Sensitivities in Abu Dhabi," *Forbes*, June 1, 2016, accessed April 11, 2024, https:// www.forbes.com/sites/dominicdudley/2016/06/01/bmw-pulls-abu-dhabi -ad/?sh=657935c51ddc.

11. Nataly Kelly, "The Most Common Mistakes Companies Make with Global Marketing," *Harvard Business Review*, September 7, 2015, accessed April 3, 2024, https://hbr.org/2015/09/the-most-common-mistakes-companies -make-with-global-marketing.

12. M. E. Porter and M. R. Kramer, "Creating Shared Value," *Harvard Business Review* 89 no. (1/2) (2011): 62–77.

13. Deloitte Insights, "2020 Global Marketing Trends," accessed April 11, 2024, https://www2.deloitte.com/us/en/insights/topics/marketing-and-sales -operations/global-marketing-trends/2020.html.

14. Ann Landman, "BP's 'Beyond Petroleum' Campaign Losing Its Sheen," *Center for Media and Democracy's PR Watch*, May 3, 2010, accessed April 11, 2024, https://www.prwatch.org/news/2010/05/9038/bps-beyond -petroleum-campaign-losing-its-sheen.

15. Britannica, "Legal Action: Charges, Settlements, and Penalties," accessed April 11, 2024, https://www.britannica.com/event/Deepwater-Horizon-oil -spill/Legal-action.

16. Burhan Wazier, "Nike Accused of Tolerating Sweatshops," *Guardian*, May 20, 2001, accessed April 11, 2024, https://www.theguardian.com /world/2001/may/20/burhanwazir.theobse.

Chapter 7

1. 20VC, "Getir Founder, Nazim Salur on the Future of Last Mile Convenience, Who Will Win? Lessons on Driver Acquisition and Efficiency, Zone Maturity and Time to Profitability and Scaling to 300 Cities in the US in 2022," , September 16, 2021, accessed March 26, 2024, https://www .thetwentyminutevc.com/nazim-salur/.
2. "Getir Arrives in the U.S. Promising Ultrafast Grocery Deliveries Around 10 Minutes," *PR Newswire*, November 11, 2021, accessed March 26, 2024, https://www.prnewswire.com/news-releases/getir-arrives-in-the-us -promising-ultrafast-grocery-deliveries-around-10-minutes-301422449.html.
3. M. Mithat Üner, T. Cuneyt Evirgen, and S. Tamer Cavusgil, "Getir: A Remarkable Example of a Digital Disrupter from An Emerging Market," *California Review Management*, September 13, 2021, accessed March 26, 2024, https://cmr.berkeley.edu/2021/09/getir-a-remarkable-example-of-a -digital-disrupter-from-an-emerging-market/.
4. Morgan Meaker, "As Gig Economy Companies Flee Europe, Getir Is Taking Over," *Wired,* January 11, 2023, accessed March 26, 2024, https:// www.wired.com/story/getir-europe-delivery-wars/.
5. Ebru Tuncay, "Turkish Grocery Delivery Company Getir Pulls Out of Europe, U.S," *Reuters*, April 29, 2024, accessed December 9, 2024, https:// www.reuters.com/business/retail-consumer/turkish-grocery-delivery-company -getir-pulls-out-europe-us-2024-04-29/.
6. Katie Searles, "Getir Withdrawing from UK and US Markets," *Internet Retailing*, May 1, 2024, accessed December 9, 2024, https://internetretailing .net/getir-withdrawing-from-uk-and-us-markets/.
7. Philip T. Kotler and G. Armstrong, "Products, Services, and Brands: Building Customer Value," in *Principles of Marketing,* 18th ed. (Pearson, 2020).
8. Daxue Consulting, "IKEA in China: Cultivating an Omnichannel Home Décor Shopping Experience," accessed April 3, 2024, https://daxueconsulting .com/ikea-in-china/.
9. Gabriellelee, "The Reasons Behind Home Depot's Multimillion-Dollar Failure in China and What It Revealed About Globalism," *Medium*, March 1, 2021, accessed April 3, 2024, https://medium.com/writ-150-at -usc-fall-2020/the-reasons-behind-home-depots-multimillion-dollar -failure-in-china-699bcb76ec25.

10. "Profile: Red Bull," *Forbes*, accessed April 3, 2024, https://www.forbes.com /companies/red-bull/?sh=74302d2261ce.

11. Joshua Robinson and Jonathan Clegg, "He Got Bored. Built an Empire. Then Cracked the Formula for the World's Fastest Sport," *Wall Street Journal*, March 1, 2022, accessed April 3, 2024, https://www.wsj.com/sports /red-bull-racing-formula-one-horner-eacaa99e.

12. Bernadine Racoma, "How Red Bull Adapts to New Markets," (blog), *Day Translations*, February 14, 2019, accessed April 3, 2024, https://www .daytranslations.com/blog/how-red-bull-adapts-to-new-markets/.

13. Shantanu Dutta, Mark Bergen, and Daniel Levy, "Price Flexibility in Channels of Distribution: Evidence from Scanner Data," *Journal of Economic Dynamics and Control* 26, no. 11 (2002): 1845–900.

14. Certified Management Accounts, "The 7 C's of Pricing in International Markets," February 11, 2020, accessed April 3, 2024, https://cmaaustralia .edu.au/ontarget/the-7-cs-of-pricing-in-international-markets/.

15. Mei Fong, "Ikea Hits Home in China," *Wall Street Journal*, March 3, 2006, accessed April 3, 2024, https://www.wsj.com/articles/SB114132199911087764.

16. International Trade Administration, "Export Pricing Strategy," accessed April 3, 2024, https://www.trade.gov/pricing-strategy.

17. Rajneesh Suri and Kent B. Monroe, "The Effects of Time Constraints on Consumers' Judgments of Prices and Products," *Journal of Consumer Research* 30, no. 1 (2003): 92–104.

18. Frank-Martin Belz and Ken Peattie, *Sustainability Marketing: A Global Perspective,* 2nd ed. (Wiley Global Education, 2014), VitalSource Bookshelf.

19. See Thomas O'Guinn, Chris Allen, and Richard Semenik Semenik, *Advertising and Integrated Brand Promotion* (South-Western, 2011); Dean M. Peebles and John K. Ryans, *Management of International Advertising: A Marketing Approach* (Allyn & Bacon, 1984).

20. Lisa Johnson, "Nike's Next Metaverse Move Is RTFKT Pickup," December 14, 2021, accessed April 3, 2024, https://consumergoods.com /nikes-next-metaverse-move-rtfkt-pickup.

21. J. H. Pae, S. Samiee, and S. Tai, "Global Advertising Strategy: The Moderating Role of Brand Familiarity and Execution Style," *International Marketing Review* 19, no. 2, (2002): 176–89.

22. Christopher L. Myers, *International Marketing: Winning in the New Global Economy,* 2nd ed. (Cognella Publishing, 2023).

23. World Trade Organization, "Global Value Chain Development Report— Beyond Production," November 2021, accessed April 3, 2024, https:// www.wto.org/english/res_e/booksp_e/00_gvc_dev_report_2021 _e.pdf.

24. PWC, "PWC's 26th Annual Global CEO Survey, Winning Today's Race While Running Tomorrow's," 2023, https://www.pwc.com/gx/en /ceo-survey/2023/main/download/26th_CEO_Survey_PDF_v1.pdf.

25. Anne-Titia Bové and Steven Swartz, "Starting at the Source: Sustainability in Supply Chains," *McKinsey Sustainability*, November 11, 2016, accessed April 3, 2024, https://www.mckinsey.com/capabilities/sustainability/our -insights/starting-at-the-source-sustainability-in-supply-chains#/.

26. CDP Report, "Committing to Climate Action in the Supply Chain," December, 2015, accessed April 3, 2024, https://cdn.cdp.net/cdp-production /cms/reports/documents/000/000/580/original/committing-to-climate -action-in-the-supply-chain.pdf?1470053398.

27. PWC, "Connected and Autonomous Supply Chain Ecosystems 2025," https://www.pwc.com/gx/en/industries/industrial-manufacturing/digital -supply-chain.html.

28. Barry Jaruzelski, John Loehr, and Richard Holman, "Are Fashion Brands on Track to Meet the 1.5C Emissions Pathway?" *Strategy and Business*, October 15, 2011, accessed April 3, 2024, https://www.strategy-business.com /article/11404.

29. Jeroen Kraaijenbrink, "Twenty Reasons Why Strategy Execution Fails," *Forbes*, September 10, 2019, accessed April 3, 2024, https://www.forbes .com/sites/jeroenkraaijenbrink/2019/09/10/20-reasons-why-strategy -execution-fails/?sh=27a918b41ebe.

30. Kelly, Nataly, "The Most Common Mistakes Companies Make with Global Marketing," *Harvard Business Review*, September 7, 2015, accessed April 3, 2024, https://hbr.org/2015/09/the-most-common-mistakes-companies -make-with-global-marketing.

Chapter 8

1. David Edelman and Jason Heller, "How Digital Marketing Operations Can Transform Business," *McKinsey & Company*, July 1, 2015, accessed April 19, 2024, https://www.mckinsey.com/capabilities/growth-marketing-and-sales /our-insights/how-digital-marketing-operations-can-transform-business.

2. Pierre R. Berthon, Leyland F. Pitt, Kirk Plangger, and Daniel Shapiro, "Marketing Meets Web 2.0, Social Media, and Creative Consumers: Implications for International Marketing Strategy," *Business Horizons* 55, no. 3 (2012): 261–71.

3. *Ibid.*

4. Srikanta Mondal, "Top 10 Search Engines You Should Know About in 2024: Must-Known Facts," *GKBooks*, December 22, 2023, accessed April 19, 2024, https://gkbooks.in/top-10-search-engines/.

5. Sam Carr, "How Many Ads Do We See a Day in 2024?," *Lunio*, February 15, 2021, accessed April 19, 2024, https://lunio.ai/blog/strategy/how-many-ads-do-we-see-a-day/.

6. Valentina Dencheva, "Influencer Marketing Worldwide—Statistics & Facts,' *Statista*, December 18, 2023, accessed April 19, 2024, https://www.statista.com/topics/2496/influence-marketing/#topicOverview.

7. Mailchimp, "Email Marketing Benefits: 10 Ways It Can Grow Your Business,' November 1, 2022, accessed April 19, 2024, https://mailchimp.com/resources/benefits-of-email-marketing/.

8. Data Privacy Manager, "20 Biggest GDPR Fines So Far [2023],' March 17, 2024, accessed April 19, 2024, https://dataprivacymanager.net/5-biggest-gdpr-fines-so-far-2020/.

9. LinkedIn Business, "Effective InMail Example," accessed April 19, 2024, https://business.linkedin.com/content/dam/me/business/en-us/sales-solutions/resources/pdfs/effective-inmail-to-a-fellow-group-member.pdf.

10. Mailchimp, "Customer Journey," accessed April 19, 2024, https://mailchimp.com/marketing-glossary/customer-journey/.

11. David Edelman and Jason Heller, "How Digital Marketing Operations Can Transform Business," *McKinsey & Company*, July 5, 2015, accessed April 19, 2024, https://www.mckinsey.com/capabilities/growth-marketing-and-sales/our-insights/how-digital-marketing-operations-can-transform-business.

12. Josh Bernoff and Charlene Li, "Harnessing the Power of the Oh-So-Social Web." *MIT Sloan Management Review* 49, no. 3 (2008): 36.

13. Jagdish N. Sheth. "Borderless Media: Rethinking International Marketing," *Journal of International Marketing* 28, no. 1 (2020): 3–12.

14. Jagdish N. Sheth and Michael R. Solomon, "Extending the Extended Self in a Digital World," *Journal of Marketing Theory and Practice* 22, no. 2 (2014): 123–32.

15. Brian Solis, "The New Role of Marketing: Drive Business Growth by Reimagining Customer Engagement," *Forbes*, November 1, 2022, accessed April 19, 2024, https://www.forbes.com/sites/briansolis/2022/11/01/the-new-role-of-marketing-drive-business-growth-by-reimagining-customer-engagement/?sh=5160c2f9431c.

16. Jennifer Warnick, "AI for Humanity: How Starbucks Plans to Use Technology to Nurture the Human Spirit," *Starbucks*, January 10, 2020, accessed April 19, 2024, https://stories.starbucks.com/stories/2020/how-starbucks-plans-to-use-technology-to-nurture-the-human-spirit/.

17. Jyothi Subramaniam, "Sephor's AR and VR Make-Up Magic: How a Beauty Giant Is Innovating in the Digital Age," *LinkedIn*, March 31, 2023, accessed April 19, 2024, https://www.linkedin.com/pulse/sephoras-ar-vr-make-up-magic-how-beauty-giant-digital-subramaniam/.

18. Aura Consortium, "A Revolution in the Luxury Industry," accessed April 19, 2024, https://auraconsortium.com/.

19. Sales Force, "The 8th Edition State of Marketing Report," accessed April 19, 2024, https://www.salesforce.com/resources/research-reports/state -of-marketing/.

20. Kate Gibson, "7 Marketing KPIs You Should Know & How to Measure Them," *Harvard Business School Online*, February 1, 2024, accessed April 19, 2024, https://online.hbs.edu/blog/post/marketing-kpis.

21. The World Bank, "Digital Progress and Trends Report 2023," accessed April 19, 2024, https://www.worldbank.org/en/publication/digital-progress -and-trends-report.

22. The European Commission, "Data Protection: Commission Adopts New Rules to Ensure Stronger Enforcement of the GDPR in Cross-Border Cases," July 4, 2023, accessed April 19, 2024, https://ec.europa.eu /commission/presscorner/detail/en/ip_23_3609.

23. David Edelman and Jason Heller, "How Digital Marketing Operations Can Transform Business," *McKinsey & Company*, July 1, 2015, accessed April 19, 2024, https://www.mckinsey.com/capabilities/growth-marketing-and-sales /our-insights/how-digital-marketing-operations-can-transform-business.

Chapter 9

1. Brett Molina, "Burger King UK Under Fire for Tweeting 'Women Belong in the Kitchen' on International Women's Day," *USA Today*, 2024, accessed April 4, 2024, https://eu.usatoday.com/story/money/2021/03/08 /burger-king-uk-under-fire-women-belong-kitchen-tweet/4627505001/.

About the Authors

M. Billur Akdeniz, a professor of marketing at the Peter T. Paul College of Business and Economics at the University of New Hampshire (UNH), is a marketing strategy scholar with research expertise in new products and innovation, brand management, and international marketing.

Her research has been published in prestigious journals such as the *Academy of Management Journal, Journal of the Academy of Marketing Science*, and *International Journal of Research in Marketing*, among others. She was invited as a visiting research scholar by the NEOMA Business School in France, and her scholarly contributions were recognized with the Faculty Scholar Award from UNH.

Billur is an associate editor of the *Journal of Business Research* and *Journal of Product Innovation Management* and is on the editorial review boards of the *Journal of the Academy of Marketing Science, Industrial Marketing Management*, and *International Business Review*. She is recognized with Outstanding ERB member award multiple times from various academic journals and has served as a guest editor for special issues.

Professor Akdeniz has taught undergraduate-level and MBA courses at three different institutions for the past 20 years. Her main areas of teaching are marketing analytics, marketing strategy, and international marketing. Her teaching has been recognized with several accolades, such as the Excellence in Teaching Award at UNH and the Best Online MBA Teacher award.

Billur holds a BA degree in economics and an MBA from Bogazici University in Istanbul, Turkey. Her international education continued with a PhD degree in business administration from Michigan State University, East Lansing, further enriching her understanding of the global business landscape.

234 ABOUT THE AUTHORS

Sebastian van der Vegt is a founding partner at WMBV Consulting, where he leverages over two decades of experience in international communications, strategy, marketing, and business development to help organizations expand and navigate complex global markets. His career has included significant roles with various multinationals and United Nations Agencies, enhancing brand and reputation management across diverse cultural landscapes.

Having lived in 6 countries and visited over 75 worldwide, Sebastian's profound understanding of global business dynamics informs his approach to creating shared value and innovative solutions that benefit all stakeholders. Before founding WMBV, he owned Untold Communications and spent over a decade at the Coca-Cola Company.

There, he led significant projects like EKOCENTER and managed the "Every Drop Matters" partnership with the United Nations across nine countries. His efforts at Coca-Cola included training over 500 senior leaders and earning accolades such as the Golden Quill Award for Business Communications, the Effie Award for Sustainability Marketing, and the MarCom Award for Marketing Activation.

Sebastian started his professional journey at the United Nations in 2001. While there, he coauthored one of the first authoritative books on corporate social responsibility within companies, titled *Raising the Bar*, which included a foreword by then UN Secretary General Kofi Annan. His academic publications include insights on international business strategies and sustainability.

He holds an MBA from Dalhousie University, a bachelor's degree in psychology from the University of Calgary, and a diploma in strategic communications from Columbia University. Currently, he is the president of the Netherlands Chamber of Commerce for the Southeastern United States.

S. Tamer Cavusgil currently serves as regents' professor, Fuller E. Callaway professorial chair, and executive director, Center for International Business Education and Research (CIBER), J. Mack Robinson College of Business, Georgia State University, Atlanta, United States. He is a trustee of Sabanci University in Istanbul, Turkey.

Professor Cavusgil has been mentoring students, executives, and educators in international business for the past four decades.

Tamer authored more than several dozen books and some 200 refereed journal articles. His work is among the most cited contributions in international business. Google Scholar lists him among the top scholars in the world in international business, international marketing, emerging markets, and export marketing.

Tamer was awarded an honorary doctorate, Doctor Honoris Causa, by the University of Hasselt, Belgium, in May 2014, and an honorary doctorate from the University of Southern Denmark in October 2017. In April 2018, Tamer was honored as an honorary professor by Atilim University in Ankara, Turkey.

Professor Cavusgil is an elected fellow of the Academy of International Business, a distinction earned by a select group of intellectual leaders in international business.

Tamer holds a bachelor of science degree in business and economics from the Middle East Technical University in Ankara, Turkey. He earned his MBA and PhD degrees in business from the University of Wisconsin.

Index